Africa Through the Mists of Time

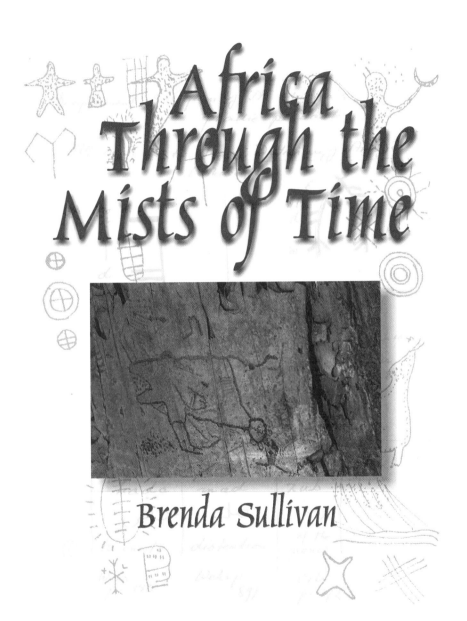

Brenda Sullivan

COVOS DAY
Johannesburg & London

By the same author:

Spirit of the Rocks
A Tale of White Rainmakers in Square Houses
The Lost Calf
Hairdo's and Don'ts of Yesteryear
Tears from the Sky
The Beer of Reconciliation
A Time to Talk
The Elephant Children
The Morogo Garden

Co-authored with George Armstrong:

Dlova
Luguma

Published by Covos Day Books, 2001
Oak Tree House, Tamarisk Avenue,
P.O. Box 6996, Weltevredenpark 1715, South Africa
Email: covos@global.co.za
Website: www.mazoe.com

Copyright © Brenda Sullivan 2001

Cover design by Thalita Harvey, South Africa
Design and origination by Jonathan Harvey, South Africa
Email: j.design@mweb.co.za

Printed and bound by United Litho, South Africa

All rights reserved. No part of this publication may be reproduced, stored, manipulated in any retrieval system, or transmitted in any mechanical, electronic or digital form or by any other means, without the prior written authority of the publishers. Any person who engages in any unauthorized activity in relation to this publication shall be liable to criminal prosecution and claims for civil and criminal damages.

ISBN 1-919874-18-6

*To my daughters
Caroline, Joanne and "Peej"
for their caring and support throughout the years
and
my husband Peter
for his patience and support*

Foreword

There is an old African saying that goes: "The wise eagle that wants to see tomorrow's brightest day must be brave enough to shake the great reptile of the Past awake", and the saying means that if people wish to create a bright future they must first look closely and clearly at their past. Today the entire world is in trouble in many ways simply because people are refusing to study their past closely and coldly and to learn important lessons from it. One of the greatest fallacies that many are shackled by is that the Past is dead and that we can safely consign it to the darkest cupboards and cellars of our existence ... that is not so, the Past is *alive* and dangerously so, and those who care to ignore it do so at their direst peril.

The Past *is* alive; it is a powerful and dark consciousness which cries out for attention, and even if, like the mad Chinese Emperor Huang-pi and the bloody-handed Pol Pot, we were to burn all books on history and palaeontology and archaeology on Earth, we would not be able to kill the Past and consign it to dark oblivion ... never; no matter what we did, the Past would fiercely attract our attention and that of our descendants; it would ooze out of the mud of great rivers at our feet in the form of ancient crockery shards and rusted metal artefacts, it would grin at us from the limestone walls of ancient caves with fossilized teeth; and it would beckon to us out of the shifting sands of man-created deserts as the golden-haired and golden-voiced Sirens of old beckoned to Odysseus, hoping to lure him and his fellow-sailors to their doom.

The Past is immortal; it draws our attention ... it demands justice and appeals to our noblest feelings, thoughts and instincts. The Past asks questions and demands fiercely that we truthfully answer them for our and our descendants' sakes. There are questions about Southern Africa's Past that have never been answered; there are mysteries in our country that have never been investigated or solved; and in this book Mrs Brenda Sullivan-Wintgen, a lady of courage if there ever was, takes the lion by the tail and answers some of these questions and makes great efforts to solve some of these mysteries for the benefit of us all.

Our leaders in Southern Africa have repeatedly called out for an African Renaissance, a great spiritual and physical rebirth of the peoples of the Dark Continent. But this Re-Birth in Africa will forever remain a mirage haunting a dead desert so long as knowledge is chained and thought wears blinkers. There will never be a Renaissance in Africa so long as people cling to palpable lies about our Past and call them the Truth. It is a lie to say that the southern tip of Africa was only rounded by Portuguese sailors during the time of Prince Henry the Navigator. No, my friends, the sea route to India was known to the bold mariners of the remotest past and was not discovered by the Johnny-come-lately Vasco da Gama and his kind. Also, the vast American continent and the many islands that float around it was not first discovered by any Christopher Columbus, but was known to ancient Celts, Libyans, Egyptians and Africans—Africans who established kingdoms and empires in many parts of Mesoamerica and South America—Africans who left African words in the languages of many Native American tribes and who also left Black gods such as Tezcatlipoca in the pantheons of Central and South American Native American gods.

I say again, my friends, the Past is alive and watching you.

Credo Vusamazulu Mutwa
South Africa, 2001

CONTENTS

Introduction x

Chapter 1   Through the mists of time. 1
Chapter 2   Ancient diamond miners?. 25
Chapter 3   Old gold 59
Chapter 4   Diamonds, sacred to the Moon Goddess 85
Chapter 5   Tsui//Goab and Heitsi Eibib 104
Chapter 6   *Isivavane* International 135
Chapter 7   *Incwala*, the ancient Swazi mid-Summer Festival of
             Regeneration 148
Chapter 8   In honour of Khulu-Khulwané 164
Chapter 9   Olulu Olulu 172
Chapter 10   Water demons and the dragons of Drakensberg 190

References. 211

Appendix   The Afro-Celtic Connection 234

Introduction

Africa, the Great Mother, is a continent blessed with many treasures. The more obvious—slaving, hunting, and the mineral wealth—have enticed daredevil explorers and exploitation, in the name of "God and Country", since time immemorial. But more important by far are the hidden treasures of historical facts woven into African myths and legends, and the physical evidence of ancient script, meaningful symbols, and fertility rituals engraved on the rocks by unknown hands in central South Africa.

Perhaps those who incised the rocks came to Southern Africa as missionaries of the Isis religion, as seekers after minerals, as slaves, or as traders. After business enterprises collapsed, through wars or changes of values, some would have returned from whence they had come. Some would have remained behind, eventually to be absorbed by African tribes. Others, the progeny left behind by traders and miners who came and went, had the opportunity of founding new communities imbued with memories of the traditional values of the homeland of their forefathers. The identity of the rock engravers remains uncertain, but there is no doubt in my mind that the symbols and pictographs on the rocks of South Africa depict the sacred animals, certain seasonal fertility rituals, and the presence of literate peoples who once inhabited Southern Africa.

Museums are well stocked with African artefacts, carefully displayed—the tools, wearing apparel, or weapons of this or that tribe. These displays give the impression that those people had always been boxed into their own small corner of the planet. And that each tribe developed art forms, religious and social customs, in their own unique style, without outside influences. While this assumption is not necessarily untrue, it is also not entirely true. People have been moving around, mixing and matching, feuding, fighting, and trading, all over the world, even before humankind discovered the use of fire. For after all, people are people. And, according to Alexander Marshack, in his book *The Roots of Civilization*, the basic function of the human brain has remained much the same since the first appearance of *Homo sapiens* in Europe.[1] Therefore, it is reasonable to suggest that, ever since humankind began making tools, hunting, speaking, singing, decorating their homes, their persons and their weapons, cultures have rubbed up against cultures. And that beliefs, ideas and technologies were continually exchanged, destroyed, or merged.

Many of the traditions and religious practices of the Old Religion, once common to the ancestors of today's so-called civilized nations in the Northern Hemisphere, have been kept alive, and continue to thrive, in Southern Africa. So, whoever sincerely wishes to gain entry into the hidden treasure trove of knowledge about the people who wove the tapestry of the past history of Southern Africa, should study the images engraved on South African rocks with the eyes of Africa. Taking careful note of whether engravings are positioned facing east—the direction of sunrise, and new life. Or if the setting sun in the west highlights them, for sunset is the time of sacrifice and the direction of death. It is also important to note how they relate to each other, and to the four cardinal points.

At certain sites are to be found rock engravings clearly depicting fertility/rainmaking rituals. While at every site are images of the revered animals of Africa, such as the eland, the elephant, and the zebra, which are linked to rainmaking and fertility. In particular, there are the enigmatic records of skilled craftsmen and women who engraved meaningful notations, ancient script, and symbols on the rocks of South Africa.

It is my belief that the rock engravings of South Africa are the records of many peoples who passed this way in ancient times, and that the engravings are in truth the archives of the land.

To date the study of the rock engravings of Southern Africa has been overshadowed by the overwhelming interest in the rock paintings. Respected European academics have even dismissed the more enigmatic engravings as the mindless doodles of Khoi herd boys, or San hunters. Yet the San, when questioned on the subject of the engravings, said they had no knowledge of the art, but that it was surely the work of the ancestors.[2] And, because it was assumed that the ancestors referred to must also have been "Bushmen", this reinforced the already established opinion that all the engravings were "Bushmen art". Thereafter, nobody ever took the trouble to look a little deeper into the matter, nor to question this assumption. And an assumption it certainly is, for the San practiced exogamy—marriage outside the immediate clan.[3] Consequently, because of the fact that for millennia they wandered throughout most of Southern Africa south of the Sahara, and that skeletons identified as "Bushman-like" have even been found in the Nile Valley dated to 12,000–14,000 BP[4], anyone from anywhere could have been their revered ancestors.

However, assuming they did refer particularly to their own kind, then it should be taken into account that the San are not all golden skinned people of small stature, speaking the same language. As with human beings all over the world, the San, or Bushmen, come in all shapes and sizes. Those living north of the Molopo River are distinctly taller than their southern relatives, and the nearer they are to the north and east, the taller they become—because the height of the northern San is due to intermarriage with other races.[5] Another physical characteristic, namely steatopygia (the fatty buttocks), is not a typical San characteristic, but one inbred as a result of miscegenation.[6] So clearly all San do not have the same appearance as the average mental image of a typical "Bushman".

The skin colour of the Auen, Naron, and Kung is a fairly constant reddish brown, but many are also yellow- or black-skinned. The !Okung vary from blackish yellow to reddish brown or copper-coloured. Others of the same group are described as almost black, but lighter in skin tone than the Nguni.[7]

Then there is the matter of language to further complicate the definition of what is a typical "Bushman", for there are four main language groups among the San, and this does not include the completely different language groups of the Khoi.[8] The only reason I mention the Khoi, at this point, is because the earlier European settlers, who colonized South Africa, claimed the San and Khoi were so similar in appearance that they couldn't tell the difference between them. The general classification was made according to whether or not the people had cattle. If no cattle, then they were "Bushmen" (San), if with cattle they were "Hottentots" (Khoi).[9] A rather unscientific classification to say the least, especially if a group of Khoi happened to have landed on hard times, and were temporarily without their cattle—to the European observers they were unquestionably all "Bushmen".

So where did this confusion start, this absolute conviction that all the rock art of South Africa, whether painting or engravings, was the work of the San? From all accounts it arose originally because everyone who was of importance in the world of letters or learning was convinced that, before the coming of the first settlers from Europe, only the San and Khoi were living in the regions where the art was discovered. This despite the fact that non-San ostealogical remains have been found at archaeological sites.[10] So if not the San, then who were they? More to the point is why those established in the fields of archaeology and anthropology have simply failed to follow up on all the evidence showing that, in pre-historic times, Southern Africa was inhabited by peoples other than the San and Khoi. In some instances evidence—such as a skeleton, and papyrus—have simply disappeared.[11] But the main contender for the role of misconception spreader, albeit it unintentionally, must be the Bleek family. For our only knowledge of the southern San is due almost entirely to the work of the Dr. W.H.I. Bleek, his daughter and sister-in-law.

Dr. W.H.I. Bleek, a German linguist, came to South Africa in 1852 originally to study the language of the indigenous peoples living in Natal. He then moved to Mowbray in Cape Town, where he persuaded the Governor Sir Philip Wodehouse to allow some of the San convicts to be released and live with him on his property, in order to study their language. Accordingly, nine San convicts (from the Kenhardt District) were released from hard labour on the breakwater, and taken to work as domestic servants at Bleek's home. To view things in context, it must be remembered that the nineteenth century was an era when, throughout South Africa, the San were classified as vermin, to be shot on sight when seen running across the veld. While Bleek worked chiefly on linguistic matters, his sister-in-law, Lucy Lloyd, transcribed their myths and their accounts of rituals and daily life. Between them they compiled 12,000 pages of verbatim /Xam text, together with literal English translations.[12] Now, while this was an astonishing achievement, it is seldom mentioned that the information in those 12,000 pages was not representative of all San, but was gathered from just nine subjects, all from the Kenhardt district, which is only one small part of the country.

The only other source of information about the San were the records of the stories told to J.M. Orpen by his San informant Qing, in Lesotho in the early 1870s. On these two sources everything today known about "the Bushmen" has been based.

By any standards, these two very limited contacts with San cannot be described as comprehensive surveys of the pre-colonial lifestyles and beliefs of the San of Southern Africa. And yet this work is now enshrined in academic circles as gospel, and preached as the full truth of all that was of the San. Included in the stories of those unfortunate, dispossessed San, is the frequent mention of "the People of the Early Race" who, the San claimed, did the most extraordinary things. What I find extraordinary is that, although everything recorded by the Bleeks is today regarded as the final word on the pre-colonial life and times of the San in general, not one academic has taken the mention of people of an earlier race seriously. It is as if any suggestion that other peoples were around before the San arrived is simply not to be entertained.

This despite the physical evidence, such as the ostealogical remains which have been classified as "other than Bushmen", and the results of archaeological investigations which have established without doubt that the San were indeed preceded by others, of whom very little is known.

The treasures of Africa are the treasures of information concealed in the legends, the social and cultural customs, and the art of the people. The past makes us what we are today. If we come out of ignorance, or are even indifferent about our heritage, then we are co-conspirators with those who cling tenaciously to misconceptions, which are often propounded as absolute truth, and jealously defended against all dissidents.

The importance of searching through legends for clues pointing to historic invasions and migrations, and studying rock engravings with a mind untrammelled by the confines of passionate nationalism or rigid religious beliefs, is to discover we all share a common heritage. Regardless of race, colour or creed, people are people.

People the world over cling to the dogmas of their religious beliefs, without giving much thought to the fact that all religions evolved from the primeval reverence of Earth as the Great Mother, Giver of Life. No, I am not suggesting that everyone would be better off if they relinquished their religious beliefs and return to paganism. But, whatever your religion, I am reminding you that God, by whatever name the Presence is called, is God. And God the Creator, Who made all things, certainly did not create "religion". God could never have created anything as hideously destructive as "religion". Religions, and the even more terrible aspect of faith, religious dogmas, were all man-made. In every case, the original inspired messages of great men and women of Spirit were quickly latched onto, and manipulated by power hungry, greedy human demons gloriously cloaked in the garments of great sanctity.

Early Christian missionaries in South Africa are known to have encouraged their converts to physically attack those who had been persuaded into following the Lord through the gates of rival Christian churches. Good Christians all! [13]

The African pagans never had those problems. Believe it or not, there is no such person as a godless heathen. To the pagan peoples of Africa God is God—God is of everything and in everything on land and in the rivers, oceans, and the sky—human, animal, mineral, plant and insect. The great unifying need of all pagan peoples was to ensure the fertility of all life, and to invoke the harmonious continuation of the cycles of

Life—birth, living, death, and re-birth, they prayerfully inscribed their invocations on the rocks. And, whereas the upholders of western standards of civilization are hell-bent on destroying this planet for secular, monetary, or political gain, our mutual pagan ancestors at least had the grace to respect their environment—so there is a great deal to be learned from their past. Even the Sacred Kings of the Matriarchal era who were annually sacrificed, specifically to take away the sins of their people, served the community better than the average monarch, or wily, amoral, self-gratifying politicians of the post-pagan era.

But first it is necessary to shake off the shackles of a biased mind.

A good way to start is to take an honest look at one's own blood group, because blood is the one substance linking generation to generation. As part of the research I delved into for *Spirit of the Rocks* and this book, bloodlines were lightly investigated.[14] Researching into one's own blood group requires courage, because blood has the power to tie a human being to a whole new spectrum of unsuspecting relatives. Knowing my own group is B Positive, I naturally read that section more carefully. To discover, with some initial consternation that, in the whole world, the people with the highest percentage of B Group blood are the Mongolians, and the Congo Valley pygmies. They are my ancestors? The how, where, why and when were not too difficult to resolve. My father's line was Hagen of Ireland. Descended from Hagen, of Viking stock. (In Germanic/Norse lore it was Hagen who killed Siegfried). The Vikings were travelling and trading along the Amber route, and widely throughout Russia for hundreds of years, and had plenty of time to acquire Mongolian bloodlines, through encounters of the sexual kind. My mother's family, and the family of my paternal grandmother, were from Scotland, another Viking homeland, and possible source of B Group blood. The Congo Valley pygmy connection is a little unclear but, according to Robert Graves, the Picts of Scotland were small, dark, tattooed people, said to have originated somewhere in Libya.[15] Libya was the ancient name for all Africa so, as the description of Picts applies also to Congo Valley pygmies, I could have inherited a dose of B Group blood from Picts through the bloodline of my maternal family as well. Knowing who the ancestors were might, as in my case, be something of a cultural shock at first, but it does break down fixed ideas about who are, or who are not, socially or politically acceptable. The inbred barriers about "them" and "us" crumble.

In the same way as I inherited B Group blood, so did the Zulu inherit one of the great health scourges of their people, namely *scrofula*.[16] Now the Celts, too, are known to have been particularly afflicted with scrofula. The Mongolian sacral spot is another inescapable pointer to a shared ancestry. The Mongolian spot is a dark bluish spot which is present at birth, at the base of the spine, but which later disappears. Mongolian babies are born with it, so too are the babies of the Maya Indians of South America, and the Kung San of Southern Africa.[17] The spots are genetic, they can't be caught, and they don't go away with a spoonful of medicine.

From modern translations of ancient documents, there is ample evidence to show that explorers and traders were sailing the oceans of the world at least 4,000 years ago. To believe that in antiquity the people living around the Mediterranean sea had only a very limited knowledge of the world beyond the Mediterranean, and little or none of the Indian and Atlantic oceans, is to deny history. The Egyptians viewed themselves as living on a great island, surrounded by water—the island of Libya. And there are references to "the Great Encircling Sea" engraved on the obelisk erected at Karnak by Queen Hatshepsut of Egypt (c. 1500 BCE).[18] From this inscription it is clear that during her reign long sea voyages were commonplace. The records of the time relate how the ships of Hatshepsut sailed the world in search of botanical specimens and other rare items, and she was not the first, nor the last, Egyptian monarch to encourage maritime exploration and trade.

Rameses II (c. 1304–1237 BCE) considered himself the ruler of Africa and the oceans. On a granite statue in the temple at Luxor is engraved his claim to "the Great Encircling Sea", as well as to "the Columns of Heaven" and "the Borders of Darkness". The mention of "darkness" has been taken to refer to a record of the length of a day at the Antarctic (see Chapter 3).

The maritime fortunes of the Egyptians rose and fell in rhythm with the successes and defeats of the successive pharaohs, invading kings, upstart generals, and princes. By the time Pharaoh Necho ascended the throne (c. 609–593 BCE), Egyptian sea trade was once again brisk, but the royal profits had dropped alarmingly because of the instability in the Middle East. The Medes sacked Nineveh; Nebuchadnezzar sacked Jerusalem; and the principal port of Ezion Geber (on the Red Sea) seethed with pirates. The situation was not helped by the fact that the Phoenician ships of Tarshish had to unload their valuable cargoes in Ezion Geber, and transport all onward bound merchandise by camel caravans, which were a prime target for supporters of the anti-Phoenician, and anti-trade, policy of Ahab's successors. Hoping to circumvent these annoyances, Pharaoh Necho sent out an exploratory convoy to circumnavigate the Island of Libya, from east to west.

Ships of Tarshish III

The discovery of the so-called Pedra Lavrada inscription in Phoenician script engraved on stone occurred in Parahyba Province, Brazil, in 1886. A translation by Da Silva Ramos was published in French in 1939, and the following is an English rendering:
"This stone monument has been cut by Canaanites of Sidon who, in order to establish trading stations in distant lands, mountainous and arid, under the protection of the gods and goddesses, set out on a voyage in the nineteenth year of the reign of Hiram [i.e., 536 B.C.] our powerful king. They departed from Ashongaber in the Red Sea, after having embarked colonists in ten ships; and they sailed in company along the coast of Africa for two years. Subsequently they became separated from the flagship, and carried far away from their companions. Ten men and three women arrived here on this unknown coast. Of whom I, the unhappy Metu-Astarte, servant of the powerful goddess Astarte, have taken possession. May the gods and goddesses come to my aid."
This document, of which the original stone inscription is now apparently lost, has been declared a forgery by Professor Frank Cross of Harvard University. On the other hand, Professor Cyrus Gordon maintains its genuineness, and has issued a more recent translation. Since hundreds of obviously genuine inscriptions found in the United States have similarly been declared to be forgeries or marks made by plows or roots of trees, by persons who have not studied ancient inscriptions, there is no obvious reason at this time for doubting the authenticity of the Parahyba text.

Ill. 1. Parahyba inscription. Photo: Professor Barry Fell. (America BC, *Simon & Schuster, New York 1978, p.111*)

According to their records, they departed from a port on the Red Sea, and sailed south. When autumn came they landed, sowed grain, waited for the harvest, and then continued their journey. They returned to the Nile Delta, via the Pillars of Hercules (the Straits of Gibraltar), in the third year after leaving Egypt, and reported that on the voyage, as they rounded the southernmost tip of Libya (Africa) they had the sun on their right. This last detail, the reversed position of the sun, has been accepted as clear proof that this journey did in fact take place.

The success of this expedition was such that Pharaoh Necho instructed his engineers to build a canal connecting the Mediterranean with the Red Sea.[19] Accordingly a route was planned from the most easterly point of the Nile, near present day Es-Zahazig, to the sea near Ismailia. From there the canal rounded the Bitter Lakes, following roughly the course of the modern Suez Canal. The work commenced some time after 600 BCE. Shortly before this gigantic undertaking was completed, Pharaoh Necho was warned by an oracle that he was working for "the foreigner". Thinking that the Tyrians (the Phoenician traders of Tyre and Sidon) might derive greater benefit from the canal than his own fleet, which would indeed have been the case, he gave orders for the project to be abandoned. But it was never completely forgotten. In the 3rd century BC Ptolemy II put the canal in working order, and gave it a lock.[20] The last ruler to have the canal cleared of sand and put into workable condition was the Muslim general Amr ibm al-As, who conquered Egypt in AD 640.[21] Finally, in the 8th century AD, Necho's visionary enterprise fell into disuse. The inscriptions relating to this incredible feat of engineering, which was undertaken 2,400 years ago, are bluntly matter of fact. The task does not appear to have aroused the emotional response which attended the opening of de Lessep's modern Suez canal on 17th November 1869, with music by Verdi specially composed to commemorate this "epoch-making" event.

Earlier evidence of voyages around Africa is found in the Parahyba inscription, discovered in Brazil in 1886 (Ill. 1). Translated and published by da Silva in 1929, it was published again in an English translation by Dr Cyrus Gordon in 1971, with only minor differences. The text reads:-

> We are sons of Canaan from Sidon, the City of the King. Commerce has cast us on this distant shore, a land of mountains. We set (sacrificed) a youth for the exalted Gods and Goddesses in the nineteenth year of Hiram, our mighty king. We embarked from Ezion-Geber into the Red

Sea and voyaged with ten ships. We were at sea together for two years around the land belonging to Ham (Africa) but were separated by a storm (literally: from the hand of Baal) and we were no longer with our companions. So we have come here, twelve men and three women, on a ... shore, which I, the Admiral, control. But auspiciously may the Gods and Goddesses favour us.

Historically the reign of Hiram of Tyre who, in partnership with King Solomon, maintained a harbour for their fleet in the Comoro Islands, and a station on the island of Madagascar, is given as 970–936 BCE.[22]

The mention that the ship's company included men and women is in accord with what is known of those early sea voyages. It was routine for a priest (but more probably also a priestess) to accompany the maritime fleets, to attend to the essential offerings of prayers and sacrifices. The fact that other women were aboard was standard procedure, as Charles Boland explains in *They All Discovered America*: on long sea voyages women were always included in the ship's complement "for biological reasons".[23] And probably for the very practical reason that, should the vessel be forever stranded on foreign soil, at least the company would be in a position to propagate a new branch of the Motherland, with an unbroken continuation of traditions, language, culture and bloodline. A second inscription has been found near Rio. Three thousand feet up, on a vertical wall of rock are inscribed the words:-

Tyre, Phoenicia, Badezir, Firstborn of Jethbaal ...

This inscription is dated to the middle of the 9th century BCE.

By c. 500 BCE the descendants of the original Phoenicians who founded Carthage had destroyed the last Greek stronghold in Spain, and Carthaginian ships were in complete control of the entire western Mediterranean. For the following few centuries, until the Punic wars when the power of Carthage was finally destroyed, the Carthaginians prevented all foreign vessels from sailing past the Pillars of Hercules (the Straits of Gibraltar) into the Atlantic Ocean. They propagated a story that, beyond this point, the world came to an end. So convincing was the lie, that even the lyric poet Pindar, a contemporary of the voyaging Hanno, who sailed down the west coast of Africa, firmly believed it to be the truth.[24] In the meantime, in 470 BCE, the Carthaginian King Xerxes gave orders that the circumnavigation of Africa should be repeated, in the opposite direction, from west to east.

This was accomplished, apparently without undue effort.[25]

The main reason why so little is known of these early sea voyages of exploration and trade is because the sea routes were the lifelines of the economy. Every possible twist and turn was used to protect the trade routes, and the knowledge of sea-lanes, shoals and harbours was guarded as a sacred trust. The Phoenicians were masters of deception. They never revealed the sources of merchandise, and rarely left durable records of their voyages. Strabo tells of a Phoenician ship, which was being trailed by a Roman vessel, whose captain was determined to learn the location of certain Phoenician tin mines. The Phoenician captain deliberately sailed his ship into rocky waters, and both vessels were destroyed. The State rewarded him full compensation, the value of both his ship and cargo, for his dramatic action in countering industrial espionage.[26]

A relatively recent attempt to circumnavigate Africa was made by Eudoxos, a Greek mariner of repute from the Propontis island of Cyzicos. He was last heard of around AD 100, when he set out on his second attempt to reach India, by sailing around the Cape of Storms.[27]

The first Medieval European to sail around the infamous Cape was Bartholomew Diaz de Noveas (August 1487 AD), and the records of his voyage show his was not a journey into the unknown. He could only have accomplished what he did with the aid of well-prepared sea charts, and a map of the entire African coast. Unfortunately, by the time he reached present day Mossel Bay, he had a bad case of mutiny on board, and was obliged to return to Portugal in a hurry.

The theory that maps of the entire African coastline were available to those with the means to acquire such useful information is proven by the recent discoveries of very ancient but accurate portolanos (*portolano:* a book of sailing directions with descriptions of harbours, etc.). So accurate are these maps that, according to Professor Charles Hapgood in his *Maps of the Ancient Sea Kings,* they could only have been compiled from much older sources. The exploratory expeditions of Portugal's Prince Henry the Navigator down the west coast of Africa had only reached the site of present-day Lagos by 1471.[28] The cartographers took a further three years to reach Cape St Catherine, which lies only 8 degrees farther south of this point. Working at this rate, they could never have completed the detailed charting of the rest of the coast of Africa all the way around the Cape of Storms, to the east coast port of Sofala, lying near present day Beira, in Mozambique, by the date of 1487.

The next Portuguese mariner to round the Cape was Vasco da Gama. He set sail from Lisbon in July 1497, with four ships supplied by

King Emanuel of Portugal. His orders were simply to reach India. The records of this voyage mention that Bishop Diego Ortiz supplied him with books and maps. Also mentioned is that Abraham Zacuto—the brilliant Jew who had written the highly technical *Almanach Perpetum* in Hebrew, ten years earlier—trained the ship's officers in the art of making observations. The order given to da Gama was to reach India and to return home as soon as possible. There does not appear to have been any mention of surveying the coast, nor instructions to undertake any other kind of exploration, as would be expected of an expedition into the unknown. He and his fleet left Cape Verde Islands with the seasonal winds and, instead of hugging the coast, he sailed well out to sea, in a wide sweep to the west. He was out of sight of land from the Gulf of Guinea until only a few degrees north of his first landfall at St Helena Bay. He drew into land less than 300 kilometres north of the southernmost tip of Africa. Rounding the Cape, he too put in at Mossel Bay, and his crew also mutinied, but da Gama was a man of purpose. And his purpose was to reach India.

Accordingly he tricked the three chief seamen, the master, and the pilot, into signing a warrant for him to present to the king absolving him from blame for not completing the journey as planned. Completely satisfied, the officers signed, and the crew cheered. Vasco da Gama promptly ordered the pilot, the ship's master, and the three chief seamen to be clapped into irons for the remainder of the voyage, declaring that henceforth the ships would be steered by himself, and God, to India.[29] His diary details the voyage up the east coast of Africa, which he travelled with the confidence of a man who knew exactly where he was going. In 1498, en route to India, he visited Khor Fakkan, Dibba, and Ras Al-Khaimah in the Persian Gulf, and his report is the first known record of the area by a European.[30] He hired the renowned Arab navigator and seaman Ahmed Bin Majid, as pilot, reached India, and returned to Portugal in July 1499.

We know of da Gama's voyage because his records survived the voyage and were preserved with care. Unfortunately for science and historians, the records of earlier civilizations, and of their trade and maritime expeditions, were rarely found. Partly because mariners and merchants were very secretive about their routes, and partly because what was recorded has been lost, or deliberately destroyed, in the many wars of the past millennia. One of the most serious losses of historical material occurred when the library of Alexandria was destroyed.

The great library of Alexandria is said to have housed one million books. It was founded, around 300 BCE, by Alexander the Great, and is believed to have contained documents of the greatest antiquity, which had previously been jealously guarded in temples and vaults throughout the ancient world. These books contained the entire knowledge of antiquity—the technology, science, literature, and of course all the archaic esoteric, historical and commercial records of Egypt since earliest times. All this wisdom, and knowledge, was utterly destroyed. Hapgood states there must have been at least three burnings. The first, when Julius Caesar captured Alexandria, and met with stiff resistance from the citizens. In retribution, he burned the library, and then called a public meeting to explain to the enraged population that it was all their own fault because, by resisting him, they had caused the library to be burned. The second burning is thought to have taken place after the library had been restored and enlarged. According to Hapgood, the vandals this time were a mob of Christians who had been roused to mindlessly destructive hysteria by a most virtuous bishop. He claimed the burning of all those pagan teachings would be their salvation. Finally the library was thoroughly razed to the ground by the Muslim Arabs, after their invasion of Egypt in the 7th century AD. One of the stories relating to this catastrophe is that the newly installed Caliph said the Koran already contained all the wisdom of Islam, and that any other literature was of the infidel, and fit only for the inferno—so into the inferno the library went. [31]

Destroying the knowledge and wisdom of the enemy has ever been the pious duty of conquering heroes and prelates of all nationalities and sects. History records how the magnificent city of Carthage, the scourge of the Roman Empire, was totally destroyed by Roman troops in the year 146 BCE. The library was a prime target. This library was believed to have contained about half a million rolls of papyrus manuscripts recording the scientific, esoteric, historical and maritime knowledge of the ancient Phoenician and Carthaginian trading empires.[32]

The only reason we today know of the terrible destruction of the libraries of Alexandria and Carthage, is because somebody recorded the event, and this information was preserved for the future. How many other records have been lost, and are today unknown, because the records of their destruction have also been destroyed?

Nobody knows.

It is not even possible to guess at what has been lost through the damage regularly inflicted on historical places by religious, social, political, or military upheavals throughout the ages. Only tantalizing, and often unrelated, fragments of past achievements remain. Some of these fragments are physical objects, such as pottery, ruins, jewellery, weapons, tomb treasures and inscriptions, laboriously excavated by archaeologists, or unexpectedly unearthed one way or another, by chance.

Other knowledge is stored in the heart of folk tales and legends. Many an ancient city and many an answer to the purpose of a puzzling artefact, have been revealed by unravelling the threads of facts woven into half-remembered fables.

In the hallowed halls of conservative learning the unorthodox that approach history in this way, are contemptuously dubbed "lunatic fringers". A true "lunatic fringer" is rarely disturbed by the intended insult—there are so many things of interest going on in the life of a "lunatic fringer" that they can ignore the rumblings of jealous wrath from the Establishment. Not only do "lunatic fringers" defy convention by believing what is academically unacceptable but, with equal enthusiasm, they thrive on the theory of cultural diffusion. "Lunatic fringers" accept that no culture developed entirely independently of contact of a trading or raiding kind. Even if the trading was done by banging a gong to alert the customer, and then placing the goods in an open clearing, and retreating rapidly by ship, or behind a sheltering tree, in the manner of the Phoenicians—or the Papuans trading with their deadliest enemies.[33] Money is money, if it's a thing, it's got value, and these acts constitute a form of alien contact, and an interchange of ideas.

"Lunatic fringers" contend, if a tribe were technologically more advanced than other nomadic or settled groups whose paths they crossed, inevitably something of their own culture would rub off on the others whenever they made contact. It is a fallacy to assume that, simply because people appear less developed, they are less intelligent. Furthermore, this acceptance does not necessarily presume the cultural diffusion to be only from the so-called "superior" culture to the less developed one, but infers that a diffusion of ideas and ideologies, between migrants and others is inevitable. Each subtly alters his own concept as an exchange takes place through marriage, serfdom, trade, or observation of a different way of life.

Established archaeologists, and other academics, often attribute all widely separate cultural developments to an independent evolution, and usually hail the Collective Unconscious. One serious stumbling block to this overall theory of explaining every unexpected, or unusual, "primitive" development as the Collective Unconsciousness is that Cosmic, or telepathic thought, cannot be assimilated by those not able to comprehend the given mystery. The invention of the wheel is but one example of the failure in the system. Humanity's most useful

Ill. 2. Geometric patterns—zigzags, concentric circles, geometric patterns, and other apparently meaningless designs are, at worst, dismissed as "pre-school art, childish doodles". At best, they are passed over, and seldom recorded. These engravings are indeed enigmatic. They were intended to be enigmatic to all but initiates of the higher grades.

invention, the wheel, which was such an asset to the compulsively travelling Celts, was never put into practice by equally migrating Amerindians, the ever-wandering Maori, nor the San or Khoisan of Southern Africa. The Amerindians, at least, used a fire-wheel in rituals, but either never thought to put it to any further practical use, or believed such an invention could only cause disharmony among the people. It is nonsense to suggest they did not invent the wheel because they had so few possessions they were able to carry everything they owned on their backs, or piled on their hand/dog-drawn sleds. A more logical explanation is that the amount of property they owned was, of necessity, limited to what they could physically carry. This state freed them from the clutter of material possessions as status symbols, above all else, and allowed space for deeper spiritual awareness.

The majority of archaeologists are completely out of touch with pagan ways—many are downright agnostics. On the whole, they have no reverence for the Earth Mother, and cannot comprehend the esoteric purpose behind seemingly simple artefacts—in particular, the images engraved on rocks. Zigzags, circles, concentric circles, geometrical patterns, and other apparently meaningless designs are, at worst dismissed as "pre-school art, childish doodles". At best, they are passed over, and seldom recorded. These engravings are indeed enigmatic. They were intended to be enigmatic. For, like the truths woven into legends, these notations were, for the most part, sacred secret symbols intended to convey a meaning to the initiated only. In some places, they were designed to release the powerful Earth Forces (Ill. 2).

In *The Secret Country* Janet and Colin Bord have described Russian and Czech experiments with the concentric and zigzag patterns so often found on ancient stones throughout the world. The results of these experiments suggest the stones so engraved were once used as psychic generators. In addition to causing small wheels to turn, and to charging a rod, so that it is able to pick up non-ferrous metals and minerals, the energy released by these enigmatically engraved stones has been used in tests to increase plant growth, and even to slightly alter the molecular content of water. These engraved stones have also been used successfully in telepathy experiments.[34]

Further proof that engravings on rocks were not merely the doodles, or games, of bored herdboys, or a hunter's record of passing food, is provided by the fact that many stones were engraved where the carvings cannot be seen. At Newgrange (Ireland) and other sites in the British Isles, excavators found many stones that were first carefully engraved, then, equally carefully, buried. An association between secrecy and engravings on stone is not confined to pre-Celtic and Celtic engravings of Ireland and the British Isles.[35] Deliberately buried engraved stones, and large, polished boulders with engravings below surface level, or hidden in shadowed niches, are also a feature of many of the engraving sites of South Africa (Ill. 3).

The engraved slab illustrated here is but one of a pile of similar broken slabs of engraved rock which I saw, dumped to one side of a desecrated engraving site, near Maanhaarrand. On enquiring of the owner of the farm I was told that, despite his protestations, one of the university professors had stripped the site of "anything of worth", leaving behind virtually nothing but large boulders. And as he had been told that "nothing of worth" remained, the farmer ploughed out the remaining rocks, to uncover engraved slabs buried beneath some of the boulders. These, he said, had been broken during the excavations and, believing them also to be of no value, he dumped all the pieces on the perimeter of the ex-site. For all I know, they may be lying there still.

Who engraved these slabs, and when? For what purpose were they inscribed, then so deliberately buried? Only to be thrown away as "rubbish" thanks to the ignorance of a respected academic hell-bent on amassing "Bushman rock art" to the exclusion of knowledge. So often has this kind of mindless stupidity happened in the past, that it is no wonder so many misconceptions about the pre-colonial history of South Africa abound.

Therefore, to put perspective and truth into the things of Africa, to motivate a movement among historians and researchers to correct accumulated misconceptions about Africa, I have written this book. *Africa Through the Mists of Time* is about treasure-hunting into the past, through the medium of legends and rock engravings, to find the truth about the past.

Ill. 3. Fragment of but one of the many engraved slabs broken—and discarded as "rubbish"—when the farm owner ploughed out the remaining boulders at an engraving site, desecrated after a respected South African academic had removed "everything of value", despite protestations from the land owner. What wealth of historical records lie thus discarded throughout Southern Africa?

Chapter One

Through the Mists of Time

Even today Africa, the Great Mother, hides her secrets well. It is said, "There are many ways of telling a white man what he wants to know, without revealing the truth." Perhaps it was always so. Or perhaps it is because the missionaries, explorers, traders, hunters and colonists from the northern climes were, on the whole, so motivated by avarice, so blinded by prejudice, they were incapable of looking at the peoples and traditions and legends of Africa with the eyes of Africa.

The Portuguese were the first to trade with West Africa. In 1441, Antam Goncalvez was sent out, not to explore the African coastline as other captains had done for several years before him, but with instructions to ship a cargo of the hides and oil of the sea lions previous expeditions had reported sighting off the coast of Africa.[1] At that time Portugal was full of Moorish captives, but the market was still a good one. And so, hoping to please his royal master still further, Goncalvez and nine of his crew went ashore to capture some of the inhabitants of this unknown land. They succeeded in kidnapping a man and a woman, whom they presented to Prince Henry of Portugal. Thereafter, the need to know more about the resources of Africa led very quickly from the taking of prisoners for information, to the kidnapping of Africans to be sold for profit.

Sufficient to say, after a second successful raiding expedition, Prince Henry sent a special envoy to the Pope, explaining his plans for further raids and even conquest. The Pope, welcoming this new "crusade", granted "to all of those who shall be engaged in the said war, complete forgiveness of all their sins".[2]

The island of Arguim soon became famous in Portuguese slaving annals, and it was not long before this profitable trade caught the attention of Good Queen Bess of Merrie England. Never one to allow the Portuguese or Spaniards to corner a market, Queen Elizabeth I encouraged her seamen to muscle in on the Portuguese monopoly, on condition that the royal coffers received a right royal share of the profits of the Guinea trade.[3]

Up until this time, captured Africans were traded along with ivory, pepper, palm oil and gold, for the markets of Europe. It was not until the Portuguese and Spanish "liberation" of the West Indies and Central America that the demand for slave labour to work the new mines and sugar plantations, grew with frantic speed. The French were soon in the market, closely followed by the Dutch, Danes, Swedes and, later, the Prussians. An international battle for "African black gold" began. After 1640, with the expansion of European colonization of the Americas, a far larger work force was urgently required on which to build the newly established cotton plantations—which kept the mills of Britain turning. The market was bottomless, because the faster the survivors of the infamous "blackbirding ships" died while labouring in the fields or in the mines, the greater was the need to replace these human chattels. And so, from around 1450 to 1850, an estimated fifty million Africans were uprooted, shackled and shipped, mainly to the slave markets of the Americas.[4] The full story of the rape of Africa by slavers is to be found in *The Black Mother* by Basil Davidson. Sufficient to say, the breakdown of traditional values as Africans were "harvested" over a period of four hundred years, is incalculable. Time enough to bring about devastating moral decay and loss of oral history for the peoples of the west, central and southern areas of Africa.

On the east coast of Africa, the Portuguese, ever searching for the fabled Christian kingdom of Prestor John, destroyed the fabric of African life as far as they penetrated into the interior.[5]

In the south, the Dutch East India Company pragmatically built up their supply station, with the help of slaves from Angola and Malaysia, who lasted out the rigours of subjugation better than the Khoi or the San. While it is true there was almost no traffic in the sale of Khoi and San by the Dutch and German servants of the Dutch East India

Company or the Free Burghers, this was, again, a matter of economics, not Christian charity. Whereas slaves who had been purchased were relatively well cared for to protect the material assets of their owners, captive Khoi and San were expendable, because replacements were easily obtained. So for the most part they were indifferently treated, and often simply worked to death. In the Cape, slave owners were guided by the precepts of the Dutch Reformed Church. Slaves were to hear the Christian message, and it was customary for all the members of a household to gather together daily, to listen to a Bible-reading and prayers by the master of the house. But it was not permitted to allow slaves to be baptized, nor to teach them to read and write. Again, the reason was one of economics. For once slaves were baptized, and could read even a small portion of the Bible and write their name, they were effectively Christian, and must therefore be granted their freedom.[6] This policy was fiercely upheld and, until the takeover of the Cape by the British (1795 and again, for the second and last time, in 1805) missionaries, other than those of the DRC who abided by the rules, were effectively discouraged from visiting the settlement at the Cape. The Moravian missionary Georg Schmidt from Wuppertal (Germany) who, in 1737, set up his mission station at Genadendal, ran foul of the DRC when he not only taught his Khoi converts useful skills, and reading and writing, but baptized them as well. After ten years of struggle he gave up, and returned sorrowfully to Germany.[7]

As a direct result of the colonization of the Cape, in 1713, 1755 and 1767 three major smallpox epidemics swept through the settlements. The worst was the epidemic of 1713, caused by infected linen sent ashore from a ship returning from Batavia, to be laundered by the slaves of the Dutch East India Company.[8] Against this disease the Khoi were defenceless. How far inland the smallpox epidemic spread was never recorded. Smallpox could well have decimated the Khoi and the San living beyond the settled villages and outlying farms of the Dutch at the Cape. Perhaps the disease was even carried far into the interior, beyond the banks of the Orange and Vaal rivers, leaving vast areas of almost uninhabited country for later hunters and trekkers to pass through.

Thereafter the remaining independent clans in the southwestern Cape virtually disappeared. Some fled to the interior and joined renegade freebooters. Others returned to a hunter-gatherer existence, and many entered the colonial labour market. Thus forced to abandon their traditional way of life, these survivors became penurious and subservient guides, domestic workers, postmen, stock herders, transport riders and farm labourers.[9] The few who clung to their land and traditional way of life soon ran foul of the authorities. After the second occupation of the Cape by the British in 1805, more often than not these dispossessed unfortunates ended their days as convicts condemned to hard labour on the breakwater.

In 1870 nine San convicts, all from the Kenhardt district, were released from breakwater servitude and allotted to the German linguist, Dr W.H.I. Bleek, to serve in his household so that he could study their language. Dr Bleek worked chiefly on linguistic matters while his sister-in-law, Lucy Lloyd, transcribed their myths and accounts of traditional daily life. Together they compiled an astonishing total of 12,000 pages of research.[10] This work is today revered as the ultimate authority on the life and times of pre-colonial San, simply because it is virtually the only information on record. But the fact remains that the study was conducted on only nine San, all from the same district, two hundred and eighteen years after the first European settlers landed at the Cape, in 1652. In other words, the San and Khoi had already experienced contact, and trade, with Europeans for two hundred and eighteen years before Dr Bleek wrote the first of his 12,000 pages. In short, we know very little about the lives led by any of the indigenous peoples of Southern Africa, and their forefathers, before the advent of European exploration.

While for the most part the details of the daily life, beliefs and rituals of those pre-colonial peoples remain veiled, thanks to the research of Professor Westphal, in 1960, we now know there are no less than four distinct "Bush" languages, and several "Hottentot" languages. But relevant to any research into the identity of the people who engraved the rocks is the fact that Professor Westphal noted one previously unrecorded language, *Kwadi*. *Kwadi* is neither San, nor Khoi, nor is it related to any of the languages spoken by the black peoples of modern South Africa.[11] Who these people were, where they came from originally, or what happened to them, has apparently never been researched. But they too played their part on this stage. As did the Biri-kwa.

Towards the end of the 18th century, the explorer Hendrik Hop travelled northwards and reached a point one hundred and forty miles beyond the Orange River. The cattle- and sheep-owning Khoi, whom he met on the way, described a black-skinned, goat-keeping people in the further interior, who were named Biri-kwa (the Goat People). Further explorations to the north reached the site of present-day Kuruman, and the Biri-kwa, a Bechuana clan, by 1796.[12] Other records mention that by 1750 the Batlhaping were becoming a powerful group north of the Orange River, and that the most southerly chiefdom was the T'haping (or "Briqua", the Khoi name meaning "people of the goat"). From them the Khoi came to know, and tame, the boerbok. Until the beginning of the nineteenth century, the T'haping were a large, very wealthy chiefdom, with a great number of livestock, and they learned the use of bows and arrows from the San. These little snippets of history could well go unnoticed, but for the fact that on a hillock not far from Vryburg is an engraving depicting a procession of tall men, with very muscular legs. The central figure wears a tall headdress, and carries a bow. Behind him strides a much smaller male, possibly pygmy or San. All are naked, except for the tailed human male figure bringing up the rear (Ill. 4).

Ill. 4. A procession of naked males, the central figure wears a towering headdress and carries a bow. Traditionally, men and boys always wore a penis covering of some sort specifically as a protection against the entrance of "evil". The only exception was if the men were engaged in ritual practices, certain funeral rites, or magic.

Elsewhere, on the apex of the hillock, is a most enigmatic engraving depicting a five-horned female rhino in association with several, lithesome, naked youths. African youths and men never went about

Ill. 5. Youth wearing a round penis covering, a pointer perhaps to the possibility that this engraving site, at least, was a centre for rituals such as the traditional circumcision schools when youths were instructed in the law and lore of their society. Initiation ceremonies and circumcision schools are traditionally linked to the cycles of the moon, and start with a new moon. In addition to the physical ordeal of the removal of the foreskin, the purpose of the initiation schools was to give the youths full sexual instruction, to teach them the laws of their people, and to leave them in no doubt about their place in society as the responsible parents of future generations.

totally naked. They always wore a penis sheath of some kind, to prevent the entrance of evil. Amongst the Khoi and San, complete nudity was certainly not the norm among adults, and even children over the age of one year wore genital coverings. The exception to this practice was when people were engaged in ritual practices, certain funeral rites, or magic. Therefore the pictures of naked youths and men on the rocks cannot, by any stretch of the imagination, be interpreted as a record of simple herders or hunters[13] (Ill. 5).

Relevant to the mention of the goat-keeping Biri-kwa or Briqua, on the same rock but to the right of the rhino above, is the engraved image of a naked youth who, unlike the San, has large hands and feet. He is surrounded by baboons, and in a corner of the slab is clearly engraved the head and raised foreleg of a goat. Other pictographs at this site leave no doubt that here was a centre where fertility rituals were conducted, by African peoples, who are certainly not in the likeness of the San from Kenhardt studied by Dr Bleek (Ill. 6).

The concept created by researchers in the field of rock art that the engravings of animals were hunting magic practised by primitive San or Khoi hunter-gatherers, slipped easily into general acceptance. So too the belief that the San did not practise fertility rites.

Researchers claimed that the lack of rock art depicting mating, human pregnancy, or birth, was proof that the San never practised rituals for the increase of life. Maybe this was true of the San—but if so, then who were responsible for the very graphic engravings of human male and female copulation, and the pictographs clearly depicting pregnant animals? Not to mention the many symbols relating to the cycles of the moon, giver of rain and of life (Ill. 7, 8, 9, 10)?

It is most curious that all the rock engravings are officially, and definitively, described as "Bushman art". For, according to the records, the San themselves said they did not know who the early rock engravers were.[14] A most likely response, as the life of truly nomadic hunters is not favourable for art, which requires rest and a semi-permanent home.[15] Perhaps this misconception arose because Europeans noted that many of the engravings portray animals, and because the San are classified as "hunters and gatherers", the images of animals caught the eye. Therefore it was assumed that the images of animals could only be the work of hunters whiling away their time, while waiting for a meal to wander past. At this point, after declaring "the Bushmen" rock engravers supreme, the collective academic mind stalled— "don't confuse us with facts, our mind is made up!"

On the surface, to a Western mind unconditioned to seeing things from an African viewpoint, this assumption is logical. But nothing could

Ill. 6. Although not central to the many images engraved on this large rock, the head and raised foreleg of the goat – right foreground – could surely have been the signature of the Biri-kwa or Briqua, otherwise known as the "Goat-people". In early Crete a goat cult preceded the bull cult, and in Greek myths the centaurs are said to have been goat-men originally. Note the baboons surrounding the youth, and his flat head. In African lore the baboon was greatly respected for its wisdom.

Ill. 7. Virility and fertility is what the continuation of all life is all about. Despite denials from the majority of rock art experts that fertility rituals were not practised by the San, because no such evidence exists in their rock art, yet life must go on however blind the academic world. Clearly the annual spring/new year mating of the High Priestess and the Sacred King, or the Earth Goddess and the Sky/Sun god is depicted in this graphic engraving.

Ill. 8. After conception, pregnancy.

Ill. 9. Birth, the natural completion of pregnancy after the completion of the gestation period of ten lunar months, for humans, cattle and eland. In ancient times, throughout the world an image depicting birth was recognized as a powerful symbol of the Great Mother. Birth scenes are rarely found at South African engraving sites, but here the final stage in begetting life is clearly illustrated.

Ill. 10. The birth of young completes the triad of mother, father and child. This engraving, worked on a pelvis-shaped rock, and incorporating as it does the image of a family group, includes an inscription, which has been recognized as Ogam. But there could be much more to this picture, for the shadows of the human figures converge into an image of a person lying as if dead, or the emergence of spirit. For in Old Africa many people visualized God the Creator as a trinity – God the Father, God the Mother, and God the Son.

be further from the truth. Because of the dangers to be faced, and the possibility of the accidental death of the hunter, many taboos and rituals were linked to hunting. In addition, before a hunt the spirit of the animal chosen to die was prayerfully, and respectfully, propitiated, to prepare it for death. Then an impermanent image of the animal to be killed was drawn on the sand, with the invocation that the animal anticipates its death.[16] It is said such an animal often turned from the herd, and walked deliberately towards the hunters, as if self-chosen to die.

After a successful hunt, portions of the liver and skin of the slain animal were laid respectfully down within the sand drawing, covered over, and the picture then wiped out with a prayer that the spirit of the slain return, in time, to repopulate the herd. Thus encompassing the pagan African belief in the endless cycle of birth, life, death, and rebirth. Not by accident were portions of the liver and skin included in this invocation, for these two organs—animal and human—continually regenerate throughout the lifetime of the body. Had the hunters engraved a permanent image of the projected prey on a rock, it would have defeated the possibility of rebirth—the return of its spirit to the herd—because the spirit would then remain forever fixed to the stone.

Deeper insight reveals that the animals most frequently portrayed are the once-sacred animals of Africa—the eland, the elephant, the ostrich, the zebra, the giraffe, the rhino, the baboon—revered, and killed ritually and respectfully (See Appendix). Traditionally, these animals were not slaughtered as food for the sake of filling empty bellies—certainly, very few eland bones have been recovered from middens. Tortoises were the commonest single item of diet in Southern Africa, and I have never seen a rock engraving depicting a tortoise.[17] Nor was there ever an African tradition of slaughtering game, European fashion, for trophies displaying the sheer pleasure of killing.

Even more important than the pictographs of animals are the enigmatic symbols incised into the hard rock surfaces. The rocks are hard, dolerite and striated amygdaloidal diabase, and allied rocks of the Pniel series predominate. Incising the surface takes time, strength, and a writing tool with a point considerably harder than the rock. The effort required to peck or gouge images into stone is surely an indication of purposeful effort on the part of the scribes. In other words, it must be accepted that the apparently inexplicable symbols were not only meaningful to the scribes, but possibly also powerful invocations for the prosperity, and regeneration, of all life—human, animal, vegetation, and mineral. Minerals, spewed from the womb of

Mother Earth, were especially prized, and to each were accorded mystical or magical properties.

In Africa, Mother Earth was envisaged as a living creature, and rocks were revered as "the bones of the Earth Mother"—a concept shared by the early Greeks.[18] In Africa the invisible world presses hard on the visible, this is one of the most fundamental religious heritages of the African peoples. To the peoples of Africa, God is in everything and of everything. And never were Africans "ancestor worshippers", but rather in the Christian sense of worshipping God through the good graces of Mother Mary, or any of the legions of saints. In traditional African religion the ancestors were, and are, envisaged as the link between those living on earth and the rising phalanx of ever more senior ancestral spirits depended on, by the living, to conduct their supplications to the Most High.[19]

To ensure the harmonious progression of the seasons, good rains in their season and fair skies for the growth of grass for the cattle, and fruit and herbs, the spirits of the ancestors, and the nature spirits were respectfully petitioned. In Australia every species of animal and plant had its own increase centres, where essential rituals were conducted to release the life essence of the various species.[20] In the Middle East the fertility deities, Ea, El, Baal, were also attached to specific centres, and not to any particular clan, as are churches, mosques and temples today. (The name *Baal* occurs in the Hyksos period of Egypt; to the Egyptians of the XIX Dynasty; and Baal was a well-known Semitic deity[21]). In Africa, too, were sacred shrines at rivers, groves, mountains and rocks where people gathered to honour and pray to ancestral and nature spirits. Rocks, the Bones of the Earth Mother, were especially favoured, for it was believed that spirits clung to rocks and rocky hillocks.[22] It is mainly on rocky hillocks, and on the outcrops of great slabs of glaciated paving, where the rock engravings of South Africa are clustered.

So, what manner of person inscribed the rocks? Well, it has been established that the older, more perfectly executed engravings were the work of holy men, priests, or as is more likely, priestesses. For among the Berbers women were the rock artists.[23] That women were the scribes is the more likely, for only men initiated into the higher mysteries would dare to break the flesh covering of a bone of the Earth Mother by engraving a rock. Before the destruction of traditional values, the men of Africa, as also the men of the Amerindian tribes, did not do mining, tunnel, dig holes, nor hoe a garden. That was women's work. Not because the men were lazy layabouts, but out of respect and fear of angering the Earth Mother, thus invoking drought and disease on their community.[24]

Even in South Africa today, men going down to work in the mines, make special sacrifices before leaving their rural homes, to ensure they do not incur the wrath of Mother Earth.[25] Evidence of the terrible fear aroused by the need to descend into the depths of the earth in order to earn money to support a family is everywhere manifest. Pushed into crevices in the underground are coins, substitute offerings to propitiate the Earth Mother, from those who were unable to make the necessary blood sacrifices before entering the mines. For this reason, in antiquity, women and children were the miners, and it has been recorded that the skeletons found in ancient mine workings are those of women and children.[26]

No "man-in-the-street" hunter-gatherer would ever have dared to scratch an image on a rock, however prayerfully, lest the whole community suffered for his arrogance. Community life was just that, the individual gave way to the needs of all. There was no concept of individual desires, ego, or self-first, in the European way. In many ways, the pagan Africans were far more civilized, in the true meaning of the word, than the settlers from abroad.

So sacred was the art of engraving in ancient times, that in Greece special sacrifices were offered before an image was made, and again after it was completed, when the engraving tool was ritually destroyed.[27] As a diviner-healer once told me, 'When I make a cut into the body of a patient, and rub in the herbs, I don't just rub the medicine in. I pray it in. I talk to the herbs telling them to strengthen the patient and fight the disease. And I talk to the disease, telling it to leave the body, making the patient whole again. It is the same with the engravings. They were not done just like that—scratch, scratch, there is the picture! No! The holy ones who made the pictures on the rocks of our land did so with prayer, madam. With prayer!'

Archaeologists have noted that the engraving sites do not appear to have been living areas.[28] Of course they weren't. Stonehenge was never a living area, nor was Callanish, the Ring of Brogar, Mystery Hill (USA), nor other ancient monuments worldwide where engraved stones have been recorded. They were sacred centres where rituals, and ceremonies for the procreation of all life, were earnestly conducted. So too, I believe, were the engraving sites of Southern Africa. The engravings attest to this. The animal most frequently portrayed in African rock art is the eland (Ill. 11, 12). Had this been a diet-related matter, then middens would have been strewn with eland bones. But it is not so, in fact very

Ill. 11. Eland, could this exquisite depiction of the revered animal of the moon really be classed as "the doodle of herd-boys and hunters"?

Ill. 12. Central to this peaceful vista of youths offering food to a pregnant animal in a sylvan setting, is the engraving of an eland on the rim of a basin deliberately worked into the centre of the rock. Rainfall in this region is limited to occasional summer squalls and thunderstorms, so there is no possibility that the depression below the eland is the result of natural weathering.

Ill. 13. (left)   Moon numerals. This small, crude engraving is surely a record of the gestation period of ten lunar months, common to humans, cattle, and eland.

Ill. 14 (right)   The zigzag symbol is internationally recognized as a symbol for water/rivers/life, and the squared rectangle has been identified internationally as an earth symbol, or symbolic grid pattern – the basic agricultural grid.

few eland bones have ever been found—one reference mentions only one set of eland bones so far discovered. And the San legends say that the eland was the first created, and the most beloved animal of Kaggen, and that when a hunter killed an eland, Kaggen did not love them. Clearly, then, eland were not viewed as prey. Therefore it can only mean that eland were hunted and killed ritually, as is evident from a rainmaking song of the Tswana, which calls for the death of an eland.[29] Other pointers to my belief that the engraving sites were sacred centres, are the many ithyphallic images, moon-related numerals, and fertility symbols (Ill. 13, 14, 15, 16).

The occurrence of moon-related notations is nothing new to Africa. A bone engraving tool, with a quartz point, embellished with notations linked to the cycle of the moon, was found at Ishango and dated to around 8500 BP.[30]

Ill. 15. Symbols identical to the South African rock engraving in the previous illustration, depicting a zigzag and symbolic grid pattern, are incorporated in this American artefact. Known as the Georgia Elephant Disc, this small clay disc—about 4 centimetres in diameter —was found in a creek eight km (five miles) north of Ludowici, Georgia, USA. This disc raised as many questions as solutions, and has been identified as of Indian or Asiatic origin. However, it is also possible that the design was inspired by an African who escaped from slavery, bringing to America African earth symbols and representations for earth/ rain/water/life—the grid pattern, the elephant, and the zigzag.

The shamans, who were the engravers, were the spiritual leaders, healers, and diviners of their peoples. In the work of the diviner, great importance is attached to sexuality and related symbols and, as I have indicated, many of the pictographs are overtly sexual.[31] After all, sexuality is what virility, fertility, and procreation are all about. And fertility rituals are not only for the continuation of the human species, but also for the procreation of all life—human, animal, vegetable and mineral—to ensure the cycles of life, in their seasons. The mineral connection is very significant because, in Southern Africa, as elsewhere in the world, the majority of the engraving sites are located near mineral outcrops.

In Scotland researchers have noted the presence of engravings close to deposits of tin or gold. In ancient Egypt, engraved rocks are found near the ancient turquoise mines of Sinai.[32]

So also in South Africa, where the greatest concentration of rock engraving sites are found in the areas of diamond-bearing alluvial gravels, or near outcrops of red ochre/iron ore, steatite/soapstone (the material most sought after for temple ware and holy statues). And, very significantly, as we shall see later, there exists a line of what has been described as "Bushman artefacts and engravings from Egypt to the Cape",[33] mostly occurring in the vicinity of diamond-bearing gravels.

Ill. 16. The ultimate fertility symbol—a male penis and scrotum. And it is pointing to the right, the direction of life. And in case of any doubt about the intention of the artist to create a representation of the fertilizing power of semen—human and animal—the figure of a virile male is positioned above and to the left.

The existence of clusters of engravings occurring in the near vicinity of mineral deposits; the presence of recognizable script; the perfection of the earlier engravings with no evidence of preliminary sketches; and the knowledge that those who incised the rocks were of the priestly caste, points inescapably to the likelihood that well-organized, literate people were profitably mining a variety of minerals in South Africa in pre-historic times. Literate they certainly were, for Professor Barry Fell translated an ancient Libyan inscription, written in Ogam, from Driekopseiland which reads:- "Under constant attack we have quit this place to occupy a safe stronghold"[34] (Ill. 17). In the hill above this site are ancient ruins, a "rock gong", which looks like a dolman, and an outcrop of hematite. Hematite was widely used for many ritual purposes, including burials with the hope of re-birth into the clan and hematite, which is used as a pigment and as a polishing powder, is also iron ore. The Ogam inscription translated by Barry Fell is not a singular occurrence, for I have recorded other examples of this most ancient script at the same site (Ill. 18).

Through the Mists of Time

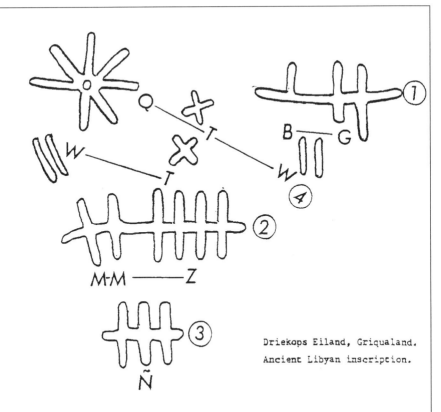

Driekops Eiland, Griqualand.
Ancient Libyan inscription.

Decipherment

(1) Inverse ogam: G-B (Arabic giba) under constant attack
(2) Inverse ogam: Z-M-M (Arabic zimam) this place
(3) Inverse ogam: N (Arabic na') have quit
(4) Numidian script: W-T-Q (Arabic wataq) a safe place, stronghold
T - W (Arabic tawa) to occupy.

"Under constant attack we have quit this place to occupy a safe stronghold."

Data from photograph by Lina M. Slack, Rock Engravings from Driekops Eiland, Centaur Press, London, 1962, p. 75).

Ill. 17. Translation of an inscription from Driekopseiland by Professor Barry Fell.

The use of Ogam, known as "the tic-tac hand language of witches" in the Medieval times, is as African as it is Celtic, and will be further discussed in a later chapter on the Afro-Celtic connection. For the moment the focus is on the suggestion that diamonds were being mined, in South Africa, in pre-historic times.

Diamonds indeed! In the following chapter the probability of ancient diamond miners in South Africa is fully explored. But for the moment let us go back to the first discovery of diamonds in South Africa, and the fable attached to it. Starting with the fact that diamonds—stones of the sun—were not unknown to the Khoi and the San, and others who used them in a most practical way.

African hunting stories tell of a time when the San drew the tall, far-seeing giraffe within arrow range by concealing themselves in a bush, and directing towards their prey sun-enlivened, glittering flashes of the "magic stone" they carried for this purpose. Unable to resist the sparkling lure, the inquisitive animals were enticed to their death.[35]

Only a rough diamond could have that attraction. Pieces of unpolished quartz, or crystal, have a nice shiny surface, but they pale against the lambent fire of a rough diamond. When diamond diggers sort the glistening, wet, gravitated gravels, they ensure that shade covers the sorting table. Because, of all the semi-precious gemstones present in the alluvial gravels in the rough state—the crystals, topaz,

Ill. 18. An as yet untranslated inscription from the same site, recorded by Brenda Sullivan.

garnets, corundum—only a diamond in its natural state shimmers with inner fire in the shade. In sunlight, no other gem has the fire of a diamond. And why should the hunters not have used these glittering, hard-but-brittle pieces of carbon for such a labour-saving purpose? So brainwashed by marketing ploys have people become, that few are aware how relatively easy it once was to find a diamond. In South Africa, diamonds of all shapes and sizes were lying around waiting to be picked up, wherever alluvial gravels surfaced, or had been washed into the rivers.

One fallacy is the naïve belief that diamonds are valuable because they are rare. Diamonds rare? Not at all! This form of carbon was spewed out of the bowels of Mother Earth, by volcanic action, worldwide. Diamonds occur in Siberia, Australia, the United States of America, India, Borneo, Indonesia, Tanzania, West Africa, Congo, Central African Republic, Botswana, Lesotho, Namibia, Angola, South Africa, Guyana, Venezuela and Brazil. The well-advertised rarity of these stones has been a market manipulating technique, conducted in earnest, since the diamond moguls, the Rand Lords, gained control of the diamond market after the first kimberlite outcrop was discovered in South Africa in 1871.

It is really only fairly recently, since the discovery of diamonds in Brazil and South Africa, that diamonds have been amassed by status-seeking socialites as outward and visible signs of their monetary wealth—the glittering entrance calculated to draw gasps of awe, and envy, from business associates and rivals. Our modern evaluation of diamonds, based on the all important three Cs, clarity, cut, and colour, is made with little thought for the mystical qualities of these "stones of the sun". In antiquity, the three Cs were secondary to the properties attributed to jewels, and many were the beliefs and legends linked to "stones of power." Certainly, diamonds have mystique, and they vibrate on a very powerful frequency. Stories, legends, beliefs and superstitions about diamonds are many, but diamonds themselves are not rare. Today clever advertising and marketing strategies restrict supplies, and keep prices high. On this matter I can speak with the authority of personal experience.

For fourteen long years, from 1970–1984, I lived as the wife of a diamond digger in Bloemhof, and later at Boskuil—literally on the residential reserve of the diamond diggings at Boskuil—of the region then known as the far Western Transvaal (today the North West Province). After the accidental death of my husband, at his claim in 1984, I continued as a diamond digger in my own right, until 1986.

Ill. 19. During the 1970s Friday was "Buyer's Day" at Boskuil (North West Province). On Fridays diamond diggers and licensed buyers converged on the cluster of corrugated iron shacks which served as the local diamond "market place", to haggle with the licensed diamond buyers for the best price for their week's "finds". Believe it or not, but on occasion hundreds of thousands of rands changed hands in these primitive offices.

Diamond selling, and buying, is like horse-trading. When I lived there, in the 1970s and early 1980s, Friday used to be "market day" at Boskuil. It was the day diggers gathered at Boskuil, to haggle with the legal diamond buyers from all over the country, who converged on this outpost of man's greed and deceit, to trade with the licensed diamond diggers, as opposed to the illicit diamond buyers, the diamond smugglers who actively traded throughout the week (Ill. 19)!

Honest diggers who were not able to "get their price" from the Friday buyers at Boskuil, headed for the Saturday morning diamond market at Barkly West, or for the offices of De Beers in Kimberley. One Saturday, disheartened by the poor prices offered for his weekly parcel of "finds", my late husband, Harry Sullivan, took his stones to the De Beers buyer in Kimberley. It had been a bad week for us, and apparently also a bad week for the mighty De Beers.

The buyer eyed Harry's "finds", and shrugged, "I don't know! What can I offer you on these? What is the parcel worth to me? What is it worth to you? Everything is relative, I tell you. Have you ever seen a shit-house full of diamonds? No? Come!" With that, he led my bemused husband down the corridor to what in normal times would have been one of the toilet facilities, threw open the door, and said, "See for yourself! We haven't any more space in our storerooms to keep the stuff." Taking up every possible space in the "shit-house" were boxes upon boxes, packed almost to overflowing with sorted, classified, uncut diamonds. To be held until such time as the overseas market prices could be induced to improve.

There is no doubt, in my mind anyway, that a close association with trading in rough diamonds definitely affects people adversely. Diamonds bring out the worst human characteristics, all of the seven deadly sins, in particular greed and unscrupulous dealings at every stage of the game. Experienced diggers seldom speak about their finds, to anyone—not to their spouses, their minister, and not even to their bank manager, for fear of gossip. So it is not surprising to find, on closer inspection, that the pretty story of the discovery of the "first" South African diamond in South Africa is just that—a pretty story based firmly on well presented half-truths. According to this tale, the stone was picked up by fifteen-year-old Erasmus Jacobs in December 1866—or February 1867, accounts differ—who gave it to his younger sister to play with. In his old age Erasmus Jacobs admitted that, when he found this diamond, a Hottentot (Khoi) who was employed by his father, was standing near by.[36]

Other sources give credit to Schalk van Niekerk of "De Kalk", a farmer who, with the encouragement of von Ludwig, the government surveyor, was already studying geology and quietly prospecting the area in the hope of finding diamonds.[37] The story relates how Schalk van Niekerk found children playing with the stone, recognized it as a diamond and entrusted it to John O'Reilly, an itinerant trader, for evaluation.

There is no doubt that van Niekerk and O'Reilly were the first to draw international attention—and later, hordes of hopeful diamond diggers from around the world—to the alluvial diamond fields of South Africa. It is a fine story indeed. But the conflicting accounts of how the first diamond, a 21.25-carat stone (eventually to be known as the "Eureka"), and the second (the 83.25 "Star of Africa"), were found, indicate that this pretty tale about the stone being accidentally picked up by children was something of a cover-up. And, because I know from personal experience that lying, cheating, and even murder, are an integral part of the "diamond game", I looked for the truth behind the reality of their discovery. Research reinforced my belief that diamonds were recognized, and valued, as "magic" stones by the indigenous peoples of Southern Africa long before the coming of the first Europeans.

Folk tales should always be viewed in context so, when reading about the discovery of the Eureka and Star of Africa, it is important to remember that the first two diamonds were found in 1866/67, a time when law enforcement in the northern districts was very difficult to implement. To go back a little earlier in the history of the country, slavery was abolished in South Africa in 1833. Embittered, slave owners claimed they had suffered considerable financial loss because the emancipation of the slaves was enforced at a time when a labour force was needed for the harvest. Angry at the British government for imposing restraints on their way of life, and loudly proclaiming that the compensation they had been offered was unrealistic, many of the European settlers began a great exodus, from the Cape Colony into the interior of South Africa, around 1835–1836.[38] Living by their own laws, taking what they wanted at will, and by force of arms, they added to the misery of all the indigenous peoples themselves already dispossessed by droughts, smallpox epidemics, and the marauding hordes of the *Mfecane* (*Difaqane* or *Lifaqune*). There followed a time of great unrest, uncertainty and upheavals. Life was even worse for the surviving remnants of the nomadic Khoi and San hunters and gatherers, who were absorbed into the households of the land-usurping settlers. Although seldom enslaved, at best they were looked upon as expendable labourers, and not infrequently simply worked to death! Things were no different around Hopetown in 1866–1867, where the infamous practice of *inboeking*, the forced servitude of captured San and Khoi children, also flourished. The children were "rescued" after their villages had been raided by the settlers, registered with the presiding magistrate as the property of whomever had captured them, hence the term "inboeking", and then they were put to work as indentured servants.[39]

While living on the diamond diggings at Boskuil, I learned from the wife of a local diamond digger how her grandfather was party to the shooting of San, as they ran across the veld. Herself the fifth generation of the first settlers who established farms in the area, she said, "Those Bushmen were just wild animals, giving us a lot of trouble." Even today few see the dispossessed San as "people".

So let us take another look at contemporary accounts of the discovery of the now famous 21.5-carat "Eureka", and the even more exciting 83.5-carat "Star of Africa" for, before they fell into the hands of Schalk van Niekerk, both are said to have been the property of San, or Khoi "witchdoctors".

The Cape of Good Hope Official Handbook, published in 1886, gives the following account of the discovery:-

> Early in the year 1867, a trader named John O'Reilly, travelling southwards from the Orange River, rested his oxen at the farm 'De Kalk', the property of one Schalk van Niekerk, in the Hope Town district: and this is Mr O'Reilly's account of what he saw there, given in a letter addressed some five years later to the Governor of the Cape Colony, Sir Henry Barkly:-
>
> "In March, 1867, I was on my way to Colesberg from the Junction of the Vaal and Orange Rivers; I outspanned at Mr Niekerk's farm, where I saw a beautiful lot of Orange River stones on his table, and which I examined. I told Niekerk they were very pretty. He showed me another lot, out of which I at once picked the 'first diamond'. I asked him for it, and he told me I could have it, as it belonged to a Bushman boy of Daniel Jacobs. I took it at once to Hope Town, and made Mr Chalmers, Civil Commissioner, aware of the discovery. I then took it on to Colesberg, and gave it to the Acting Civil Commissioner there for transmission to Cape Town to the High Commissioner. The Acting Civil Commissioner sent it to Dr Atherstone, of Graham's Town, who forwarded it to Cape Town.
>
> "Dr Atherstone wrote back to the Colesberg Commissioner—Mr Lorenzo Boyes, who is still a member of the Civil Service in another part of the Colony—"I congratulate you on the stone you have sent me. It is a veritable diamond, weighs 21.25 carats, and is worth 500 pounds. It has spoiled all the jewellers' files in Graham's Town, and where that came from there must be lots more."

The report continues:-

> It may be imagined that Messrs Boyes and O'Reilly, who shared the proceeds of this sale, were well satisfied with their bargain. They lost no time in returning to the scene of the first discovery, where others soon joined in the exciting search, but the success was so small that for another two years the existence of diamond fields in South Africa continued to be disputed. However, in 1869, van Niekerk secured from a Griqua or Hottentot a large stone for which he gave the sum of 400 pounds or livestock to about that value, and which he sold directly after to Messrs Lilienfeld of Hope Town for over 10,000 pounds. This was the famous

"Star of South Africa". It weighed 83.5 carats in the rough, and was estimated in June 1870 to be worth 25,000 pounds. It has been cut, and now figures amongst the jewels of the Countess of Dudley, its present weight being 46.5 carats.[40]

Four further sources mention that these stones had been obtained from San or Khoi. *Diamonds* by Eric Bruton relates that, in his old age, Erasmus Jacobs admitted that when he came into possession of the stone "a Hottentot who was employed by his father mainly to look after sheep was standing near by". George Kunz in *The Curious Lore of Precious Stones* writes: "It is said that the first large diamonds discovered by Europeans in South Africa were found in the leather bag of a sorcerer." Again in *The Seven Wonders of Southern Africa*, Hedley Chilvers says the 83.5-carat "Star of Africa" was "secured from a Hottentot by the same farmer who had disposed of the first diamond." In *Shovel and Sieve* Eric Rosenthal touches on the life of Scott Alexander who described the "Star of South Africa" as "the big stone that was bought from a witchdoctor, exhibited in a shop window in Cape Town."[41]

A not improbable claim, for I have heard weathered diamond diggers tell how, in the early days of diamond prospecting in South Africa, "the easiest way to get diamonds was to find the cache hidden in the walls of a witchdoctor's hut". Since ancient times, diamonds have been valued by African shamans as "Stones of the Sun"—valued not in terms of monetary wealth, but for the strange powers these brilliant pieces of carbon are believed to possess.

Surely it was not only coincidence which led prospectors to the rich deposits of diamonds near Mafikeng and Jwaneng? For the traditional names, *Mafikeng* and *Jwaneng*, mean literally *the Place of the Stones*.

Chapter 2

Ancient diamond miners?

Witchdoctors hoarding diamonds? Even if they did, or still do, what does that matter in today's world? It does matter, because the past steers the future. And to discover the truth about the past of the peoples of South Africa makes for better understanding of the present.

The past does not merely relate to pieces of broken pottery and such in museums, nor to the hundreds of ruined stone buildings and walls scattered around the country. It also includes the strange, and unexplained, objects recovered from the depths of the alluvial diamond gravels, by privately working, licensed diamond diggers. Many of those oddities certainly deserved a closer study than the brief exclamation of surprise by the digger, before being thrown away for lack of interest. For surely those "finds" were valuable evidence of the prehistoric people—"die oermense"—some of whom, I believe, worked the diamond fields long ages before the coming of settlers from western Europe. Diamonds have been valued for millennia, as is evident from the legend of the Koh-i-noor. The history of that famous diamond goes back 5,000 years, and is celebrated in the songs of the Vedas as having formed part of the treasures of an Indian raja.[1]

For the majority of people, the history of the diamond industry goes no further than a vague idea that, before new fields were opened up in

Brazil around 1717, and subsequently in South Africa, all diamonds came from India. The better to understand the complexity of the subject, let us first look at the origin of these glittering stones—kimberlite. For volcanic kimberlite, pipes are the source of all diamonds.[2] Alluvial diamond fields were formed when material from kimberlite pipes was carried from source, and spread out over the surface of the earth by the action of water. The diamond-bearing lava was named "kimberlite" after the town of Kimberley in South Africa, where kimberlite was first identified by geologists from Europe.[3]

Kimberlite pipes occur throughout Southern Africa, yet not all kimberlite pipes contain diamonds.[4] Although the majority of the kimberlite pipes so far prospected have been found to be barren of diamonds, the other minerals recovered from non-diamondiferous kimberlite—the jasper, quartz, topaz, garnets, crystals, agates, ironstones, "ertjies", "silkies" (corundum), etc.—are otherwise identical to the material recovered from diamond-bearing kimberlite. In other words, there is no easy way of differentiating between diamond-bearing kimberlite, and a "dead" pipe. Only hard work, excavating, washing, sorting—and praying, diggers are very devout—will eventually prove the pipe, one way or the other. Often, to discover the presence of diamonds, it is necessary to excavate to some considerable depth before abandoning a kimberlite pipe as unprofitable. This procedure is most necessary in sources such as the Monastery mine, where diamonds are few, and widely distributed.

If the records of the indefatigable prospector, Dr Percy Wagner, are to be believed, miners were working the kimberlite of the Monastery mine in ages past. In his book *The Diamond Fields of Southern Africa*, Dr Wagner recorded that, while prospecting the Monastery mine, they discovered the existence of ancient workings. Then, at a depth of about twelve metres, they found two human skeletons. Dr Wagner particularly mentioned that, had the Basuto been mining there for ilmenite, which he believed they used for personal adornment, or for any of the semi-precious stones associated with kimberlite—the garnets, water crystals, agates, jasper, yellow and red ochre, corundum—they could have collected any quantity right near the surface. The presence of the ancient workings, and the skeletons, completely mystified him and his report concludes, "and the true nature and object of the workings thus remains a mystery".[5]

Today the Monastery mine is considered an unprofitable source because, although the diamonds recovered are large and of good quality, they are few and far between. Therefore, the evidence of skeletons at a depth of twelve metres can only mean that in ancient times miners were able to identify kimberlite as the source of diamonds, and that people were actively engaged in working the pipe at the Monastery mine, specifically to extract diamonds.

Dr Wagner was not the only person to discover evidence of prehistoric diamond miners. In the mid-1940s, the then Director of the Bureau of Archaeology, Dr C. van Riet Louw, in association with P.G. Söhnge and D.J.L. Visser, published *The Geology and Archaeology of the Vaal River Basin (Memoir No. 35)*. It is clear from this report that Dr van Riet Louw was also mystified by rock-hard evidence of prehistoric mining of the diamondiferous alluvial gravels of the Vaal River basin. Contrary to the generally held belief that the man-made stone artefacts found in association with these gravels were water washed, or rolled, to their position in the gravels, *by chance*, this report clearly states that these artefacts do not belong to the gravels. But that the stone implements were all introduced at a later stage when the gravels, quote, "were exposed and literally turned over and 'mined' by primitive man in his search for suitable material for his needs. The indications of disturbance are clear. In one particular patch all the material in the gravel had been handled by man from bottom to top".

Again, with reference to the stone artefacts in the diamond-bearing alluvial gravels, the report continues, "man appears to have settled in the area only when he had reached a comparatively advanced stage, but once he settled he did so with a determination that is amply revealed in the unusual mass of implements he left in his tracks". The mention in this report of the "unusual mass of implements" left behind by the early miners, challenges the generally accepted picture of a country "fairly thinly populated by clans of roving hunters and gatherers".

Again, on the same track, I. Schapera in *The Khoisan Peoples of South Africa* concluded that the stone industries associated in South Africa with the San were not indigenous to the country, but constituted an invading element from the Northeast. He further suggested that this invasive culture superseded the two pre-existing stone cultures.[6]

It was these anomalies that first set me to query the official stance that prehistoric South Africa was inhabited only by roving bands of San hunters and gatherers, before the (much later) arrival of the Khoi, and even later, the Nguni. As the wife of a diamond digger, working claims at Boskuil and Bloemhof, I had first-hand knowledge of the enormous quantity of man-made stone artefacts recovered from the gravels. So numerous were these crafted rocks, I could have filled a wheelbarrow in a morning from our claims alone. At one stage I even thought of starting a business, selling genuine, prehistoric stone tools to tourists. Unfortunately, I soon discovered that, although archaeologists showed no interest in our finds, it is illegal to sell any artefact.

Nevertheless, the quantity and quality of the tools recovered from our claim fired my desire to find out at least something about archaeology. To this end, I assembled a selection of beautifully crafted stone artefacts excavated from our claims, of different shapes and sizes, some in pristine condition, as examples, and made an appointment to meet with Professor Mason at the Archaeology Department of the University of the Witwatersrand. He very solemnly told me that all the tools recovered from alluvial diggings were rolled there, water-washed to their present location. To me this explanation did not make sense. While many were indeed worn, others, found in the same area, were in perfect condition. His urbane assurance still did not explain away the quantity of tools found by diggers. If his explanation was correct, then where did they all come from in the first place? If, as is generally believed, the San did not make stone tools other than arrowheads and scrapers, then who were the people who made and used them? And where did they go to; when did they leave? Even to anyone as unfamiliar with archaeological discoveries as I was, at that time, the sheer volume of hand-crafted stones was evidence of a large number of people, living and working "somewhere", for a considerable time span—maybe even thousands of years. No, no, somewhere something did not make sense. However, after tea, he very graciously accepted a number of my beautifully knapped stone tools for the museum, and I returned home unconvinced. Clearly, the Halls of Learning were less well informed than diamond diggers on the ground.

Diamond diggers are well aware of this anomaly. Many of the old hands told me that whenever they found large numbers of stone tools—which they called "skilpadklippies" because the shape was suggestive of a tortoise—in the "rough", thrown out during the sorting process, few, if any, diamonds would be recovered there. They then had to decide whether it would be worth their while to work through that ground, until they were out of the "patch", or to pull up their claim pegs and move to another area, muttering as they did so, "Die oermense was alreeds hier!" ("the most ancient, primeval ones have already been here!"). Others, such as my late husband Harry Sullivan, were happy to find stone tools, taking the discovery as a sure sign that a "run" of payable gravel would be found not too far away.

We were also finding curiously worked artefacts at our claims at Boskuil, and later at the Donkey Rush (Bloemhof townlands). My

Ancient diamond miners?

collection grew by the month, and included a large number of perfectly worked round stone balls, and many bored stones of differing shapes and sizes. One cleaver-shaped tool had a small, perfect square, cut into one surface—a square hole is a symbolic representation of the four seasons, the cardinal points, and also of the planet Earth. At Megalopolis (Egypt), a square image of the sun stood in the precinct of the Great Goddess, and was worshipped as Heracles the Saviour. Three stone tools were found with carefully worked lines deeply cut into the surface, in the form of the three-finger "Phrygian blessing", or Ogam symbol for the fertility god, Baal. Another very curious find was an agate of unusual shape—a natural "face", enhanced by the chipping-out of a second eye, and the other side of a natural mouth. And my favourite, a small, smiling "Madonna", a classic example of the Great Mother goddess; her smile a row of tiny dots, her eyes tiny crosses. Over a period of weeks, a number of small, flat stones (or fossilized bone), each bored through at one end as if used as pendants, were recovered, and several small tubular objects, possibly beads, apparently made from quartzite crumbs. Other "finds" were sculptures of bird-like figures (Ill. 20, 21, 22, 23, 24, 25, 26, 27).

Ill. 20. Three curiously incised stone tools excavated at different times from the claims at Boskuil and the "Donkey Rush" at the Bloemhof Townlands.

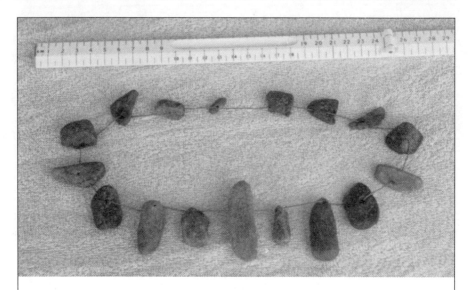

Ill. 21. A collection of bored fossilized bone pendants recovered over a period of several weeks from the diamond gravels at the "Donkey rush", Bloemhof Townlands. Of interest is the fact that here there was once a perennial mineral spring, which was subsequently destroyed through the actions of the diamond diggers. And it was close to this site where the greatest number of unusual stone artefacts was recovered from the gravels.

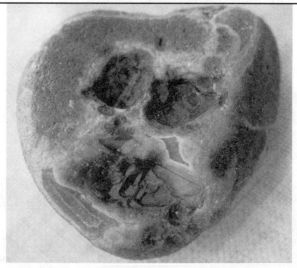

Ill. 22. An agate "face" recovered from the diamond gravels at Boskuil. The natural form of the stone was chipped away to give it a second eye and a wider mouth.

Ancient diamond miners?

Ill. 23. The Great Goddess. This small (approximately 10 centimetres high) female figurine was unearthed at the "Donkey Rush", in a claim close to the old perennial mineral spring. Her mouth is formed with dots, and she has tiny crosses for eyes. This figurine was one of the many items in my private collection that I donated to the museum at the Lotlamareng Dam Cultural Village, at Mmabatho. Unfortunately, everything there has now been destroyed.

Ill. 24. An engraved fragment of stone on display at the Barkly West museum, one of the unusual items found by diamond diggers during the diamond recovery process.

Ill. 25. A most unusual, carefully crafted quartzite artefact worked with a square hole in the centre.

Ill. 26. The collection of stone balls I accumulated while living at Boskuil. Some were crudely formed "cores", but most were perfectly worked round balls.

Ancient diamond miners?

Ill 27. Nicknamed "the Boskuil bird", this overtly phallic artifact is one of several bird-like crafted stones unearthed from the diamondiferous gravels at Boskuil. These bird-like phallic shaped stones are of dolerite, Ventersdorp lava, and quartzite, specimens of which are rarely found naturally shaped in this particular form.

The bird-like figures were all very similar in shape, as if inspired by a common thought, or theology. In later years I recorded an engraving in the same shape as those stone "birds". Of particular significance was the fact that a strung bow extended from the tip of the phallus, clearly an invocation to the androgynous Great Mother for fertility and prosperity. This engraving was located at the apex of a hillock, an outcrop of steatite/soapstone (Ill. 28).

Western archaeologists, and scholars such as Robert Graves, identify the presence of engravings and sculptures of bird-like figures as an indication of the worship of the androgynous Great Mother. Russian scholars agree. In *Archaeology in the USSR*, A.L. Mongait discusses the figures of birds found in graves, and mentions the theory that such images are the final stage in the degeneration of the crafting of female statuettes of the Great Mother.[7] There is international accord on the subject of phallic, bird-like images, and general agreement that these objects represent the fertility aspect of the Great Mother. Not so widely known is that a Griqua mother, when discussing a medical problem relating to the penis of her son, will say, 'sy voëltjie is seer'—literally, 'his little bird aches'.

Ill. 28. The pregnant womb and virile penis surmounted by a strung bow. The bow with a fitted arrow is universally recognized as a symbol of impregnation. A San courting custom was for the suitor to aim tiny "Cupid arrows" at his intended wife-to-be.

Not all of these artefacts were roughly ripped from the gravels, during the process of gouging into the earth for diamonds. My husband's method was to trench down into the gravel layer, using the long arm of the excavator, to expose a vertical cross-section from the surface to the alluvial deposits, some six to 13 metres from the surface. While working his claims at Boskuil, and again a few years later again at the Donkey-run on the banks of the Vaal River near Bloemhof, he came across three-metre-wide, unnatural, perpendicular shafts, or pits. In each case the shaft had been dug through the strata to the depth of—but no deeper than—the bottom of the otherwise unbroken "run" of the diamond-bearing deposit.

Lying at the base of each of these shafts we found a number of beautifully worked stone artefacts, all in pristine condition. Together with the artefacts found in the shaft at the Boskuil diggings was the androgynous "Boskuil bird", a small red quartzite tool, with a symbol clearly engraved on one face, and the three hand axes, each carefully worked with markings suggestive of the ancient Ogam finger alphabet sign for the Sun-god Bel/Baal/Beli, or the Phrygian blessing made with the thumb, index finger and middle finger raised and spread out. The presence of these beautifully worked artefacts, at the bottom of a shaft excavated to reach no further than the diamond bearing gravels, could serve no other purpose than that they were thank offerings to the Earth Mother.

In antiquity mining, and the digging of wells, being the forceful penetration of the skin of the Earth Mother, was a task for which atonement had to be made in the form of ritual placatory sacrifices. The Celts laid votive offerings at the bottom of shafts, and the Hindu sacrificed cattle when a new mine was opened.[8] Again, this information must be seen in context, because the mention of sacrificial cattle does not always refer to bovines, but often to human sacrifice offered as "cattle". The Carthaginians sacrificed children, calling them "calves", and in times of severe drought, the Tswana sacrificed a chosen human victim as "the black bull of the rain".[9] Therefore, the discovery by South African archaeologists of the skeletons of San women in a mine near Bulawayo, is more likely to be evidence of sacrificial offerings than death by disease.

It was also customary to fill in the excavations to avoid offending the spirits of the underworld.[10] At the time of our discovery it was obvious that the shafts, into which these pristine tools had been laid, had originally been roughly filled in, and at a later time, the whole area was submerged under overlay of sterile mud. The overlay of mud was clearly evidence of massive flooding, which not only filtered into these shafts, but also covered the then surface of the surrounding countryside with mud to a depth of nearly three metres.

The excavation of the ancient shaft at the "Donkey-rush" was unusual. The material that had been removed from the alluvial deposits at the bottom of the shaft was stacked, neatly sorted, into heaps around the lip of the shaft at the original surface level—i.e. before the tide of mud settled over the area. These heaps of sorted stones contained all the minerals usually found in diamondiferous gravels—including pebbles of red and yellow ochre used in quantity by the San, Khoisan, and the Nguni of Southern Africa—all the material, except diamonds! Important to the discovery of the heaps of sorted stones on the lip of the Donkey-run shaft, is the fact that, on either side of the shaft, this particular "run" of gravel was a rich lode—my husband's diamond register was proof thereof!

Believing we had found evidence of ancient diamond miners, we kept this shaft face open for four months, while I tried to persuade archaeologists of the University of the Witwatersrand to come down to

Bloemhof and examine the site. After holding up production for four months, in the hope that even a minor archaeologist would take note of our discovery, we worked through the ground, destroying all the evidence. Because nothing had been found in situ, and because of their firm belief that all the tools in the area had been tumbled to their present location along with the alluvial gravels, archaeologists showed no interest in any of the artefacts I rescued from the diggings. And so, after my husband's death at his claim in 1984, with only three exceptions, I donated my entire collection to the living museum at Lotlamareng Dam, Mmabatho.

Alas for the evidence of ancient diamond miners, and the months of work P.G. Söhnge, D.J.L. Visser, and C. van Riet Lowe put into *The Geology and Archaeology of the Vaal River Basin*.

By this time my first casual interest to discover more about the origin of these tools, the people who made them, and why, had become a quest. Living an almost isolated life on the diamond diggings, I had the time, and the money, to launch myself into a self-motivated, self-instructing, study programme on "the ancients". Not merely concentrating on stone tools, bones, pottery, and ruins, but more particularly on the people who made them. What were the thoughts, desires, and problems of the crafters as they made the artefacts? To whom did they pray?

During the years I was living on the diggings (from 1970 to 1986), I often visited the small museum at the Mining Commissioner's office in Barkly West. This museum houses a jumbled display of

Ill. 29. An unwieldy quartzite "chopper", but one of the many curious items recovered from the diamond gravels by diamond diggers and handed in to the Mining Commissioner's museum at Barkly West.

Ancient diamond miners?

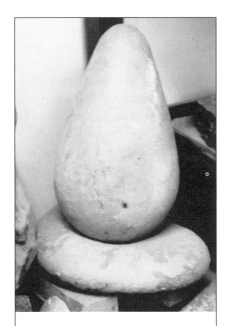

Ill. 30. A beautifully crafted and polished dolerite "cone" recovered from the alluvial gravels, and on display at the Barkly West museum. The cone is internationally recognized as a classic representation of the womb of the Great Mother, and depicts fruitfulness and good fortune.

unusual objects excavated by modern diamond diggers. Among the many curious objects on display, three in particular caught my attention (Ill. 29, 30, 31).

The collection included a large, crudely crafted "chopper"; a carefully sculptured dolerite "cone"—typical of a classic representation of the womb of the Great Mother, depicting fruitfulness and good fortune.[11] A symbol which later became an emblem of Aphrodite/Astarte when the sun-worshipping, patriarchal, multi-deity religions supplanted the matriarchal religion centred on respect for earth, the Great Mother/life, the Moon, Giver of Rain, and the eternal cycle of birth, life, death, re-birth.

Complementing the discovery of the sculptured stone cone was a wooden carving of a woman's head. The features are African. Her black hair is garlanded with red flowers; her smiling red lips are set in a silver-painted face. In every respect this small wooden head (approximately 15 centimetres) resembles a classical portrayal of a laughing Moon Goddess, or Sarah of the Sea. The face is painted silver, the colour sacred to the Moon; the hair is black, the colour of death/the dark side of the moon; the lips and floral headdress are red, the sacred colour of prosperity/fecundity/the harvest moon—happiness. The fact that the hair is crowned with a red floral headdress is most significant, for a red floral headdress was characteristic of the classic representations of a moon goddess such as Aphrodite, Astarte, or Demeter.[12] The red rose was the sacred flower associated with the orgiastic cult of Aphrodite, while red poppies were sacred to Demeter, the Greek and Celtic Moon Goddess associated with barley and brewing.[13] The priestesses of Demeter were famed for their oracles and

Ill. 31. *In every respect, this carved wooden head (approximately 15 centimetres) depicts a laughing Moon Goddess of the Aphrodite/Astarte/Ashoreth variety. The head was excavated by a diamond digger at some unknown date during the days of large-scale diamond diggings around Barkly West, and handed in to the then Mining Commissioner as a curiosity for the mining museum.*

prophetic pronouncements, which may well have been inspired by the soporific qualities of poppies, and their skills as brewers, for it is even said they carried the secrets of whisky brewing to Scotland.[14] The choice of a crown of red roses was certainly not coincidental. In *The Meaning of Flowers,* Claire Powell says that, when the Three Graces accompanied the Muses, they wore wreaths of roses, while the God of Silence was represented by a youth holding a white rose. White roses were once hung over banqueting tables, to remind guests that the confidences heard during the revels were never to be repeated, and this was the origin of the phrase *sub rosa*.[15] Later, this pagan symbol was assimilated by the Christian church, and the emblem of a rose was carved over confessionals.[16] Therefore, a wreath of red flowers, rose or poppy, on the head of a representation of a Moon Goddess, could be taken to mean that the priestess had been initiated into the deepest occult mysteries relating to the fountains of knowledge pertaining to the *here*, and the *hereafter*.

The sacred colours of the Moon Goddess, black, red, and white (or silver), *are also the sacred colours of Africa.* The features of this laughing, silver-painted head are clearly feminine, and African. How did the stone "chopper", the crafted stone "cone", or the head of the African Aphrodite, come to be buried in the alluvial gravels? Unfortunately, the records merely show that these, and many other enigmatic artefacts, were excavated by unnamed diamond diggers during the early days of diamond digging, and handed in to the Mining Commissioner, as unexplained curiosities recovered from the gravels.

But there can be no doubt that the presence of this representation of an African Moon goddess can only mean that ancient, time-honoured pagan Moon-worshipping rituals were once conducted by people working the diamond gravels of central South Africa. What other explanation can there be for the symbolic stone "birds", the polished stone "cone", and the silver-painted, wooden head of a typical Aphrodite/Isis/Sarah of the Sea?

The Moon Goddesses of fertility were also goddesses of mining and mariners.[17] Not an unlikely combination of responsibilities when the link between earth's riches, and trade over vast distances of ocean, is made. The consort of the Moon Goddess was the male fertility figure, Baal. The Baals were the spirits of fertility linked to specific locations.[18] Logically, therefore, where there was an image of Aphrodite/Astarte/Demeter there ought to be a Baal or two not very far distant. And there are indeed images typical of the ithyphallic horned god Baal engraved on the rocks at certain sites; usually these Baals are positioned to receive the morning sun, representing life and energy (Ill. 32, 33).

Ill. 32. Facing the rising sun at a site in the North West is this classic representation of the rain/fertility horned God, Baal, the consort of the Moon Goddess represented as Aphrodite/Ashoreth/Astarte, etc.

Close to the engraving of Baal and also positioned to face the rising sun, is an engraving in a more primitive art style depicting a very virile male ejaculating sperm in the direction of an eland on a rock obliquely opposite. This beautifully crafted engraving of a most regal eland is positioned to face the setting sun in the west, and is clearly symbolical of death with the promise of rebirth. In times of drought the sacrifice of an eland was called for to propitiate the Moon Goddess. A Tswana rainmaking song runs, "I speak about rain, let the eland die—let there be downpour" (Ill. 34).

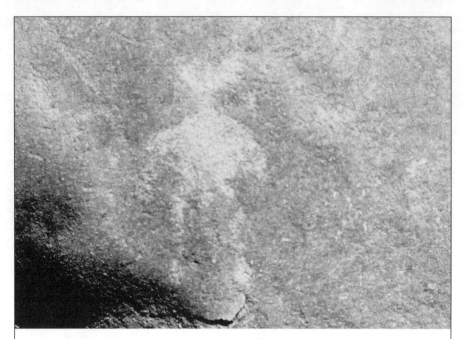

Ill. 33. Another image, which can be taken to be a portrayal of Baal, is also positioned to face the rising sun, symbol of light and life. In Egypt and the Near East the fertility god was known by many names—El, Baal, Seth, Mot, Hadad, Tshub.

The fertility rites linked to the worship of Baal and Astarte/Aphrodite/Demeter/Istar include the seasonal fertilizing of the land by the king, in his position of earthly representative of the divinity. This practice stems from the theology that originally earth was the first female to receive the semen of the god.[19] Molech was another "Baal" fertility deity, and similar rituals were practised by his followers. The prophet Moses raged against the practice of giving seed to Molech:-

"Whosoever he be of the Children of Israel, or the strangers that sojourn in Israel, that giveth any of his seed to Molech; he shall surely be put to death"(Levit. 20, 2–5).

Baal was worshipped in Egypt during the Hyskos period, and in the time of Ramses III, but the procedure of seasonally ejaculating semen on the ground was obviously a tradition in Southern Africa too. For, apart from the four very graphic engravings depicting the act I have so

Ancient diamond miners?

Ill. 34. Beautifully crafted eland, head not held proudly, but lowered as if anticipating death, as well this engraving might suggest. For it faces west, the direction of the sunset, which is the time of sacrifice and death. When severe drought threatened, the rainmaking song of the Tswana calls for the death of an eland, so that rain might bring life to the parched land. East facing, and placed obliquely opposite this eland, is an engraving of a very virile male ejaculating his sperm in the direction of the eland. An annual fertility rite of antiquity, which, I have been told, is still conducted in remote parts of Botswana to ensure the harmonious continuation of all life throughout the region.

far recorded, South African diviners have told me that even in modern times this rite continues to be practised "in remote parts of Botswana".

While I was living on the diamond diggings at Boskuil, the local Mining Inspector, Mr Frank Nienaber, was building his own private museum. This too housed an unusual collection of objects found by diamond diggers. Of particular interest was a carved stone head, identified by Dr Revil Mason (Archaeology Department of the University of the Witwatersrand) as being very similar to the stone heads found in Polynesia. This artefact had been excavated from the diamond gravels near Warrenton, at a depth of ten metres. When an article appeared in the *The Star* (Friday, 27th April 1979) about this one-eared head, the comment by Dr Mason was, "It was left there, or it was put there", meaning it was a hoax. It was certainly no hoax. Nevertheless his remark was correct —it was left, or put there, not recently, but in ancient times (Ill. 35).

To dismiss a Polynesian connection, out of hand, is to overlook known Polynesian and Malayan connections with the East African coast. A Malayan and Polynesian form of coconut grater is found in East Africa, and also a special eel pot. In addition, there is a peculiar method of catching turtles common to East Africa and Malaysia. This is not to infer that the Malayans came and instructed East Africans in the art of catching eels, or grating coconuts, for they could have learned these techniques in Africa. But it does imply a physical trans-oceanic connection. Not only domestic chores, but dogs, too. How else, other than through the means of long distance sea voyages thousands of years ago, can it be explained that the only two places in the world where the "African" hunting dog, known as the *Rhodesian ridgeback*, occurred are Zimbabwe and Siam (Thailand)? An African-Malayan-Polynesian connection brings us back to the South African rock engravings. The people inhabiting the island of Leti, Sarmata, and some other groups of islands that lie between the western end of New

Ill. 35. A one-eared stone head. Yet another curious object unearthed by diamond diggers working the gravels near Warrenton, at a depth of 10 metres, and was later handed over to the private museum of Mr Frank Nienaber in Bloemhof. It is said to be very similar to the stone heads found in Polynesia. When I asked Sanusi Credo Mutwa for his explanation, he said, "It shows the face of MaBona the Sun God. Such faces have one ear and one nostril to show the god's humanity."

Ancient diamond miners?

Ill. 36. A pagoda-like ladder with seven rungs. Many African legends speak of the mythical ladder that once joined Heaven and Earth. On the same rock but slightly to the left of this figure is the engraving of a square-armed cross, with a dot set between each of the arms.

Guinea and the northern part of Australia, practised seasonal fertility rites. Central to the ceremonies to increase the harvest, was sexual intercourse between men and women for the purpose of promoting the growth of crops, the women representing earth as the female principal, and the men the sun principal who fertilizes the women. They call the sun *Upu-lera*, or "Mr Sun". In *The Golden Bough* Sir James Frazer describes the ceremonies, and says that once a year, at the beginning of the rainy season, "Mr Sun" descends to earth on a ladder with seven rungs.[20]

At two separate engraving sites, not too far from Warrenton where the Polynesian stone head was found, I recorded two rock engravings depicting seven-rung ladders. The one very beautifully worked, in an almost oriental style, and the other a much cruder example, but together with a bull—another sun symbol (Ill. 36, 37).

In addition to the stone head, and stone tablet illustrated above, the collection of the late Mr. Frank Nienaber included a beautifully worked stone "hand axe", 60 centimetres in length. There is no possibility that

Ill. 37. Legends of the islanders of the Pacific Ocean tell of the seven-rung ladder of the Sun God. Here on the rocks of the North West Province is an engraving showing a seven-rung ladder beside the picture of a horned animal—which could be one of several species—and the two short strokes worked outward from the left leg of the ladder.

this artefact is a fake, or of modern construction. Once again, who made it, and why (Ill. 38, 39)? The same question can be asked of another stone head I photographed in the Kimberley museum (Ill. 40).

Yet another exceptionally unusual object, the front part of a female torso cast from seemingly untarnished metal, was recovered by diamond miners working on the banks of the Orange River, between South Africa and Namibia. The Orange River has its origin in the heart of the mighty Drakensberg mountains, another plentiful source of diamonds. In the late 1970s I was given an opportunity to study and photograph this female torso. But, once again, there is no explanation forthcoming about its origin or purpose, other than that it was recovered during working operations by the diamond diggers (Ill. 41, 42).

My theory that the deliberate mining of diamonds was carried out by earlier peoples, is backed by the undisputed fact that wherever numerous stone artefacts occur in the otherwise rich alluvial gravels, or alluvial deposits, no diamonds are to be found. Yet, with the exception of diamonds, all the other minerals prospectors look out for as a sure

Ancient diamond miners?

Ill. 38. The exceptionally large "hand-axe", 60 centimetres in length, is but another strange artefact excavated by diamond diggers and handed to Mr Frank Nienaber for his museum. This is unquestionably not a fake.

Ill. 39. The reverse of the unusual 60-centimetre "hand-axe". It is deeply incised with slash marks and Ogam-like notations on either side. Sanusi Credo Mutwa endorsed my photograph—"To the DANU, the Earth Mother—her sharp weapon" and "Also engraved on the axe are the names of priests who carried it over the centuries."

Ill. 40. Another unexplained curiosity is this stone head, which I photographed in the Kimberley museum.

sign of the presence of diamonds—jasper, agates, "bandoms", rock crystal, garnets, corundum, "silkies", topaz, red and yellow oxide, "groen ertjies"—turn up on the sorting table at every turn of the sieve. This confirms my belief that during the Neolithic, Bronze Age, Early or Late Iron Age, or intermittently over millennia, diamonds were being deliberately mined in South Africa. The most likely explanation is that prospectors with advanced technology, such as the early Egyptians, were after diamonds, and provided labourers with stone-hewn hand axes to get on with the job.

The evidence of "primitive" diamond mining is a fact. (I really dislike having to use the word "primitive" in this sense. For all I know those early people were far more "civilized", in the true meaning of the word, than we of the twentieth century!) Added to the evidence of early diamond miners are the tales of indigenous peoples rewarding those who pleased them, or who saved their lives, with handfuls of diamonds taken from secret places. So consistent are these stories that I believe such caches still exist. And that they were collected, at specific points, millennia ago, for the merchant/prospectors who for some as yet unexplained reason, or reasons, over many different historical periods, never returned to the "market" at the appointed time.

Perhaps life as a diamond digger's wife, living physically on the diggings, gave me a perspective different to one incubated in the hallowed Halls of Learning. At Boskuil I was in the fortunate position of being able to study an amazing variety of stone artefacts at first hand, in my own time, and at will. It was not long before I expanded my interest in crafted stones, to include a study of the engravings incised into rocks clustered together on local hillocks. In South Africa the hundreds of rock engraving sites are generally located either in areas of alluvial diamond deposits, or where other minerals, such as red ochre

Ancient diamond miners?

Ill. 41. (Left)   Another strange object recovered from the diamond diggings, which I was privileged to photograph in the late 1970s. The female torso, made of seemingly untarnished metal, was excavated by a diamond digger working along the banks of the Orange River on the South African-Namibian border.
Ill 42. (Right)   The reverse of the female torso above.

(iron ore), steatite/soapstone, occur. The rocks on which engravings have been incised are hard, amygdaloidal diabase, allied rocks of what are known as the Pniel Series, and dolerite predominate, and working an inscription or pictograph onto the surface cannot have been easy.[21]

It was Maria Wilmot who, very logically, suggested the engravers had used diamond-tipped tools to inscribe their messages on the rocks. Her suggestion has been viciously attacked by South African academics, probably because for the most part the engravings are still officially viewed as merely the doodles of Khoi herdboys, or San hunters, and therefore of little consequence. We tend to hold a one-sided view of diamonds as gemstones, while in our own industrial culture they have also been extremely useful in mining and drilling. Unhampered by too much academically inculcated preconditioning, with the help of my husband I constructed a primitive engraving tool similar to the experimental engraving tool Dr Maria Wilmot described in her book *The Rock Engravings of Griqualand West and Bechuanaland*

South Africa.[22] Using the gum of an acacia tree (*acacia luederitzii*) for glue, we affixed a well-shaped diamond (of poor quality, naturally) into the split end of a water-softened reed, and bound it securely into position with thin strips of wetted rawhide. The reed and sap dried and hardened, and with this serviceable tool I was able to duplicate the typical circular pitting, short strokes, and deep incisions of local petroglyphs on the surface of a dolerite rock.

Researching still further into the enigma of the rock engravings, and in the hopes of finding answers I could believe, I travelled to the United States in 1978 to meet with members of the Epigraphic Society. On returning to my home on the diggings, I submitted a paper to the OPES—*Ancient Diamond Miners in South Africa*—with illustrations of a few South African rock engravings. The paper was published in the April 1979 edition of the OPES.[23] By this time I had made contact with Sanusi Credo Mutwa, then living in Soweto (Johannesburg) and, hoping he would not find me presumptuous, or my theories outrageous, I sent him a copy of my paper. His reply, dated August 1979, I quote in full:

> *Greetings, Madam Sullivan,*
>   *I was deeply honoured to receive your letter dated the First of August and I took great care to read not only the letter but also the other papers accompanying it, and I also carefully studied the two photographs enclosed with the help of a magnifying glass, and, Madam Sullivan, I give you my word both as a man and as a Sanusi versed in the mysteries of my people that the rock inscriptions you photographed are neither Hottentot nor Bantu but belong rather to that fabled race of foreign people known in our legends as the Bafiki (the Strange Ones) and also the Mahiti or Mahatu.*
>   *These people worshipped the Sun, and like the Bantu they worshipped the Great Mother, but our legends say that these people were WHITE and not BLACK originally but that in later years, towards the end of their rule in Southern Africa and eastern Africa they became a mixed race of White, Yellow, and Black people. From these people we are told there descended two Black tribes which faithfully kept their strange religion and customs unchanged for generations, and of these two tribes one is still in existence while the other is long extinct. The tribe, which still exists, is the Balubedu tribe of Vendaland, which to this day still carries on rituals of incredible antiquity which it inherited from these long-vanished White colonists, and the tribe which has died out was known as the BAKWAKWA, the People of the Bronze War-Axe. Legends*

Ancient diamond miners?

say that the BAKWAKWA people were the earliest Bantu people to settle in what is today Lesotho, that they practised cannibalism and crude human sacrifices AND THAT THEY, LIKE THE MAHITI, POSSESSED THE SECRET OF WRITING MAGICAL MESSAGES ON ROCKS IN HONOUR OF THE SUN, THE EARTH MOTHER and THEIR DEAD HEROES. Even to this day the Southern Sotho of Lesotho call a battleaxe a "KWAKWA" after these long-dead Bakwakwa people. Madam, you are right before God when you say that these ancient people used diamonds to engrave on rocks, but you are a little off the mark when you say they used a reed tipped with a diamond, for our legends tell clearly how they did it, and what is more African witchdoctors still use an instrument similar to the one that these ancient people used to engrave sacred signs on slate and soapstone in various parts of Botswana, Lesotho and Zululand. This instrument is of three kinds—there is one which consists of a copper rod hammered flat at one end and then the flat end beaten into a pipe and then the stone (diamond, crystal or ordinary Zululand amethyst) put into the end thus prepared with a strong mastic. This copper rod with its stone tip is used in the same way as a "firestick" is used, held between two hands and twirled to create a series of tiny holes in the stone that forms the design. The second instrument is simply a horn of a small buck, a klipspringer say, whose hollow end is stuffed with resin with the stone held fast in this resin. I possess an instrument like this given to me by a witchdoctor in Barotseland ten years ago when I was made blood-brother of the Lunda-Luvale woodcarvers in the Zambian town of Livingstone, and this instrument is tipped with a black crystal. The last instrument is a small phallus made of hard wood with a hollow tip in which the stone is inserted and held with adhesive or bound with a thin "ribbon" of cowhide. My grandfather had such an instrument tipped with a real diamond, a very old thing which he said a Hottentot had given to him as a gift near Kimberley in the early years of this century when my grandfather travelled to the diamond fields. The Hottentot had said that the instrument had belonged to his father who had been killed by the Boers near Kuruman (Ill. 43).

I also have in my possession several stones which I could show you if you ever come to Johannesburg, stones of great value to my family which have been handed down to us to keep, stones which prove that ancient Africans used diamond dust mixed with eland fat to drill fine holes in extremely hard stones. I have a piece of TIGERS-EYE which we call "the Python Stone" which has two fine holes drilled into it. This piece of tigers-eye once belonged to the famous Sotho Queen MANTATISSE and she had worn it as a charm against injury when going into battle. I also

Ill. 43. Duiker horn writing tool. This ancient pen was once the inherited property of a Khoi medicine man and, according to its present owner it was used to engrave rocks. The delicacy of many of the earlier rock engravings shows a firmness of line that could not have been achieved by using any hand-held chunk of quartz.

have a piece of IRON PYRITES also with a hole drilled into it so it can be worn on a string around the neck for protection against lightning, and this charm once belonged to SHAKA but was said to have been of great antiquity even during Shaka's time. I also have a massive copper neckplate weighing an incredible twenty-five pounds and suspended from this ornament is a large heart-shaped lump of VERDITE as well as two carved and drilled verdite faces, all these three heavy stones having been drilled over two hundred years ago with a drill of startling precision, and my grandfather told me that these heavy green stones had been carved and drilled with the help of diamond dust mixed with fat many, many generations ago and had been found in the grave of a long-dead chief desecrated by marauding Zulus in the north of Basutoland (Lesotho). I wear this copper ornament on ceremonial days only. Today witchdoctors prepare a mixture of eland fat and powdered crystal or amethyst and give it to clients to bring them good luck in money affairs. Such a mixture was once used for drilling stones and even polishing the HEALING STONES that ignorant scientists say were polished by wild animals rubbing against them. This patent ignorance shown by some scientists in South Africa nauseates me, Madam Sullivan; they say that the many polished boulders and stones you find scattered in various parts of Southern Africa were polished by wild animals and yet every witchdoctor worth his salt knows that these were HEALING STONES on which Bantu and Hottentot people practised one of the oldest healing rituals on earth, a ritual which I will describe to you one day if you wish

Ancient diamond miners?

AND WHICH INVOLVES POLISHING THE SACRED BOULDER. *Our people used this Healing Stone ritual for thousands of years and legends describing it abound; it was a form of sympathetic magic AND IS STILL USED TO THIS DAY RIGHT HERE IN SOWETO!*

The polished Healing Stones are known by the Sotho as "Latlabolwetsi" which means "Throw-away-illness" rocks and their history is very beautiful and touching.

Madam, I fear this letter might become too long and too bulky to fit the small envelope I have, so I shall hasten to tell you about the photographs that you sent me, which I am returning to you with comments written on their backs. I regret I could not decipher one of these, the photograph is NOT CLEAR COULD YOU PLEASE SEND ME A SKETCH OF IT IN INK? *But the other photograph shows a hoofed beast with the sign of lightning within it and the beast is either a* BULL *or a* WILDEBEEST BULL. *This is obviously a personal name "Thunder Bull" or "Thunder Beast", and legend has it that the white Strange Ones and the Bakwakwa warriors loved to give themselves dramatic nicknames like this amongst which were "Far-Traveller", "Friend of the Thundergod" to name but two. I would say that the stone with the Lightning-beast on it marks a grave or is a record of some explorer who travelled where the stone is and engraved it for several days as a message for other wanderers of his kind to find.*

Madam Sullivan, the engravings on Driekopseiland and those of the Stowland site all belong to this shadowy part of our country's long history, THEY CAN BE READ BY ANY WITCHDOCTOR OF MY CLASS FROM ANYWHERE IN SOUTHERN AFRICA, *and I am asking you in our country's holy name to please show these interpretations I shall give you to Professor Fell who wrote the letter you sent to me to you. The veil of ignorance that covers our country's scientific world has got to be broken. You may not realize it but you are involved in momentous discovery but like me, you stand a chance of being ridiculed into silence by ignorant and bigoted men, so please be strong of heart. Yet more startling discoveries await you for the places you are exploring are clearly mentioned in our legends. Madam, it is true that the* MAHITI *and the* BAKWAKWA *mined diamonds in various parts of the Cape, Free State, Lesotho and Transvaal and even northern Botswana and the reason for mining these stones was partly commercial and partly religious because the diamond was associated with Sun Worship, and even today the diamond, crystal and amethyst are known as Sun-stones by our people. It was not only the Bushmen who carried diamonds for luck but chiefs and witchdoctors of both the Hottentot and Bantu races as well, and legend has it that long after the Strange Ones and the Bakwakwa had died out Bushmen and Hottentots continued mining for diamonds though they no longer knew WHY they had to, and they were still mining them when White people came to South Africa. Let us take a few of the signs that appear on your paper (this is a reference to my paper published by the Epigraphic Society) beginning with the ones from Driekopseiland; we shall take only the following* (Ill. 44—illustrations, with Credo Mutwa's interpretations).

Unfortunately there is a noticeable lack of "beautiful and touching" empathy between South Africa's academics and Sanusi Credo Mutwa. And the healing power of the *Latla-bolwetsi* cannot be recharged in the spiritless sanctuaries of our modern universities, where few academics desire to be welcomed into the confidence of shamans and tribal historians. So it is that archaeologists continue to claim diamonds were unknown to the Bronze Age and Iron Age peoples of the world, in general, and to the San, Khoi, and Nguni-speaking peoples of Southern Africa, in particular.

The belief that the engraving sites of South Africa were merely vantage points of San and Khoi hunters, gained acceptance when the main groups of European colonists trekked through the diamond-and-engraving-rich interior. Observing the surviving San and Khoi sitting atop the hillocks of the engraving sites, the migrant Europeans presumed they were hunters lying in wait for game. A supposition that was "confirmed" when the new arrivals noticed, but could not appreciate the meaningful representations of the engraved portraits of the sacred animals of Africa on the rocks, the elephant, rhino, giraffe, eland, zebra, baboon, ostrich and serpent. It would never have occurred to those worthy burghers that the people they considered to be "primitive animals" had the slightest comprehension of the Most High, nor that the engraving sites were to them sanctuaries in the truest sense—Sacred Places where violence and killing were taboo. European trekkers and hunters regarded all the San and Khoi with great distaste and mistrust. Quite naturally this feeling was very mutual, therefore the esoteric mysteries of these indigenous peoples were never revealed. So, because the ceremonial importance of the sites was not appreciated, in later years many were stripped of engravings to provide museums with examples of this form of "primitive art". And no attempt was ever made to record the position of engravings in situ, to survey the sites before desecrating them, nor to plot the position of engravings before removal.

Ancient diamond miners?

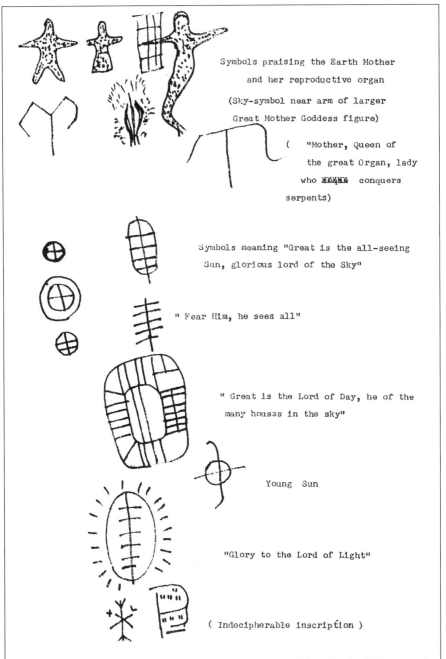

Ill. 44. Sanusi Credo Mutwa's interpretation of the South African rock engravings illustrated in my paper Ancient Diamond Miners in South Africa, published by the Epigraphic Society (1979). (Continued overleaf)

Moon-Goddess, bringer of health and love
(Signs from Stowlands and Wonderstone Mine")

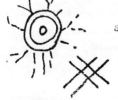

Sun at dawn on a spring day, i.e. the New Sun

Very old sign of the Earth Mother

Father Sun

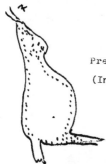

Pregnant Earth Mother
(Invoked by women seeking babies)

"Earth Mother, bringer of grain"

Copper or gold ingot (Prayer for good trade or thanksgiving for good trade)

Sign of Earth Mother.

Credo V. Mutwa

Ancient diamond miners?

Whether these centres were first created by "foreign devils", or by the mixed descendants of the many visitors to this sub-continent in ages past—the miners, traders, refugees, people who formed tribes and settled here—is presently known only to the few surviving Sanusi who jealously guard the legends of Africa's past.

Who they were can only be guessed at, as yet. Answers will only be forthcoming when all researchers, and archaeologists, put aside their pride, and meet trustfully with the traditional guardians of African history, and listen with respect to what they have to say about the past. Not only to resolve the question of whether people were deliberately mining diamonds, hundreds, maybe even thousands, of years ago in South Africa. But also to determine what happened to the miners, and traders, as well as their reason for mining diamonds—obviously there had to be a need, for diamonds are not edible. For myself, the principal question was not how diamonds could have been discovered at an early historical date, but who needed these hard but brittle chunks of pure carbon, and why? Gold and ivory have been important trade goods for millennia, but diamonds?

Who *needs* diamonds anyway? Diamonds are not even investment material. If you doubt this assertion, test the market yourself. Buy a few thousand rands/dollars/pounds/yen worth of diamond jewellery at retail prices and then, a year later, try to recover your money by offering the jewels for sale at the price you paid! Not a chance, but you will have learned an expensive and bitter lesson.

To identify what regal power, or governing force, could have motivated this industry, I felt I had to find a group, or a nation, with a need for large quantities of diamonds hundreds, or maybe even thousands, of years ago. At least as far back as the Bronze Age, which should more truthfully have been called the Age of Gold, for it was the obsession and relentless searching for gold, the metal sacred to the Sun God Apollo, which goaded mankind into the Bronze Age. Historically, it was during the Bronze Age that prospecting for gold was undertaken on a global scale. And there can be no doubt that those early prospectors would most certainly have discovered diamonds while searching for gold, because diamonds are often found with gold in alluvial deposits. Although not naturally occurring together, diamonds, gold, and other heavy minerals gravitate towards each other in certain alluvial deposits as the result of the action of winds, flooding, and rain over long periods of time.[24]

Diamonds, as mentioned, although the hardest natural mineral found on planet earth, are nevertheless very brittle. Which means they chip or pulverize easily. Because of this characteristic, many large stones recovered by inexperienced diggers working the diamond fields in South Africa during the late 19th and early 20th centuries were utterly destroyed. Inexperienced diggers, believing diamonds were so hard they could withstand any blow, when in doubt about the veracity of their "find", particularly when it was a large stone, hit it with whatever heavy instrument was to hand. One hard whack and, pouf! No more diamond. Modern diamond diggers drop their finds into hydrofluoric acid. Dangerous stuff, but effective, and at least it cleans a diamond's surface of all impurities and eats away anything that is not gem or industrial quality, such as boart or quartz.

But even diamond dust had its uses in days gone by. In the Middle Ages diamond dust was used, with success, to kill off unwanted royals. It is written that Emperor Frederick (1194–1230) died after a dose of powdered diamonds.[25] And it is on record that Selim, the son—who was presumably also the heir—of the Turkish Sultan Bajazet (1447–1513), mixed a large amount of pulverized diamonds into his father's food, after which repast the Sultan expired, and was buried with the mourning and pomp befitting his state.[26] English aristocracy were not above using diamond dust to eliminate enemies, either. Sir Thomas Overbury made a deadly enemy of the Countess of Essex, because he opposed her marriage to Robert Carr, Viscount Somerset, a favourite of James I. Shortly after the marriage, the Countess arranged for Sir Thomas to be imprisoned in the Tower. She then persuaded apothecary James Franklin to procure diamond dust which, mixed with a little mercury, cantharides, etc., was added to Sir Thomas' diet, effectively ending his life.[27] The infamous Catherine de Medici, too, was a dab-hand with diamond dust. It is said that the *poudre de succession* she favoured, as a poison, was diamond dust with a pinch or two of arsenic.[28]

Going further back in time, Russian archaeologists have established that, as early as the eighth to third centuries BCE, the Sacae tribes of south-eastern Kazak were wearing perforated diamonds from India, where alluvial gravels were being worked for diamonds as early as 800 BCE.[29] This finding is very relevant to my research. It proves, without doubt, that as early as the 8th century BCE engravers had already discovered the fact that all diamonds are not of equal hardness.

Diamond does not automatically cut diamond. To perforate or engrave a diamond it is necessary to select a "hard", or twinned, diamond—such as those found in India and Borneo—for the engraving tool, and a "soft" diamond—such as those more commonly

Ancient diamond miners?

found in South Africa—as the stone to be engraved. Because only the dust, or points, of harder diamonds can be used to perforate, drill, polish, or engrave, softer diamonds.

But all the above-mentioned uses were limited, and cannot account for the demand for these useful chunks of carbon evinced by the volume of stone tools recovered from the alluvial gravels in South Africa.

Researching further back in time, I learned that recent excavations show that diamonds were used in Egypt to cut stone as early as 4000 BCE. Further research revealed that the Egyptians were using diamond- and corundum-tipped copper, or bronze, saws, and jewelled tubular drills, during the time of the Archaic and Old Kingdoms (c. 3200–2723 BCE). One of the hardest minerals, diorite, was drilled and polished by ancient Egyptian craftsmen. It is said that such was the skill of the craftsmen, they were able to cut huge blocks of granite to an accuracy of 1/50th of an inch (0.5 millimetres).[30] So, here we have an established industry using diamond dust to polish and cut slabs of granite. This I felt was at least a logical answer to the question, "Who needs diamonds?" An answer that in turn led directly to the question, "Could Egyptians have been the early diamond miners in South Africa?"

Unlikely as this notion may at first appear, the possibility that Egyptian prospectors were active in central and Southern Africa by 4000 BCE, or even earlier, should not be curtly dismissed. The gold-mining ventures, which later took the Egyptians as far afield as Sumatra, Borneo, India and China, have been well documented. And they are known to have been great stonemasons who used diamond-tipped tools, so clearly the Egyptians, at least, *needed* large quantities of diamonds to tip the tools used by the craftsmen sawing, and polishing, the blocks of stone required for their many building projects, and templeware. I am not suggesting they were the only people to mine gold, diamonds and other minerals in Africa, but that it was the Egyptians who hacked, hewed and gouged the first prospecting trail through the continent, leaving behind evidence of their presence engraved on the rocks of South Africa—images such as the Egyptian symbol for Life, the Ankh (Ill. 45)—and imagined portraits of the fertility god, Baal, whose worship was common in Egypt at the time of Ramses II and III, of the 19th and 20th dynasties, around 1186–1085 BCE.

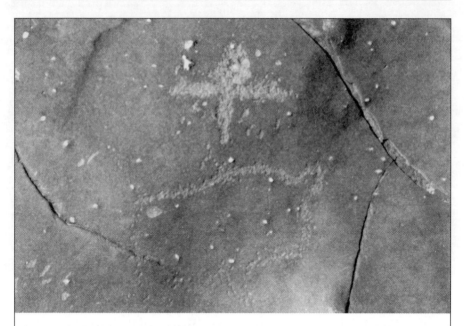

Ill. 45. An ankh, the Egyptian symbol for life engraved on a rock in the centre of South Africa. I have recorded two other engravings of the ankh, one single representation as above, and the other together with a pregnant eland with young in her womb, and to the upper right of the rock, a baboon. In African lore the baboon is known as "the father of wisdom", and to the Egyptians the baboon was a symbol of Thoth, a moon-god who was also the god of time-division, as in the ten-moon-month gestation period for humans, cattle, and eland.

Chapter 3

Old Gold

Once the Portuguese had cleared the Arab traders from their ancient strongholds on the East Coast of Africa, they were determined to find the fabled gold mines of King Solomon.

With the knowledge that they were seeking a place known to the local African peoples as "Fura", and to the Arabs as "Aufur", a great company of Portuguese under the leadership of Francisco Barreto set out along the banks of the Zambezi River in November 1569. The expedition was a disaster.[1] The Portuguese never located "Fura", or "Aufur", and the whereabouts of the Biblical Land of Ophir remains a mystery to this day. But had they reached the Lozi kingdom in the Zambezi, they would have heard of the Queen of the South who, as joint ruler of the Lozi, announced, 'I am transformed into a man,' in honour of an ancestress who usurped a patriarchal throne.[2] The Ethiopians called the Queen of the South *Makeda*. And the royal name of the Egyptian queen Hatshepsut, also lauded as the Queen of the South, was mentioned throughout the Punt reliefs as *Make-ra*.[3]

Queen Hatshepsut, reigning as co-ruler with her nephew Tuthmosis III, proclaimed herself "king" and pronounced, 'I am changed into a man,' when she entered the council chamber.[4] So there is every possibility that the "ancestress" of the queen of the Lozi was none other than the Egyptian queen, Hatshepsut. Queen Hatshupsut emphasized her androgynous standing by covering her body with electron dust—an admixture of gold and silver.[5] Other African royalty, the Ashanti kings and queens, dusted their bodies with gold or silver according to sex. The kings covered their bodies with gold dust and the queens with silver.[6]

It was during the rule of Queen Hatshepsut that great journeys to the Land of Punt were undertaken and recorded by her scribes. "Her fame encompassed the Great Circle" was an Egyptian term for the oceans first travelled by Egyptian prospectors and traders.[7]

Perhaps the truth about those early prospectors and traders from Egypt is to be found at the heart of African legends about the Bafiki/Mahatu/Mahiti, the Strange Ones. Or perhaps some hard facts about those legendary Strange Ones will be revealed once the papyri, found in a Southern African ruin by a Lieutenant Colonel A.L. da Costa in the 1920s, are rediscovered. It is said that there is now no trace of the papyri, but the find was well documented.[8] Another significant link with the past was discovered in 1972 when two young boys, searching for scorpions on the Northcliff hills in Johannesburg, found a stone engraved with meaningful symbols, which appeared to be script. This discovery, although surely of great importance, attracted no interest at the time, and was soon forgotten.[9]

Other indications of a "vanished race" were noted by the Register of Mining Titles, Mr D.S. van der Merwe who, in the 1920s, explored the northern region of South Africa during the course of his duties. He carefully recorded the many unusual things he came across, including evidence of an ancient irrigation system "of enormous extent"; remnants of a large dam; sacrificial graves of an entirely new type; a "sacrificial altar" which pointed due north and south which he described as being "approximately five feet high and nine feet long", approached by ceremonial causeways; stairways that he said could only have been used by pygmies; and "guideposts" hitherto unknown to science. In particular, he learned of the tradition among the Africans living along the Limpopo River about the "people with a white cloth around their head", who travelled there on camels, in ancient times.[10]

The Limpopo River is navigable for a great distance inland, so travelling through sub-tropical bush country on camels would seem a waste of effort and energy, considering the logistics of transporting camels from Egypt, or Arabia, to the banks of the Limpopo River. But a camel caravan would have been the most practical way to travel if the "people with a white cloth around their head" were *passing through* the Limpopo River valley, en route from the ancient east African port of

Sofala, to Namibia. And even beyond the copper, tin and diamond wealth of Namibia, to mineral-rich Angola. A camel caravan route from Sofala to Angola would certainly have been possible, because an ancient migration route crosses Southern Africa from the former Lake Ngami to Namibia.[11] And in Africa, where there are migration routes, there are also traders on the trail.

Although this hypothesis would seem to be wildly imaginative, it is nevertheless based on sound reasoning. During the 1960s, when my late husband Harry Sullivan was prospecting for diamonds in Angola, he was astonished to see herds of wild camels in the south of the country.[12] He also described the strange carved "grave-stones", and the stone-lined river banks he saw—the stones weighing several tons each—running for about 15 kilometres, just beyond the town of Caitou. For wild camels to be roaming the countryside of southern Angola means that someone, at sometime, must have introduced these useful riding and pack animals into the region. Certainly they are not likely to have migrated down Africa on their own, to settle eventually only in southern Angola.

Equally certain is that they were not introduced by the ancient Egyptians, for the small numbers of camels which had been introduced into North Africa during the period of close Afro-Asian relations, soon died out. Camels were not reintroduced into Egypt again until the Persians conquered, and ruled, Egypt during the Late Period 663 to 332 BCE (or 525–404 BCE, opinions differ).[13] The official language of the Persians was Aramaic, and texts in Aramaic have been found throughout Egypt, these include papyri, ostraca, and rock graffiti—which means they too engraved meaningful symbols on rocks. It was also during this period of Egypt's history that the canal connecting the river Nile to the Red Sea, started by the Assyrian vassal Pharaoh Necho I (672–664 BCE), was completed by the Persian Pharaoh Darius, and put into use as the direct route from Egypt to Persia.[14] Thus putting into Persian hands a rapid and easy access to the Indian Ocean and the east coast of Africa. Which, together with the control over all the ancient records of Egyptian prospecting and trade links throughout the regions, must inevitably have led the Persians to the mineral resources of Southern Africa.

The Persians are mentioned in papyri as *p-r-s-tt*, and are therefore said to have been the formidable Pereset. The Persians, or Pereset, were notable for their wealth and luxurious lifestyle, and wore very distinctive crown-like helmets made of metal plates fashioned to imitate feathers, as may be seen on the bas-reliefs in the palace of Darius at Persepolis.[15]

A similar headdress to the high-crowned Persian helmet is pictured in a South African rock engraving close to the Harts River, near the South African town of Taung (Ill. 46). This very small, but detailed, engraving shows a man wearing a high-crowned helmet. To the right of, and almost touching, the man is a geometrical symbol similar to an "ithyphallic dancing man", except that it most probably does not represent anything like that. This symbol is found worldwide—in Hawaii; West Iran; Indian rock art of Canada; Hopi Indian art at Springsville, USA; as Polynesian predial vowels "ha-a"; in New Zealand it represents the letter "h"; it is included in ancient Chinese script; and worked in beads on the gala cloak of Ndebele brides of South Africa.[16] And an Egyptian connection—maybe only a race memory, but a connection nevertheless—is certainly indicated by the simple five-pointed star above, and to the left, of the man.

A single five-pointed star was a symbol of the god Baal, and the five-finger open hand was also an emblem of the goddess Tanit. In particular, the symbol was used in connection with Creation and the sacred kings of ancient Egypt.[17]

Ill. 46. The tiny figure of a crowned, lamed male. To his right a geometrical symbol found in many places throughout the world, and left above a simple five-pointed star—symbol of Egyptian kingship, the god Baal, and his consort Tanit. The five-pointed star is also a symbol for the sacred pentagram.

Egyptian murals of the Creation story traditionally depict the Sky Goddess *Nut* as a female figure covered by simple five-pointed stars. Simple five-pointed stars were the symbol of the gods, and of Egyptian royalty and kingly priests, whose ceremonial garments were decorated with simple five-pointed stars.[18] In reality there was nothing simple about this star, for the symbol reaches far back in time to the lore relating to apples, pentagrams, sacred geometry, and the *phi* ratio. The pentagram was a sacred symbol of the Pythagoreans, as it contained within it references to the mathematical measurement known as the "Golden Section", or *phi* ratio—and is often depicted as man with outstretched arms and legs representing the symbol of perfection, the power of the circle.[19] On meeting a stranger a Pythagorean would offer an apple. If the stranger was also an initiate, he would cut the apple laterally across the core to reveal the pips laid out in the shape of a pentagram. The secret sign, the "cutting of the apple", was the transmission of non-verbal shared wisdom, the knowledge of the universal language of mathematics.[20] In ancient times the five-pointed star was sacred to the Moon, Sea, and Mining goddess Aphrodite, and an apple was the gift by which the priestesses of Aphrodite destroyed the sacred king at the end of his term with love songs[21]—shades of Adam and Eve, and Snow White.

The early Egyptians knew the value of *phi*. By the First Dynasty (3100 BCE) they had measured the circumference of earth, and had established their own measures of the remen and cubit as functions of this circumference.[22] Small wonder then, that the ceremonial robes of kings, and priest-kings, were decorated with a simple five-pointed star, symbolic of the pentagram. Which brings us back to the smallish rock near Taung engraved with the symbol of a simple five-pointed star, above and to the left of the male figure wearing a crown-like helmet.

Below this isolated star, and to the right of it (the right is the side of the male in African lore, the left is the side of the female), is the tiny figure of a man. The attention to detail is extraordinary. On his head is a high crown-like headdress. Both arms are raised, as if rejoicing or imploring the heavens, and the way in which his feet have been drawn indicate that this figure could depict a king or a chief. The shortened left leg ends in an exaggerated foot with five tiny toes. His right leg ends in a foot resembling the paw of a lion.

In ancient times, in Africa and elsewhere, the sacred kings, and also the metallurgists/smiths, were ritually lamed. The sacred kings of the Lunda, Nyamwezi, and Baganda were prevented from placing both feet on the ground at all times, for fear their solar powers might escape and ruin the crops and health of their people. Metallurgists and magicians were sometimes deliberately lamed to prevent them from running away.[23] Furthermore, the left foot was once known as the "hostile" foot, and never used to enter a friend's house, and when going off to war, soldiers used to take the first step with the left foot.[24] Muslim worshippers enter a mosque on the right foot, and honour the right hand and foot above the left.[25] That the man's right leg ends in a foot resembling the paw of a lion, shows his royal station in life. And, as this engraving is obviously not of the same quality as the earlier art, it is more than likely that it is the heritage of the Baralong who once occupied the Taung region, and whose chieftains were hailed as "Tau", "the Lion".[26]

Historically, the ancestors of the Tswana, and the Shona, were the first African peoples to have crossed over the Zambezi River into the southernmost regions of Africa.[27] So it is more than likely that, in one way or another, their ancestors had experienced prospectors, miners, and traders from Egypt. And that customs and rituals originating in Egypt and the Near East had been absorbed by the ancestors of the Tswana and Shona over the millennia, to be preserved for all time in an enigmatic engraving on a sun-bleached rock near Taung.

There could even be a link between an engraving on the red sandstone outcrop at Twyfelfontein (Namibia), which has a high iron ore content, and another at an engraving site in the vicinity of Vryburg, South Africa. The engravings at Twyfelfontein have been dated to around 5,000 years ago. While on a visit to the area I photographed an engraving of a lion, strangely drawn—each foot turned to show the underside, and the underside of a paw engraved at the tip of the tail. Similarly, at a site near Vryburg, to the north of Taung, I photographed an engraving of an elephant, also with the feet turned to show the underside of the pads. The lion and elephant are both royal beasts (Ill. 47, 48).

The lion, the symbol of kingship and magic; and the elephant, symbol of wisdom, stability, moderation and pity, but also a symbol of the queens of Africa who, as keepers of the rainmaking hereditaments of the nation, were lauded as the "Lady Elephant".[28] As mentioned, the rocks are hard, and working this kind of detail takes time and effort. One can only conclude that these pictographs conveyed a message of great importance to those initiated into the mysteries of the symbols, and that literate people with similar knowledge were to be found at both Twyfelfontein and Vryburg around 5,000 years ago.

Old records testify to the extent of Egyptian mining activities, as early as the 2nd Egyptian Dynasty, and towards the end of this chapter

Ill. 47. Figure of a lion from Twyfelfontein (Namibia) with upturned paws and a paw on the end of its tail.

Ill. 48. A similar figure, an elephant with upturned feet, worked on a rock in the district of Vryburg (North West Province).

excerpts from *Egyptian Gold Seekers and Exploration in the Pacific* by Professor George Carter, relating to Egyptian gold seekers on the African continent, have been included. As background material, a brief look at early Egyptian history makes for better understanding of the subject.

Historically, around 3000 BCE, the peoples living in the Nile Valley were very much the same as their neighbours to the north, on the Nile estuary. In other words, the Egyptians of 5,000 years ago were most likely as definitely African as people of ancient Numidea or Mauretania before the Carthaginian traders or Romans came.[29] In *Races of Africa* Charles Seligman points to the evidence of less than friendly relations between the north and south inscribed on the proto-dynastic slate palettes, from around 3200 BC. These records show dead and captive enemies of Egypt, with the spiralled hair of the true Negro and the same form of circumcision that is still practised by the Masai and other negroid tribes of Kenya and Tanzania.[30]

In ancient times Egypt had many connections with Africa to the south and west, and the Egyptian influence permeated southwards from Nubia through the grasslands of the Sudan.[31] A fresco of the time of pharaoh Akhnaton shows one head unmistakably middle or south African.[32] The Nubians to the south had a civilization comparable to that of their northern neighbours, they had developed a belief in an afterlife, and in gods with different personalities, and their fertility rites included offering a young girl to the river god.[33] There is a parallel here with the traditional Venda practice of sacrificing a pregnant girl at the end of the Domba ritual, which lasted the full human, cattle and eland gestation period of ten lunar months. Before the missionaries censored this traditional rite, at the start of Domba, to demonstrate the mysteries of Life, a pre-selected girl was ritually impregnated. At the end of Domba, ten lunar months later, she was sacrificed to the crocodiles of the sacred lake Fundudzi.

Around 3000 BCE trade between Nubia and Egypt was brisk. The name *Nubia* means *El Dorado*, the Land of Gold, and Seligman notes the finding of typical pre-dynastic Egyptian objects of the finest type, including a gold-handled stone mace, in Nubian graves. The finding of a 5,000–4,500-year-old stone mace decorated with gold clearly shows that not only did those early people value the metal, but that by 3000 BCE mankind—men and women—had already mastered the techniques of mining, smelting and crafting gold.[34]

At the beginning of the Old Kingdom (2780–2270 BCE) Egypt was a well-organized country, divided into provinces, or nomes. During the

3rd Dynasty (2780–2723 BCE) the pharaoh Imhotep built the first stone step pyramid at Saqqara, and sophisticated theological systems were established at Heliopolis and Memphis. In addition, at Memphis was built the Great Forge of Ptah.[35]

In an age when gods and goddesses were neither few nor far between, a temple to one named Ptah—the Egyptian equivalent of the Canaanite god Kathir-and-Khasis—attracts little attention. But Ptah was essentially the god of craftsmen, and his priests were jewellers, smiths, metallurgists, and mathematicians.[36] Now, because knowledge is power, in antiquity the mysteries of metalworking and mathematics were closely guarded secrets—and since time immemorial secret knowledge has ever been hidden under a cloak of sanctity.

The greater the potential for power, the more important the secret. The more important the secret, the bigger the temple they built around it.

A point one must always bear in mind is that religions—all religions—are manmade. God, the Creative Spirit, Divine Intelligence, call the Presence what you will, never created a religion, least of all one regulated by dogmas, or rituals. But mankind did, lots of them, and every one a winner, for behind the façades of dogma and ritual lies a most ungodly grasping for wealth and power. Religious dogmas were either built up around politics, or created to veil scientific discoveries that enabled the inventors to corner a market, and become wealthy beyond the dreams of avarice. Take the political-religious chicanery of Emperor Constantine as an example. Although Emperor Constantine never converted to Christianity himself until his deathbed, yet he could well be called the Father of Christian dogma because he summoned the Council of Bishops to Nicaea in AD 325, to unify the Christian faithful. Not because he had been transformed and saved suddenly by Christianity, but because he had a war coming up and needed the support of Christian Bishops and Christian recruits to fight his battles.[37] And to give but one example of scientific discoveries cloaked by many layers of misrepresentation—the storytime tales which relegate swineherds to the lowest station in life, and describe them as filthy creatures unfit to mix with respectable people. In truth, in antiquity, the keepers of pigs were a priestly caste kept apart from common people by reason of their knowledge of magic and metallurgy.[38] The priestly Celtic and Egyptian swineherds, in addition to being keepers of the sacred pigs, were also metallurgists and magicians.[39]

Throughout the world, among earlier peoples, mystery and magic surrounded the forging of metals. The incantations and magical rites practised by the priestly swineherds hid a very practical, non-superstitious purpose. The exclusion of the keepers of the sacred pigs from the rest of society served to conceal the fact that the use of the fat and bones of pigs greatly improved the quality of the metals they were refining.[40] Human fat and bones were equally good for the purpose and, even as recently as the Middle Ages, human sacrificial victims are known to have been dropped alive into seething cauldrons containing metals destined to become church bells—specifically to give the bells a voice to cry to heaven. The smiths of the Venda (South Africa) also had this knowledge, for in earlier times they also added human sacrificial victims to the metals in their forges.[41] Behind this seemingly brutal practice, lies the fact that the bones of pigs and humans have a very high calcium content, and calcium is an excellent flux. In this case the sacred secret, the ability to refine superior metals, equalled political and material power, because whoever possessed this knowledge held the key to the manufacture of stronger weapons with which to conquer, and despoil, greater numbers of enemies.

The fact that a great temple was raised to the glory of the Ptah, during the 3rd Dynasty, can only mean that at Memphis were gathered the most brilliant of Egypt's mathematicians, jewellers, metallurgists and scientists. There they worked their "magic" by transmuting gold-bearing and other ores into malleable metals under the sanctuary of sanctity. Very likely astronomers and cartographers were there as well, for Memphis was also the location for the House of Yah (Yaw, or Yam), the Sea God, which, it is said, was built with the help of Ptah.[42]

A temple to Yah, at Memphis, built with the help of Ptah, points to the very likely possibility that the needs of the priests controlling production at the Great Forge of Ptah, were dependant on shipping to supply the minerals necessary to keep the forges operating profitably. Iron is not known to have been used in Egypt at that time, so the main need of these metallurgists must have been the sacred metals of the Great Goddess, namely, gold, silver (electron), tin, copper and lead.

The expertise of the early Egyptian prospectors is well documented. If their means of conducting business, or of getting the rights to prospect, were in any way similar to the hunter/killer methods used by modern prospectors, then they certainly would not sit idly around after locating gold on Egyptian territory.

Gold fever is unquenchable. The thirst for this metal can only be slaked by the discovery of more, and more, gold—over the highest mountains, and through the most inaccessible and impenetrable terrain, if necessary. On and on they go, relentlessly searching as long as there is the slightest chance of a "strike". It wasn't only the Egyptians who needed gold. Around 3000 BC, the Assyrians, Mesopotamians, Tuatha dé Danaan (the People of the Goddess Danu, the early Celts), and others, also craved the metal. Therefore, it is logical to assume that the earliest Egyptian prospectors turned first towards the south, where they would be less likely to run across competitors.

Egyptian military trophies of dead and captive Africans indicate that Egyptian explorers must have reached that section of the Nile which is today known as the Albert Nile.[43] Here, a little to the west and about 200 kilometres from the entrance into this region, in the Watsa area between the Kabili and Bomolandi rivers, there is gold in quantity.

There is evidence that the Egyptian expeditions had indeed reached the great lakes of central Africa by 3000 BCE. One saga refers to the journey of an Assiut nobleman, Harkhuf, who transported a "dancing dwarf" to delight the Pharaoh Neferkere (Neferirkare). Modern Egyptian sources refer to this dwarf as "a pygmy, from the Land of the Spirits". Very clear instructions for the care of this pygmy were sent to Harkhuf, and those orders included preventive measures to ensure the pygmy did not fall into the water during his journey, by ship, to Lower Egypt.[44] Seligman states that the pygmies at the Egyptian court were not from the Congo valley. Therefore it is very likely they were taken from the pygmy regions between Watsa and Mongbwalu, and between Mongbwalu and Mabana, and transported to Egypt on the Nile River.[45]

And not all that glitters in Africa's mineral deposits is gold. Once a prospector reaches the interlacustrine (great lake) region, he or she must succumb to an incurable infection of "mineral fever"

Mongbwalu fringes on a gold area; deposits occur between Mongbwalu and Nizi, to the west of Lake Albert. There is gold on the Ituri River, at Bomili (to the west of Mongbwalu); gold between Mbana and Manguredjipa. Gold seekers who continued due south would have found gold deposits between Lubero and Lutunguru, and prospectors moving in an easterly direction would locate copper between Kilembe and Budoyne. There are tin deposits to the southeast, at Kakitumba; more tin south of Lake Edward, at Masisi, and near Kabunga; large deposits of tin around Kingombe and Kalima. There is more gold to be found on the other side of Lake Victoria, on the shore near Musoma; inland, at Tarime; and again a little to the south, at Buhemba. Almost due south from Buhemba lies the famous Williamson diamond mine, and the region has alluvial gravels as well. To the southeast, there is gold at Sekenke and at Geita.[46]

Few mineral deposits are known to occur around Lake Tanganyika—where the glorious scenery would probably be unnoticed by a frustrated prospector—but at Manono, to the southwest, there are deposits of tin. And to the east, near Chunya, there is even more gold. From Manono, overland prospectors had the choice of travelling either up or down the Lualaba River; those making use of the waterways most probably travelled via the Ulindi or Elia rivers. The Lualaba leads directly to the great copper deposits, and diamond fields, of Kolwezi and Jadotville. Diamond-bearing kimberlite occurs on the Kundelungu plateau, and at Tshikapa, Bakwanga, and Luashi, more diamondiferous deposits have been found. These are mainly Congo boart, but diamonds nevertheless, and most useful as material for polishing, or inscribing, rocks. Southeast from Jadotville it is copper all the way down to Roan Antelope.

Continuing down Africa, the next major discovery had to be the Zambezi River. Once there, explorers had three choices. They could turn left (east), and work their way down river to the Indian Ocean, and return to Egypt via the East Coast. They could turn right (west) and find a little tin and copper, farther to the west at Kamativi and Wankie (Hwange). Or they could to cross the river, there to discover rich gold, copper, tin, and diamond deposits. Most probably they made thorough explorations in all directions.[47]

The geologist, Dr P.A. Wagner, compiled a map of ancient mining ventures in Africa, and it clearly indicates that the early prospectors followed much the same routes as I have indicated. He pinpointed 23 known ancient mine workings in Zaire; 13 in Zambia; over 100 in Zimbabwe; and more than 60 in South Africa. These only show the copper, tin, and iron mines known to Wagner. The list does not mention ancient diamond workings, nor any of the many ancient workings on private farms, which were not known in 1914 when his research was carried out. Neither does this list include information relating to the mining of other materials, such as antimony.

In his book *Peoples, Seas, and Ships*, Dr Ziv Herman researched deeply into the subject of ancient sea voyages. In particular he tried to identify the exact position of the mysterious Land of Punt. He discovered that a German professor of chemistry had analysed the cosmetics used by Egyptian women of the 6th Dynasty (c. 2423–2263 BCE), and found antimony was one of the ingredients of kohl. Kohl is the black eye cosmetic used in Egypt since ancient times, to give accent to the eyes of women of high rank. As antimony was not to be found in Egypt, and the antimony mines of Persia and Turkey were not discovered until much later in history, he concluded that the antimony so prized by the Egyptian court women could only have come from present-day Zimbabwe. At that period (2400–2300 BCE, the VI Dynasty) the Egyptians were making frequent voyages to the Land of Punt. Knemhotep the sailor, visited it eleven times and the distance is known to have been about 2,485 km or 4,000 miles.[48]

In *The God Kings and Titans* James Bailey mentions the 30,000 tons of bronze, which he believed was manufactured, and removed, from the neighbourhood of the Rooiberg tin mine (North West Province, South Africa).[49] In particular, he notes an important fact, which is often overlooked—some of the bronze artefacts found in Southern Africa contain traces of nickel. Traces of nickel occur in much of the bronze-ware found in ancient Egypt and Sumatra (the connection between Egyptian prospectors and Sumatra is explained later in this chapter), but nickel is rarely present in the raw copper of the Near East. He concluded that Zambia and the Transvaal might well have been the source of the metal used in those artefacts.[50]

The countryside of Zimbabwe and the Transvaal was once littered with the debris, and other evidence, of ancient mining operations. It is an acknowledged fact that early prospectors were known as "blanket prospectors" because, instead of scientifically prospecting an area, they gave blankets to the indigenous people living in the area in return for information about old mine workings. In his *Origin of the Zimbabwean Civilization* Gayre of Gayre writes, "75,000 ancient mine workings have been found in Rhodesia alone", and it has been calculated that the ore which had been extracted totalled 43 million tons. Which, on an average yield of 10dwts per ton, gave the gold recovered as 21,637,500 ounces.[51]

The thousands of tons of gold and other minerals removed from those ancient African mines did not remain in the area of the workings. Neither was all the gold accumulated in the coffers of local African chiefs. Had this been the case then every Southern Africa monarch would have had his own Fort Knox. But by the time the first colonial prospectors moved northwards in search of precious metals and minerals, they were told they could have all the "yellow metal" they desired as it was of no value to the people they met. Local Africans called the ancient mines "the womb of the devil". Not only did they not value gold and silver, they did not even have indigenous names for them.

A denial that there was ever contact between the indigenous inhabitants of Central and Southern Africa and Bronze, or Iron Age invaders, miners, refugees, or traders from abroad, will have to include a logical explanation for the fact that, to this day, the Nguni-speaking peoples associate gold and shining metals with people of other races—people of a frightening or bedazzling nature—and with the Sun-god. According to Sanusi Credo Mutwa, in Old Africa the *unsayable* name of the Sun-god was *Thusi*. He listed for me the Zulu words for:-

gold = ithusi
silver = ithusi
brass = ithusa
copper = ithusa
to frighten, or bedazzle = ukuthusa

According to Sanusi Credo Mutwa, this awe-full fear of the metals was introduced into African speech as the result of the unfortunate experiences of the African peoples with "foreign devils", long ages before the arrival of the Portuguese or Dutch explorers.

When the Portuguese, and later the British, Dutch, and other explorers penetrated Africa, they found that the gold recovery conducted by the indigenous Africans was limited to alluvial panning, and trade with the Arabs of the East Coast of Africa.[52]

The Zulu historian, and Sanusi, Credo Mutwa explained the ingenious method of gold-washing the Khoi were using when the first Nguni-speaking peoples came down to Southern Africa, and said this method was later imitated by the Nguni. According to African oral history, the Khoi recovered the gold from the eastern rivers, and traded with the Arabs on the East Coast. In order to catch the fine particles, and gold dust, after the removal of the nuggets, the gold-containing sand was placed in a large stone basin. Such basins are described as "tools" of the mining process, and specially designed for this step in the production line. The gold-containing sand was covered with water, a quantity of the herb known as *bulawu* was added, and the muddy mixture was then beaten until very frothy. The frothy "meringue" was left to dry overnight, and in the morning the fine particles of gold were rinsed out of the dried bubbles—shades of the Golden Fleece! He told me that the herb *bulawu* is known to this day as "that which belonged to the Khoi", and it is now used in the ritual vomiting for purification practised by diviners and others to "regain the spirit of the gold".

The significance of the gold-processing methods of the Khoi, and later Nguni-speaking peoples, is that their gold recovery was limited to alluvial surface gold and river panning. Neither had any knowledge of shaft mining.[53] Nor did they tunnel for the metal. Yet researchers have

Old Gold

Ill. 49. Ingot symbols are to be found at several engraving sites in mineral-rich South Africa, and arouse no interest at all because they are interpreted as being only the hide tally of a successful hunt. Yet in southern Europe, the Near East and the islands of the Mediterranean, the ingot symbol represented currency and trade. In early times metal was transported in similar ingot forms, and the shape represented the fertility of the Great Mother, giver of wealth and minerals from the depth of her womb.

found that ancient miners of Southern Africa tunnelled, gouged, and shafted into the earth in order to reach the mineral-bearing strata. Clearly, neither the Khoi nor the Nguni-speaking peoples were the original miners in Southern Africa. Mainly, one supposes, because they had no great need for gold, antimony, tin, and other more sophisticated metals and minerals, other than iron and copper. Yet the mines exist, there they are, and obviously a great deal of effort went into their construction and maintenance.

The question of how and when the deposits of gold and other minerals were first discovered in Southern Africa has never been seriously addressed by archaeologists. Most likely the earliest discoveries took place, as I have suggested, by Egyptian prospectors who, in the manner of prospectors everywhere, continued searching and finding until they reached the Zambezi River. Once this great waterway was discovered, all their transport problems were resolved. No longer would it have been necessary to portage ore and equipment to the Great Lakes, thence overland between the waterways, until the Nile River was reached. The Zambezi was a potential highway between the Great Forge of Ptah and Africa's mineral wealth, and this may well have been how the Zambezi and Sabi rivers were named. For *sam* and *sab* were Egyptian words for gold.[54] It is significant that the expansion of Egyptian maritime power received great impetus during the Old Kingdom (Third Dynasty, c. 2780–2270 BCE). Gold and other metals were transported as ingots, usually in the shape of animal hide for convenient portage, and such ingot shapes have been engraved on the rocks of South Africa, at places close to mineral outcrops (Ill. 49).

The Middle Kingdom (2133–1785 BCE) reached the zenith of Egyptian power with the conquests of Palestine and Nubia, down to the 2nd Cataract. In 1879 BCE a law was proclaimed forbidding the entry of Negroes into Egypt beyond the 2nd Cataract, unless on trade or a special mission.[55] Egyptian maritime power again reached a new peak during the reign of Queen Hatshepsut (New Kingdom c. 1575–1085 BCE), and Ramses II (XIX Dynasty, c.1308–1186 BCE) when the foreign cults of Baal/Astarte continued to develop. The cults of Baal, and his consort Astarte (alias Aphrodite, etc.), reached a climax during the reign of Ramses III, who is said to have kept a large colony of Egyptians in Southern Africa, to work some of the mines, and to send the gold to Egypt by ship.[56]

Sanusi Credo Mutwa brought an important fact to my notice during the course of one of our conversations relating to foreign influence on Zulu culture:-

'Now you see, Mam, here is something which is very, very funny!' ("funny" in this instance meaning "curious", not "humourous") 'The Zulu people have a name for a ship. See? You know what it is called? *umKhumbi*! The name does *not* apply to a modern European ship. The name *umKhumbi* means, literally, a rope spine. It means a huge rope spine! Does this mean anything to you? No?' He paused. Then, speaking slowly, and giving emphasis to every word, said, 'Ancient Egyptian ships had a rope spine across them! They had a huge rope, which went from bow to stern, and was supported by supports in the middle. Now this rope is what we are referring to when we say *umKhumbi*. The word *umKhumbi* we also use not only to denote a ship but to denote a very strong-willed man. In other words, a man with a spine of rope. Our name for a ship goes back very far, to the first ships we knew. The ships with rope spines!'

Thus, although the Zulu may never have been a seafaring nation, there can be no doubt that long, long ago, farther north in Africa, their ancestors had contact with reed or papyrus ships often enough to coin a descriptive word for this mode of travel.

Another word, the Zulu word for a writer, *umBhali*, relates to the Sun-God Baal, or Bel, and is said to have been introduced into the language of the peoples of Southern Africa long ages ago. Sanusi Credo Mutwa gives the literal meaning of *umBhali* as "a symbol maker", a servant of the Sun-god. And, because everything associated with the craft of writing was sacrosanct, only priests of the Sun-god were allowed to engrave the sacred symbols on stone.

The engravings on the rocks of South Africa depicting typical representations of the fertility god Baal have already been mentioned. And although other sources agree that the Holy Ones, priests or priestesses inscribed the rocks,[57] Sanusi Credo Mutwa is the first to point out the link between the Zulu word for a writer, *umBhali*, and the devout scribes in the service of Baal and Astarte.

In *Circles and Standing Stones* Evan Harding mentions the work of researcher Ronald Morris who found that the distribution of rock carvings coincides to a remarkable degree with the deposits of copper and gold in southern Scotland.[58] In ancient Egypt, rocks near the turquoise mines were engraved with images of the falcon and other symbols. Rock engravings are also to be found in the gold- and diamond-producing areas near Irkutsk, in Siberia. The established link between mining and rock engravings in Scotland, Egypt and Russia, does not say the practice was confined only to those three countries. More than likely it was general practice to incise rocks with meaningful symbols wherever mining operations were conducted, so too in Africa. Yet to date little, if any, heed is paid to the fact that a trail of rock art and stone tool industries accompanies the line of gold, copper, tin, diamond and other mineral deposits, from Uganda to the Cape of Good Hope in South Africa.

As I have suggested, the discovery and extraction of Africa's mineral deposits was most probably the catalyst which led to the transfusion of legends, religion, language, rock art and stone artefacts, and to the miscegenation that produced the Khoi and Koranna races. But significant is the fact that the engraving sites of Southern Africa relate for the most part to the diamond fields, as tabled below:-

Tanzania
Between the engravings at Mwanza on the southern shores of Lake Victoria, and the painting area near Kondoa Irangi are the

gold mines of Senenke, the Williamson diamond mine and alluvial diamond fields near Shinyanga.[59]

Zambia
The engraving sites at Chifubwa are located at the source of the Lualaba River, near the Katanga diamond deposits around the source of the Lualaba, and near Kolwezi on the Mutendele River.[60]

Zimbabwe
The Bembezi group, to the northeast of Bulawayo, has four occurrences of kimberlite pipes, two of which are diamond-bearing. A considerable area of detrital deposits occur in the Somabula forest, along the N'gamo River (west of Gweru). There are kimberlite pipes on the Shangani River, and near Insiza, Colossus, and Wessels. Alluvial gravels occur approximately 20 miles below Rhodes drift, on the Limpopo River; on the Mkumbura River to the north of Darwin; and in the valley of the Mnyati River, northwest of Chivu. These deposits of diamondiferous material are all within reasonable distance of the engraving sites at the Matopos, and also those near the Zambezi.[61]

Namibia
The engravings in central Namibia are found relatively close to the huge alluvial diamond deposits along the coast, and the southern engraving sites correspond to the diamond fields of Gibeon, Berseba, Bethanie and Keetmanshoop. Relevant to a link between engravings and ancient mining activities, is the very important fact that Twyfelfontein is situated at a perennial spring, and the vast rock engraving site is on the massive outcrop of red sandstone. And that this sandstone has a high iron ore content![62]

South Africa
By far the greater majority of South Africa's approximately 350 known engraving sites are concentrated in the Northern Cape, North West Province, and the Free State—the areas where the greatest concentration of kimberlite pipes, and alluvial diamond-bearing gravels are found.[63]

Many of these rock engravings are obviously of great age. Nevertheless, distinctly different styles of artistic expression, from the earlier beautifully executed examples, to later crudely chipped images, are found together at the majority of engraving sites, and this suggests that successive groups of artists, from different, maybe even conflicting, cultures, left notations or invocations on the rocks.

African rock art in general, and the rock art of Southern Africa in particular, is regarded as a record of the life and times of the prehistoric hunter/gatherer tribes who inhabited the regions. Interpretation is therefore confined to explaining the art as depicting hunting, fighting, food gathering, and dancing for pleasure—pleasure only, no mention is made of dancing in empathy with ancestral or nature spirits. Or it is said they represent people in a trance state, full stop. Again the concept has not been taken further, such as the pre-hunting rituals, entering into the animal to be hunted, and so forth. If the mining activities are taken into account, then certain examples of the rock art could depict scenes related to mining, or the transporting of minerals and equipment to and from the mines.

In his article *Later Stone Age Research in the Motopos*, N.J. Walker states that the rock art of the Motopos usually shows people walking or resting. He particularly notes the lack of festive scenes, which, he says, could be interpreted as dancing, and the unusual rarity of hunting scenes. He mentions that the men carry small bags attached to the arms, or small of the back, and that women carry larger bundles and small bags. He further notes that groups of up to 60 people are portrayed in one picture.[64]

In ancient times, large quantities of gold and other minerals were mined in Southern Africa—43 million tons of gold ore extracted, what happened to it? The bulk of the material did not remain in the country, so, before the use of camels, the only practical way to move merchandise from the mines to waiting ships would be to load it onto porters. If the blinkers of conventional assessment are momentarily removed, and the subject is regarded with impartial judgement, then these paintings of groups of people could be seen as records of the "back-pack" transport system of early African mining operations.

Despite the lack of scientific research into the history of Southern Africa's ancient mines, old manuscripts nevertheless testify to the extent of Egyptian mining ventures as early as the 2nd Egyptian Dynasty and, as one of these records makes specific mention of Egyptian gold mining activities in Southern Africa, I quote in full the paper *Egyptian Gold Seekers and Exploration in the Pacific* (The Epigraphic Society Occasional Publications. Vol. 2 No. 27, 1975) by Professor

George Carter (Distinguished Professor of Geography at Texas A & M University, and Fellow of the American Geographical Society):

With the work of Barry Fell of Harvard in translating the material in the Maori alphabet in North Africa and his finding that this is the key to reading inscriptions in the Indian Ocean, and on into the Pacific Ocean and even to America, it becomes desirable to review some aspects of the Egyptian record as voyagers, explorers and gold seekers. For this purpose I have translated Quiring's "die Goldinsel Des Isador Von Sevilla, Aegypter Der 20 Dynastie Als Entdeker und Kulturbringer in Ostasien". Quiring, as the bibliography shows, had previously written on the oceanic discovery of the Egyptian and Phoenician prospectors and on the oldest evidence for iron and steel. I have abbreviated parts of the manuscript and have appended a note on voyaging time in the early seventeenth century.This paper is intended as a supporting piece to the footnoted reference, which includes a review of earlier papers in the "Occasional Publications" dealing with inscriptions in the Libyan dialect of Egyptian, one of these from an American site. The gist of Quiring's work is that the Egyptians had long been familiar with the Indian Ocean and the western fringes of the Pacific Ocean, especially the China Sea.If Fell's hypothesis that the Egyptians in about 232 BC sent out a fleet to seek gold and to circumnavigate the world to test Eratosthenes' determination of the size of the world, then their earlier acquaintance with the Indian Ocean and its farthermost reaches might explain why the fleet set out on an eastward circumnavigation instead of a westerly route.

Quiring begins by commenting on the fact that there was a persistent legend of a Golden Island in the East Indies and he tells of expeditions being sent out as late as the early 16th century to try to find this magical golden island. He states that in the whole circumference of the Indian Ocean, Sumatra is the only island for which gold mining is demonstrable. We may pick up direct translation here. Within the translation, my comments are placed in brackets.

"If we wish to answer the question of whether the Golden Isle legend can be verified, we must shift our viewpoint back into great antiquity. The 2nd Egyptian Dynasty (c. 2890–2686 BC, in the chronology of the British Museum, 1971; Quiring's dates being adjusted throughout Carter's translation – Ed.) had abandoned the usual placer mining of river gold for it wasn't bringing in enough, and had gone over to hard rock mining in the "desert" between the Nile and the Red Sea. Gold hunters from earliest times had sought out the gold dust in the rivers, and this had led them to mining the pediments and finally to hard-rock

Old Gold

mining. Under Sahure (5th Dynasty, c. 2494–2345 BC) the results of the first great sea voyages from the Red Sea to the gold and antimony land of Punt (Pwenet) were recorded. These voyages yielded 6,000 deben (1 deben = about 91 grams) of electron, probably river gold derived from the Zambezi and the Sabi rivers. The journeys to Punt were pursued with energy during the 6th Dynasty (c. 2345–2891 BC). A tax man tells the story in his epitaph, that he with his men, had luckily travelled the long route to Punt, which required three years, not less than eleven times. In the same way, the Pharaohs of the Middle Kingdom gave leave for these journeys to be carried on. Not only has Herodotus recorded that they set out from the Red Sea in long ships for the Indies, but so have inscriptions by two ship captains from the south of the Wadi Gasus in the Red Sea. (Note shift from Africa to the East Indies). *These voyages must have required courage, otherwise the tax people and captains would hardly have put such high praise in their records. After the expulsion of the Hyksos, Thutmose I (c. 1525–1512 BC) again took up the voyages to the Indies. In the cliffs of the Isle of Tombos, his inscription claims that he is ruler of the islands of the Great Encircling Sea. Clearly the search for gold in Africa (and elsewhere) had led to the discovery of the oceans surrounding Africa and of the possibility of sailing completely around Africa. The Egyptians were by this time well acquainted with the Red Sea and the Indian Ocean.*

Thutmose I's followers vigorously continued these flourishing trade voyages. The magnificent reliefs of Hatshepsut (c. 1500 BC) in the temple of Dair el Bahri show this particularly well. Likewise, Rameses II (c. 1304–1237 BC) considered himself the ruler of Africa and the Oceans. On granite statue in the Luxor temple he claimed the Great Encircling Sea as well as the southern Negro land as far as the marsh regions, and to "the borders of the darkness" and "the columns of heaven." (The Mediterraneans viewed themselves as living on an island encircled by the world ocean. Their frequent reference to islands in the encircling sea can be taken to refer to continents for that is how they referred to their own continent.)

Thus the Punt travellers over whose success the Egyptian History exclaimed for an era of almost 1,400 years had discovered coasts and islands in and around the Indian Ocean, apparently as far as the Southern Polar Circle. (This southern extent of exploration is based on the reference to "darkness", seemingly a record of Polar day length.) *Under Ramses III (c. 1198–1166 BC) the voyages to the Indies first became great expeditions. The Harris Papyrus claims that on such a voyage up to 10,000 seamen and merchants were sent* (see notes) *and probably expert miners and prospectors were included. The fortuitous ending of the Trojan Wars and the defeat of the Sea People by Ramses III had given back to the Egyptians their freedom of movement on the seas. Upon the Mediterranean Sea and the Red Sea swarmed not only the fleets of the Pharaoh but also fleets of the temple hierarchy of Amon, Re, and Ptah, in order to deliver the products of Phoenicia, of Syria, and of the coasts of the Erythraean Sea (Indian Ocean) to their treasure vaults. The shipping probably expanded at this time to a greater measure than ever before. These were seagoing ships built of cedar and were up to 67 metres long. The purpose of these great expeditions in the Indian Ocean was apparently in the main the combining of the predominant placer gold washing on the Zambezi and Sabi with a multiform mining operation from the hard-rock bearing areas in the great dykes of Zimbabwe, the tin-bearing areas of Roiiberg, and the copper-bearing regions of Katanga.*

When, 2,700 years later, the British Corporations in AD 1893 began to work these ore bodies they demonstrated that all mineable gold-, tin- and copper-bearing lodes had already been worked vigorously in antiquity with just such tools as were used in Egypt and Nubia in antiquity. Ferner found a barbaric clay figurine of Thutmose III in the Zambezi gold district and in Zimbabwe a gold ingot formed in the style of the ingots portrayed in the Temple of the Nedinet Habu during the reign of Ramses III. After extraction of about 5,000,000 kilograms of gold, the ancient miners suddenly abandoned their mines in the 9th century before Christ.

In AD 1896 ancient hard-rock gold works were found on the western coast of Sumatra. When prospectors of the Redjang Lebong Company searched over the gold-bearing area in AD 1897, they found in the old mine tailing dumps in the villages of Lebong Donak pieces of ore that assayed 180 to 200 grams of gold and up to 1200 grams of silver per ton which had been carried as far as 10 kilometres. In this ancient mining region therefore, there was as in Upper Egypt, Nubia, and South Africa separation of the preliminary extraction and ore dressing from the final extraction of the metal.

It was not only the shallow parts of the Lebong deposit, but also the richer zones of the neighbouring deposits, such as those of Lebong Solit and Tambong-Sawak that were mined and sometimes to depths of 30 metres.

It was first assumed that the Chinese had undertaken the mines at the beginning of the 19th century, but this is improbable. The Chinese did not do deep mining. About 1500 BC in India a gold mine in Mysore was undertaken but it was abandoned, forgotten by man for 3,400 years until the English had it reopened in AD 1880. It may be that dreadful working conditions and fear of underworld demons deterred primitive men from deep mines. In any case the people of South and East Asia at least until the end of the Middle Ages restricted themselves to surface mining and washing of gold, magnetite and gem stones from river sands.

During the course of writing my "History of Gold" I came to the conviction that the ancient gold mines of Sumatra belong to the era from 1200 to 500 BC. No East or South Asian people could have stimulated the operation or could have undertaken it. Within the circumference of the Indian Ocean in those days only one people, the Egyptians, carried out large-scale mining of gold. Without Egyptian influence there were only placer gold operations.

That just as in South Africa, so too in Sumatra, it was the Egyptians that implemented gold mining becomes almost a certainty if one considers a published report by Pauthier and Bazin, according to which in 1113 BC, the Chinese Emperor Tschoking received ambassadors from the kingdom of Ni-li, probably Egyptians, who made long voyages in "swimming houses" and who could determine their position by means of "observation of the sun and heavenly bodies" in order to identify the regions and realms. Also F. Freise, without knowing of the ancient mines of Sumatra, concluded that these ambassadors were Egyptians. This ambassadorship requires that the Pharaohs—only the Ramessidean kings of the 20th Dynasty come into question—had knowledge of the existence of the Chinese realm. The Egyptians obviously had some activity in East Asia, and this could only have been the gold mines of Sumatra.

Long Ships with gold hunters were probably already sailing under Ramses III not only on the southern (Monsoon to South Africa), but with the summer monsoon to the East to reach the northern coast of Sumatra. With the Southwest monsoon sailboats of only 10 metres length and 2.7 metres width have traversed the distance from Aden all the way to the west coast of Sumatra in 12 days. Since the gold deposits of Benkoelen are less than 40 kilometres distant from the coast of Sumatra and the gold-bearing alluvium extends to the sea, the energetic and experienced prospectors could hardly have missed them. Sumatra produced about 100,000 kilograms of gold at this time. During this period of exploitation the Egyptians established relations with the kingdoms of intervening regions. They were also the first people of the Mediterranean to pass through the Straits of Malaca according to east Asian records, and the first to travel the South China Sea to the Huang Ho River and up it to the capital of that era at Singanfu in Shensi province.

That the mines were soon abandoned is probably to be explained by the decline in Egyptian world power already evident at the end of the 20th Dynasty (1085 BC). The Egyptian cultural influence on East Asia did not disappear however, for their influence had broad effects. Thus in Cambodia, which had been dominated up to this time by Palaeolithic cultures, there suddenly appeared bronze tools. These included axes (Tullenbeile) of almost Mediterranean-European type. The Tullenbeile era coincides with the Bronze Age Stage III and corresponds chronologically with the Egyptian 20th Dynasty. It was not possible until this time to explain the sudden appearance of these axes in Southeast Asia. Menghin postulated a roundabout route through Russia and Siberia. If we may now reckon with an Egyptian cultural influence in Southeast Asia, we gain a solution for the difficult question of the sudden jump from the Neolithic to the Bronze Age and can attribute the cultural revolution to outside influences. The particular axe forms appear in the Near East and Egypt around 1850 BC and remain in use until about 700 BC and the Southeast Asian materials appear to be of the same age.

Under Egyptian influence, the gold-washing operation on the Malacca peninsula, the Golden Chersonese of the Periplus of the Erythraean Sea (the Indian Ocean) may have begun. Ptolemy recorded place names in Inner India, which are linked with SAB and SAM (Egyptian, SAM meaning river gold). Similarly, in South Africa the Egyptians left behind names related to the gold-washing operations, such for example as Sabi and Zambezi (Gold River).

However, after the death of Ramses III (1166 BC) the Egyptian decline loomed. The relationship with the East was broken soon thereafter, probably by 1090 BC."

Professor Carter comments as follows:-

Quiring shifts from Punt-in-Africa to Punt-in-the-East-Indies. If Punt referred to the distant gold-yielding lands, it could have been both, or perhaps first one and then the other. The subject has long been debated.

It is widely accepted that the Egyptians sent out a fleet that successfully circumnavigated Africa. We tend to forget that for every recorded event of this sort there were possibly ten to 100 more unrecorded. Note for instance the Canaanite inscription in Brazil, a chance record of an otherwise unknown voyage around Africa. (Cyrus Gordon, 1969; Cross, 1968).

The number of people sent on these trips is highly significant. It has been said of the presence of the American military in some of the Pacific

Islands during World War II that they virtually changed the racial make-up of the population. Ten thousand Egyptians sent out to gold districts must have had a sizeable biological impact on the native population. The biological shift must have been more abrupt and effective than the cultural change for a native woman bearing an Egyptian child might well rear the child wholly in the native culture, but biologically the child would be half Mediterranean.

No doubt other nations eventually learned the whereabouts of the apparently inexhaustible supply of mineral wealth, and they too infiltrated Central and Southern Africa from the Indian Ocean and along the waterways. The foreign intervention in Egyptian politics began as early as the First Intermediate Period (2263–2040 BCE), when social unrest erupted and the first wave of invaders entered the land. Over the ages Egypt was conquered, and ruled, by foreigners from many countries—all of whom were thus placed in the position of control over the country's mining interests.

Bronze Age miners were dependent on tools of stone, and their productivity was geared to hewing tunnels, and lifting bales, with manual labour. The extraction of metals by splitting rocks with fire, digging out earth with stone tools, and carrying away the rubble on the backs of porters in an age long before the wheel was discovered, was a lengthy process, and must surely have necessitated a very large work force. One unit would have to be employed to dig into the earth to extract the minerals or ore, others were surely used to carry away the rubble and debris, another group would have to clear and prepare ground to be worked. And this is only the middle part of such an operation. Toolmakers would have to be employed to craft stones into digging instruments, and holed stones, as loom weights in the weaving of cloths. Hunters were needed to feed the work force. And unless all haberdashery was imported from the home, or they all wore skins, then weavers were required to supply clothing, bedding etc., and this entails a need for the fleece of sheep or goats, and shepherds. It is interesting to note here, that a sheep tooth was found near Kimberley dated to the 11th to 10th centuries BCE, which is a considerable time before the accepted date for the arrival of the earliest black tribes to the region.[65] Water-carriers and fruit gatherers, root diggers, and planters of grain were necessary, for even if the labourers were lowly slaves, they still had to be fed and watered. As mentioned, in Southern Africa there is evidence that the ores were smelted into ingots, on site, for easy transport to their ultimate destination. This satellite industry required priest/magician metallurgists, specialists in forging, the maintenance of the fires, the building of bellows, for which specially treated skins, usually goat skins, were necessary. And so goatherds or hunters had to be employed. Stone basins for the grinding of grain, earthenware jars, ostrich eggs, or calabashes were essential for storing food and liquids. All these had to be made on the spot, or obtained by trading. Even skilful trading is a job that is best left to experienced hagglers.

Efficient production is dependent on all these essential services, and this suggests that the early mining ventures operated in much the same way as they do today, where the staff—men, women, and children—are housed and cared for within the complex. Therefore, near the mines, but at a distance from the mine compounds, would be found initiation centres, sanctuaries and graves. Sanctuaries, where the ceremonies for the regeneration of all forms of life—human, animal, vegetable, and mineral—were conducted, to ensure that all earth's creatures and minerals might prosper, were in the charge of the priests who controlled the daily lives of kings and workers alike. We know very little about the physical acts performed, or the chants used during the pagan rites and rituals, but we do know that certain invocations required the priests, or priestesses, to inscribe rocks with mystical symbols. And to do that successfully, they needed a writing tool such as the diamond-tipped one inherited by Sanusi Credo Mutwa.

Now, Moses recorded the Laws of the Twelve Tribes on stone tablets, and it is said he supervised the engraving of the stones of the Breastplate of Judgement with a *shamir*.

One of those twelve stones was a diamond, and although many learned arguments have been put forward to prove that, when the scholars recorded, "and the second row shall be an emerald, a sapphire and a diamond" (Exodus 28:18), the word "diamond" was a mistranslation, I believe there is nevertheless a very strong possibility that Aaron's sacred vestment was indeed embellished with a genuine diamond—one that could have been recovered, in ancient times, from the alluvial gravels of South Africa.

Chapter 4

Diamonds, sacred to the Moon Goddess

The Biblical description of the Breastplate of Judgement clearly states that the jewel allotted to the tribe Zebulun was a diamond:-

"And the second row shall be an emerald, a sapphire, and a diamond."
(Exodus 28:18 & 39:11)

An enduring modern assumption is that diamonds were unknown to Bronze and Iron Age peoples, and that every reference to "diamond" in lore or literature referred to crystals, or white sapphires, but never to diamonds.

For generations the translation of this Biblical passage has given rise to considerable discussion, and scholars are in agreement that somewhere an error, or misunderstanding, has arisen. Many insist that, whatever the stone might have been, it could not have been a diamond. One of the main objections put forward against the possibility that a diamond was engraved with the name Zebulun and set in the breastplate, centres on the value of the diamond above "lesser" jewels, such as agate or jasper. There is a belief that, had this "most precious" of gems been bestowed on one tribe only, the other eleven tribes would seethe with envy and hatred because they had been allocated so-called less worthy gems.[1]

Those who put forward this argument overlook the important fact that, in antiquity, no jewel was less valuable than another. There were no "precious stones", in the modern sense, more worthy or of greater monetary value than "semi-precious" jewels, by virtue of appearance alone. Each gem had its own unique worth. The talismanic and therapeutic value counted more than beauty or availability. There is even a Talmudic reference to the gems in Breastplate of Judgement, and the observation by the Jewish historian, Josephus (c. 3795 BCE) is most pertinent to this discussion.[2] Josephus said the stones were not only rare and of exceptional size, but that each stone possessed wonderful and miraculous powers. Which means in fact that the gems were allotted to the Tribes of Israel, each to its own need and character.

The practical worth of diamonds was probably recognized long before these stones were used in jewellery. As mentioned in a previous chapter, Egyptian workmen (2300–2723 BCE) cut stones with diamond-tipped saws. A diamond-tipped tool could cut, or engrave, a stone surface with greater speed, and less mess, than the rock crystal (quartz) or sapphire-tipped engraving tools the Assyrians are known to have used.[3] Engraving tools tipped with quartz would have been of little use as a means of cutting the stones most often incised for seals or jewellery, because quartz has a hardness of 7, which is equal to the hardness of agate, onyx, jasper, carnelian, and most of the other jewels valued by the ancients for their therapeutic, or talismanic, properties.[4] To obtain the high standard of workmanship they did achieve, the scribes must have used tools tipped with harder material, such as sapphire, jade, corundum, or diamond.

The *shamir* with which the stones for the breastplate of Aaron, High Priest of the Hebrews, were engraved, must have been such a tool. In *The Curious Lore of Precious Stones* Dr George Kunz describes how the names of the twelve tribes were first written on the jewels, in ink, then the *shamir* was passed over the writing, and the inscriptions were graven into the stones. He states that the word *shamir* means *emery*, and that the magical quality of this operation lay in the fact that no particle of the jewel was seen to have been removed in the process.[5] Only a diamond-tipped tool could cut with such precision.

Another scholarly argument for substituting anything other than a genuine diamond in the High Priest's breastplate is that all the stones selected for this talisman had to be approximately 5 x 6.5 centimetres in size.[6] Biblical scholars have expressed great disbelief that so large a diamond could ever have existed. Most likely their doubts are based on the assumption that, until the discovery of diamonds in Brazil c.1825, India, where large diamonds are rarely found, was the only known source.

The mining of diamonds in India goes back at least 5,000 years, when the Koh-i-noor was mentioned in the songs of the Vedas.[7] However, as miners and traders throughout the ages have always been extremely secretive about the source of their merchandise, it is more than likely that the Egyptians—and later, others—carried African and Indonesian diamonds to India, where diamond mining and marketing was already a long established business. Once there the stones were sold on the open market, India's reputation was made—the word went out, "all diamonds come from India".

To believe India was the only source of diamonds, prior to the opening of the mines in Brazil in AD1825, and later in South Africa, is to overlook the many anomalies lurking in dark corners of the records. India is credited with producing every one of the coloured historical diamonds. Yet "fancy stones", or coloured diamonds, are only rarely recovered from Indian mines. On the other hand, the bulk of the diamonds from Borneo and Angola (at Hanha and Mucope) are yellowish, or canary yellow in colour. And in the short time the diamond fields have been worked in South Africa, many fabulous coloured diamonds, and diamonds of exceptional size, have been found. It may even be said that large diamonds were relatively common in the early days of digging and prospecting in South Africa—as may be seen from the list of magnificent stones recovered during the past hundred years[8]:-

The Cullinan weighed 621.2 grams (slightly over one and a quarter pounds, or half a kilogram). This fabulous gem displayed only three natural facets, and its shape suggested that it was merely a portion of an enormous stone, more than double its size.

The Excelsior weighed 995.2 metric carats in the rough.

The Jubilee weighed 660.8 metric carats

The Victoria or **Great White** weighed 469 metric carats

The du Toit weighed 250 metric carats

The de Beers weighed 440 metric carats

The Red Cross weighed 370 metric carats

The Jonker turned the scales at 726 metric carats and measured 3.8 x 6.3 centimetres—almost the size needed by Moses.

The fact that modern diamond diggers, working the alluvial gravels in the 20th century, recovered very few large diamonds can be attributed to lack of experience and education. Believing that very large diamonds were only a myth, the mesh of their largest gravitating sieve measures only seven eights of an inch. In other words, any stone larger than about 2.5 centimetres was automatically thrown out onto the rough. In recent years it became very profitable to work over the digging heaps of the early 20th century, to recover the fortunes thrown away through sheer ignorance. Therefore, the fact that alluvial diamond diggers—as opposed to miners working the kimberlite—rarely recovered large diamonds, cannot be taken as an indication that no large diamonds were ever present in the alluvial gravels.

Today, the biggest known diamond in the world, owned by de Beers, weighs 1,463 carats, far greater than the size said to have been required for Aaron's Breastplate of Judgement! Sumatra and Borneo, which were prospected by the Egyptians (c. 1198–1166 BCE), were also recognized as diamond-rich regions. A pure white stone of 367 carats, was found near Landak, in Borneo,[9] but this gemstone is small by comparison with the large diamonds recovered in modern times in South Africa.

In addition to the stones listed above, the South African mines have produced many others, all of which are nameless, and have no historical importance. In his book *The Genesis of the Diamond*, Alpheus Williams gives a long list (with dates) of diamonds of at least 100 carats weight. It suffices here only to mention that the list contains sixteen between 400 and 500 carats, and fourteen that exceed 500 carats.

A very real perplexity confronting Biblical scholars is the vexing problem of how Bezaleel, the craftsman who assisted Moses (Exodus 35:33/38:22), was able to engrave a diamond when, according to archaeologists, the tools of the trade were tipped with sapphire or corundum.

Not all the engraving tools of antiquity relied on semi-hard nibs. Jeremiah was one scribe who utilized the magical properties of a diamond when he, too, railed against backsliding Hebrews, *"The sin of Judah is written with a pen of iron, and with the point of a diamond: it is graven upon the table of their heart, and upon the horns of your altars"* (Jeremiah 17:1).

Admittedly Jeremiah (c. 610 BCE) lived in a more advanced age than Moses, but the craft of engraving with a pen designed for the purpose, has been practised for at least 8,500 years. In *Roots of Civilization* Alexander Marshack describes in detail the quartz-tipped bone engraving tool from Ishango (on the shore of Lake Edward, Central Africa) which is known to date from 6500 BCE.[10] Which means that industrious, literate people were already scratching away with quartz-tipped tools 8,500 years ago. Industrious people are always looking around for easier ways of doing whatever it is they have to do. Therefore it is not unreasonable to suppose that some of the scribes, at least, must have switched to using diamonds as soon as the prospectors sent samples of this new material back to headquarters. It is more than likely that the scribes were using diamond-tipped tools long before the diamond-tipped saws were invented. Naturally they wouldn't gossip about their new technology, for otherwise the miraculous *shamir* would lose its virtue, and they their prestige.

The difficulty of engraving a diamond is overcome by simply using a harder diamond to engrave a softer one. Diamonds from Borneo and New South Wales are unusually hard. This is because the majority of Borneo diamonds are "twinned", or "knotted". By comparison, as diamonds are judged, the average South African diamond is soft, although "twinned" diamonds are not uncommon in South Africa.[11] Therefore Bezaleel, the craftsman instructed by Moses to engrave the stones to be set in the breastplate of the High Priest, could have inscribed the name "Zebulan" on a large diamond from South Africa, using a *shamir* tipped with a "twinned" stone from South Africa, Borneo or New South Wales.

Only one further question remains to be resolved before a diamond may safely be re-inserted into the Breastplate of Judgement. And that is the question of how the Hebrew hordes, trailing through arid, semi-desert wastes, or so the story goes, could possibly get hold of a 700–800-carat diamond.

Now, whether the Biblical story of Moses and the Twelve Tribes of Israel is a true historical record of the times, as some scholars aver, or merely a story about a legendary folk hero told, with little or no regard for the facts, to boost the morale of the nomads as they wandered through the wilderness, as others claim, is neither here nor there as far as this book is concerned. At the heart of all legends and folk tales lies a core of truth—either a revelation of an otherwise obscure esoteric mystery, or factual information about an historical happening. So, whether you agree with the Biblical story, or not, I am asking you to bear with me. For, whatever the origins of the tale, I believe that when the Israelites departed from Egypt, they carried away a bounty of jewels, one of which was a genuine South African diamond large enough to have been engraved, and inserted in the breastplate of the high priest.

The answer lies in the Biblical story of how Moses was found, and raised to manhood by the daughter of the Pharoah:- *"And the child grew, and she brought him unto Pharaoh's daughter, and he became her son. And she called his name Moses: and she said because I drew him out of the water"* (Exodus 2:10).

As the adopted son of the Pharaoh's daughter, who no doubt held the rank of high priestess, Moses must have received a temple education, one which included initiation into the mysteries of metallurgy, geometry, astronomy, geology (he knew which rocks to strike to find water), etc., etc., for the Egyptian priests were even then mathematicians and scientists, although it is said the earlier priests were in possession of greater knowledge.[12]

There can be no doubt that he was initiated into the craft of the scribe, for:-

He recorded the Laws of the Tribes, on slabs of stone.
He used a *shamir*.
He supervised the engraving of the stones of the breastplate.

Regardless of the arguments that the story of Moses could be something of a blending, or distorting, of a number of legends or historical facts, it cannot be denied that the character known as Moses had been initiated into the esoteric, and scientific, mysteries of the Egyptian priesthood. For otherwise he would never have been allowed to marry the daughter of Jethro, a Midianite priest. The Midianites/Kenites, who worshipped *Yahweh* at their sacred mountain, were metallurgists, and as such guardians of the sacred knowledge of refining and forging metals—and that was a very closed society indeed.[13]

The problem he faced in obtaining a 5 x 6.5 centimetre diamond was surely no less than he must have encountered in finding a sardius, topaz, carbuncle, emerald, sapphire, ligure, agate, amethyst, beryl, onyx, or jasper, of that size. For those stones made up the balance of the jewels required for the breastplate.[14] That he did obtain these huge gems, with no apparent difficulty, may be attributed to the desperate generosity of the Egyptians when the Hebrews fled the country.

According to Biblical records, the Exodus of the Israelites happened at the time when Egypt was being bombarded with a succession of the most dreadful plagues and pestilences. It is written that the Egyptian people were traumatized, and all they could think of was to get rid of the Hebrews, whatever the cost, before things got worse. As there appear to be no Egyptian records of the Exodus, we again turn to the Bible for a description of the events immediately preceding the Exodus:-

"Moreover the man Moses was very great in the land of Egypt, in the sight of the Pharaoh's servants, and in the sight of the people."
"And the children of Israel did according to the word of Moses; and they borrowed of the Egyptians jewels of silver, and jewels of gold, and raiment.
And the Lord gave the people favour in the sight of the Egyptians, so that they lent unto them such things as they required. And they spoiled the Egyptians" (Exodus 11:3 /12: 35,36).

No doubt there was also a "borrowing" of cattle and sheep—*such things as they required*—which, in normal times, might well have been viewed as stock theft. The Bible makes particular mention of the many sheep, goats and cattle the Israelites took with them when they departed:-

"And the children of Israel journeyed from Rameses to Succoth, about six hundred thousand on foot that were men, beside children. And a mixed multitude went up also with them; and flocks, and herds, even very much cattle" (Exodus 12 – 37:38).

These Biblical records leave no doubt that the Israelites removed goods and valuables to the extent of despoilment.

Royalty, and the godly, have ever hoarded wealth, from generation to generation. One only has to look at the British Crown Jewels, and the fabulous treasures of the Vatican, to have some idea of what the Egyptian priesthood and pharaohs must have accumulated over the millennia, since the earliest dynasties. Which brings us back to Moses, an initiate into temple secrets and *"very great in the land of Egypt, in the sight of the Pharaoh's servants, and in the sight of the people"*. As the adopted son of the Pharaoh's daughter, Moses must have known the whereabouts of the hoarded wealth of the palaces and temples.

Therefore, as he was leaving the country, and had no intention of ever returning, there is the hitherto unmentioned possibility that he selectively raided royal and temple coffers, and carried away a quantity of fabulous jewels. Fabulous jewels, among which must surely have been at least one of the largest diamonds ever recovered from the ancient diamond mines of Southern Africa by the Egyptian gold seekers and prospectors since earliest times. Very likely the pharaoh sent his troops pounding after the fleeing hordes to recover stolen goods, rather than to prevent the departure of the tribes.

If my supposition is correct, it was the spoils, borrowed from the Egyptians on a permanent basis, that Moses used for the building of the Ark and the Tabernacle, and the first priestly vestments, including the ephod and breastplate to be worn by Aaron. The ephod was an upper garment worn by the high priest. It was one of the six sacred vestments that he was required to put on when about to conduct the worship of God. It was made of gold, blue, purple and scarlet, and fine-twined linen.[15] The ephod went closely about the body, and was supported by two straps which passed over the shoulders. Onyx stones were enclosed in filigree settings of gold and set at the top of each of the shoulder straps of the ephod, and the command makes specific mention of:-

"Onyx stones, and the stones to be set in the ephod and in the breastplate"
(Exodus 25:7/35:27).

The word diamond is said to have come from the Greek *adamas* but, because the early Greeks are not thought to have known the true diamond, many authorities aver that when the word *adamas* is used, a stone other than a diamond is intended. Referring to Adam, first man, Robert Graves identifies this translation as an Homeric epithet borrowed from the Death Goddess, his mother, and given to the Biblical Adam, and suggests the original hero at Hebron was the Danaan Adamos, *Adamas* or *Adamastos*, "the unconquerable", "the inexorable".[16]

Of all white stones, only the diamond may be called unconquerable and inexorable. The term could never honestly be applied to a white sapphire, zircon, crystal, or moonstone, beautiful though each is in its own way.

The Arabic word for diamond is *Mâs*.[17] And a link between Arabs, diamonds, and diamond-rich Southern Africa is evident from the onomatopoeic Zulu word for diamond, *meijwane*.[18] *Adamas*, *Mâs* or *meijwane*, a bond with *Dam, Ama, Ma*, the Great Goddess is clear. But when the sun-worshipping, patriarchal hordes swept into Europe from the northeast, destroying the sanctuaries of the Earth Mother/Moon Goddess matriarchal society, which had held sway for thousands of years, they claimed the diamond as the stone of the Sun.

The Assyrian word for diamond is *elmêshu*, the word *el* means God, and in Egyptian mythology *Shu* was the god of air and light (a very descriptive mental connection, for diamonds are an element, and vaporize to nothing when subjected to great heat). The Hebrew word for diamond is *yahălōm*, and *Yah* or *Yaw* are Hebrew words for God, so the Assyrian and Hebrew words for "diamond" clearly show how highly the ancients valued diamonds. Judaism is a patriarchal religion but, in earlier times when *Yahweh* of the Midianites and the Israelites was still identified with the fertility gods, El and Baal, the deity associated with the diamond was the Moon Goddess, Astoreth/Astarte/Aphrodite/Asshur—the consort of the Baals.[19]

Clear and colourless, with the radiance of moonlight on water, diamonds were once held to be self-dedicated to the Moon Goddess by virtue of their appearance. Gems associated with the moon were accredited with the same enigmatic qualities, sometimes baleful and associated with madness, in other aspects, able to dispel dark and evil spirits.[20] And there is indeed something very enigmatic about the fact that the Lady Moon, giver of rain and life, in the guise of the love and fertility goddesses, was also the patroness of mining and mariners. Which brings us to the blessing bestowed on the tribe of Zebulun, by Jacob.

The future of Zebulun was decreed by Jacob, as follows:-

> *"And Jacob called his sons, and said, Gather yourselves together that I may tell you that which shall befall you in the last days. Gather yourselves together, and hear, ye sons of Jacob; and hearken unto Israel your father."*
> *"Zebulun shall dwell at the haven of ships; and his border shall be unto Zidon"* (Genesis 49: 1,2,13).

Zebulun was the tenth son of Jacob, and the fifth by Leah. Although Jacob, in his farewell address, pictured Zebulun as dwelling at the haven of the sea, and having a territorial border up to and including Zidon, in practice, things did not turn out quite like that. Zidon was the early name for Sidon, later to become the sister city to Tyre. The tribe of Zebulun was eventually allotted territory in the vicinity of the sea, and enjoyed the markets of the towns of the coast, but it was separated from the Mediterranean Sea and the city of Zidon by the tribes of Asher.[21]

Jacob's prophesy for Asher was, *"Out of Asher his bread shall be fat, and he shall yield royal dainties,"* which certainly happened when the tribe of Asher took over the seaports of Sidon and Tyre.

It is evident from the pronouncement by Moses before his death that, although the tribe of Asher occupied the city of Sidon, it was the people of Zebulun who were the seafarers and miners:-

> *"And of Zebulun he said, Rejoice Zebulun, in thy going out. They shall call the people unto the mountain; there they shall offer sacrifices of righteousness: for they shall suck of the abundance of the seas, and of treasures hid in the sands"* (Deut. 33:18 – 19).

Whether Moses or Jacob did in fact make these pronouncements on their deathbeds is not in question here. It is nevertheless most significant to note that only after the Israelites settled among the coastal Canaanites, did those relatively unimportant trading and fishing villages on the Eastern Mediterranean develop into the great commercial centres of the Phoenicians—or "red men of the sea". I suggest the impetus that led to the rise in power and wealth of those seaports was the direct result of the involvement of members of the tribe of Zebulun. And that it was the tribe of Zebulun who carried with them the inherited knowledge of the sea routes of Egypt's early mining ventures, and became the mariners and traders today known as the Phoenicians

Information about the exact location of the ancient mines could well have been procured or purchased, during the time the Hebrews lived and traded in the fertile Nile delta—the Land of Goshen—and handed down from generation to generation. That the migrating Children of Israel under the leadership of Moses had lived well during their sojourn in Egypt is evident from the Biblical record of a lament for the good life they had left behind in Egypt:-

> *"... on the fifteenth day of the second month after their departing out of the land of Egypt.*
> *And the whole congregation of the Children of Israel murmured against Moses and Aaron in the wilderness:*
> *And the children of Israel said unto them, Would to God we had died by the hand of the Lord in the land of Egypt, when we sat by the fleshpots, and when we did eat bread to the full"* (Exodus 16:1 – 3).

Jacob was surely aware of what he was doing when he pronounced that the stone of Zebulun in the Breastplate of Judgement was the diamond because, as mentioned, the diamond was the stone sacred to Astarte/Astoreth/Aphrodite, the Moon Goddess of mariners and mining.

The link between the Phoenician traders of Tyre and the Children of Israel was very strong indeed. When Solomon ascended the throne, he set up meetings with Hiram, King of Tyre, and together they sent ships as far down the east African coast as the Comores and Madagascar.[22] In *Ages in Chaos* Velikovsky quotes Joseph Flavius who recorded that King Solomon had many ships stationed in "the Sea of Tarsus". The ships carried merchandise to "the inland nations" and from the sale of these goods the king received "silver and gold and much ivory and *kissiim* (negroes) and apes"[23] That they explored the African coast further is evident from an inscription discovered in Parahyba Province, Brazil, in 1886. An English translation of this inscription, published in *America BC* by Professor Barry Fell, is as follows:-

> *"This stone monument has been cut by Canaanites of Sidon who, in order to establish trading stations in distant lands, mountainous and arid, under the protection of the gods and goddesses, set out on a voyage in the nineteenth year of the reign of Hiram (i.e. 536 BCE) our powerful king. They departed from Ashongaber in the Red Sea, after having embarked colonists in ten ships; and they sailed in company along the coast of Africa for two years. Subsequently they became separated from the flagship, and carried far away from their companions. Ten men and three women arrived here on this unknown coast. Of whom I, the unhappy Metu-Astarte, servant of the powerful goddess Astarte, have taken possession. May the gods and goddesses come to my aid."* [24]

King Solomon and Hiram of Tyre would not have gone to all that expense and trouble of sending fleets of ships down the African coast simply to show the flag by exercising their maritime power. For kings and merchants, time has always been money, and with their inherited knowledge of the trading and mining activities of the early Egyptians, the crews were certainly not stationed off the African coast on a pleasure cruise. The earlier Egyptian fleets to Sumatra and Borneo carried prospectors, miners and traders. So it stands to reason that the ships of King Solomon and Hiram of Tyre were sent off to return with gold, ivory, slaves, and other valuables such as rare plants—for in those days plants were valued as sources of medicine. There can be no doubts that their merchants travelled along the trade routes, which have criss-crossed Africa since ancient times. A point to ponder is why, according to Biblical sources, this trading partnership began only after

King Solomon had completed his hugely expensive building operations. The Bible makes it quite clear that Solomon must have been somewhat cash-strapped for a while, and in debt to Hiram of Tyre:-

> *"And it came to pass at the end of twenty years, when Solomon had built the two houses, the house of the Lord, and the king's house, (now Hiram the king of Tyre had furnished Solomon with cedar trees and fir trees, and with gold, according to his desire,) that then king Solomon gave Hiram twenty cities in the land of Galilee. And Hiram came out from Tyre to see the cities, which Solomon had given him; and they pleased him not. And he said, What cities are these which thou hast given me, my brother? And he called them the land of Cabul unto this day. And Hiram sent to the king sixscore talents of gold. And this is the reason for the levy which king Solomon raised; for to build the house of the Lord, and his own house, and Millo, and the walls of Jerusalem, and Hazor, and Megiddo, and Gezer"* (1 Kings 9:10 – 15).

The materials Solomon needed to build the Temple—the gold and silver; the copper and tin required for the huge bronze, molten sea basin as described in II Chronicles (4:1 – 5), even the amount of ivory required for his great throne—were more than likely brought from Africa by the ships of Hiram of Tyre. Which clearly shows that the Phoenicians—the descendants of Zebulun and servants of Hiram of Tyre—were by that time well acquainted with the African markets. But that, for some reason after the completion of all his building projects, in partnership with Hiram of Tyre:-

> *"King Solomon made a navy of ships in Ezion-geber, which is beside Eloth, on the shore of the Red sea, in the land of Edom. And Hiram sent in the navy his servants, shipmen that had knowledge of the sea, with the servants of Solomon"* (1 Kings 9:26 – 27).

The wealth and style of the Phoenician towns of Tyre and Sidon brought upon the inhabitants the wrath of Hebrew prophets. Ezekiel became particularly upset:-

> *"Thou shalt die the death of the uncircumcised by the hand of strangers: for I have spoken it, saith the Lord God. Moreover the word of the Lord came unto me, saying, Son of man, take up a lamentation upon the king of Tyrus and say unto him, Thus saith the Lord God; Thou sealest up the sum, full of wisdom, and perfect in beauty. Thou hast been in Eden the*

garden of God; every precious stone was thy covering, the sardius, topaz, and the diamond, the beryl, the onyx, and the jasper, the sapphire, the emerald, and the carbuncle, and gold: the workmanship of thy tablets and thy pipes was prepared in thee, in the day that thou wast created" (Ezekiel 28:12,13; 20 – 21).

Clearly, the Phoenician inhabitants of Tyre and Sidon must have been backsliding Hebrews, for otherwise why should the prophets, who had quite enough to worry about at home, have taken the trouble to upbraid uncircumcised, pagan foreigners? I believe the Phoenicians were indeed descendants of the tribe of Zebulun who did not put their trust in the monotheistic religion honouring Yahweh—which had only been introduced to the Children of Israel after Moses married the daughter of Jethro, a Midianite (Kenite) priest, and worshipped their God Yahweh at the sacred mountain but split their loyalties between the Egyptian sea god, Yaw (Yam), and the Moon Goddess, Ashur/Astarte/Aphrodite, the patroness of sailors and miners, to whom diamonds were sacred, and who controlled the tides.[25]

Historically there were many connections between the Phoenician enclaves of Tyre and Sidon and the island of Crete, and between Crete and Africa. Cretan culture is said to be of Libyan origin, which could have originated anywhere in Africa, for in antiquity the entire continent of Africa was known as Libya.[26] As Phoenicians were known as "red men", and Minoan Cretans were also called "Phoenicians", or "red men" by the Greeks, Cretans may well have been included as crewmembers for the fleets of King Solomon and Hiram of Tyre.[27]

In Southern Africa the Nama Khoi, and the Herero, claim their first ancestor was a "red man". However unlikely a meeting of those cultures would appear, nevertheless a singular link exists between the Phoenician/Cretan "red men", and South African rock art.

A famous mural in Knossos, Crete, depicts three people, one of whom is somersaulting over the back of a bull (Ill. 50). The explanation given by local tour guides is that they were acrobats or bull fighters. On the outskirts of Bloemfontein, at a badly damaged engraving site, I photographed a similar engraving. In this case the animal is also a bull. The crudely worked glyph depicts a single male figure somersaulting high in the air, above the bull. The concept here portrayed is not unique to one South African engraving site only.

On a sun-baked, west facing rock in the North West Province of South Africa is a rock engraving depicting people somersaulting over an eland (Ill. 51). This most evocative picture will no doubt be of great

Ill. 50. "Bull jumping" depicted on the mural at Knossos on the island of Crete. In Greek myths the sacred bull was symbolically dominated by the Moon Priestesses who personified the Moon Goddess, and who were the rainmakers of their people. Acrobatic scenes are characteristic of Cretan and Libyan art, and in Mesopotamia the god Naramsin was portrayed with bull-like horns somersaulting over the back of a bull. I have also recorded an engraving, from an almost destroyed site on the outskirts of Bloemfontein (South Africa) of a lone male figure somersaulting over the back of a bull, not an eland.

interest to Shamans the world over. The pictograph centers on an infibulated male figure completing a somersault at the peak of his swing over the back of the eland. His hand touches the horn of the eland, and he is deformed, he has a missing right leg. Not commonly known is the ancient rainmaking ritual once practised in the Northern Hemisphere, during which ceremony the crippled sacred kings of old grabbed the horn of the sacred bull, forcing its head to the earth, until the horn touched the ground.[28] In rural England, some people still bury the horn of a cow, or bull, in their gardens to ensure good rains. Behind the central figure, another human figure is pictured balanced with one foot on the hump of the animal. In front of the eland, a figure is shown standing in much the same pose as held by the person standing behind the bull in the Cretan mural. In the South African engraving, a number

Diamonds, sacred to the Moon Goddess

Ill. 51. Human figures somersaulting over the back of an eland. The central, infibulated, male figure is lamed. All are naked, as is essential during rituals of power raising, rainmaking, etc. Unlike the San, the people portrayed here have large feet and hands.

of people, evidently waiting their turn, are grouped behind the eland. Sanusi Credo Mutwa has said leaping over an eland was a most ancient African rain and fertility invocation, and that this ritual is still practised in remote areas of Botswana.

Eland were in plentiful supply, and well represented throughout Africa, as may be seen from the hundreds of rock paintings and engravings of these antelope. Yet, if the lack of evidence of eland bones in middens can be believed, eland were rarely eaten. This suggests the killing and eating of eland was done only ritually, and that the artistic reproductions of eland were executed because the eland was self-dedicated to the moon, giver of rain by virtue of its fertility—eland produce young every year—and its cloven hooves. The gentle, easily tamed eland is revered throughout Africa. Like cattle, and humans, it has a gestation period of ten lunar months, and has been successfully crossed with cattle by Russian scientists.[29]

The presence of "red men" as mariners, or traders, who were sent "inland" on behalf of King Solomon to exchange goods for gold, silver, ivory, and African slaves, suggests that the African rituals of eland

Ill. 52. A typical representation of the Egyptian god Seth portrayed as an animal-headed ithyphallic red man carrying "something" in his left hand (if he is facing the entrance), 22-centimetres high, painted on the sandstone grotto ceiling, to the left of the entrance.

propitiation were learned, and adapted by the devotees of bull cults in Crete. And that, far from being a pretty picture of acrobats frolicking over a bull, the mural in the palace at Knossos is the record of a Cretan adaptation of the ancient African eland-propitiating ritual. The rite is intended to invoke the harmonious forces of nature, through the good offices of the rain-giving moon, a deeply religious ceremony, and one that necessitated the total identification of the celebrants with the invisible spirit/element of air. For, by somersaulting, the participants pass through a moment when they are suspended, free to absorb and to be filled to ecstasy with the blessings of Heaven.

In early Egyptian art Seth, the Red One, the spirit of the waning year, and the god of Storm and Thunder, was usually represented as an ithyphallic red man with an animal-like head.[30] Some sources describe his head as dog-like, or as resembling a giraffe, but all agree that the figure has rounded, not pointed, ears. These details perfectly describe a rock painting I recorded on an ancient embankment of the Vaal River, in the heart of the diamond-digging areas of the North West province. The location of the painting is unusual; for rock paintings are rarely

Diamonds, sacred to the Moon Goddess

found where rock engravings occur. Rock paintings are almost exclusively confined to the caves and shelters of the great mountain ranges. The engravings are found mainly in the interior of the country, clustered on rocky hillocks, invariably close to a river, vlei, or saltpan (Ill. 52, 53).

In this instance the figure of a red man had been painted on the upper, left-hand side of the curved ceiling inside a very small, womb-shaped grotto in a sandstone outcrop, and faces south. The outcrop once formed the bank of the Vaal River, which now flows along a channel some distance away. The entrance of the grotto faces west, into the setting sun, the direction of death. Opposite this entrance, on the eastern wall, a circular "window" allows the rays of the rising sun to penetrate the womb-like cavern (Ill. 54).

The position of the painting of the male figure to the left of the entrance is of interest when it is related to African customs. In Zulu society, women are generally associated with the left, and men with the right. In his book *Zulu Thought Patterns and Symbolism*, the Reverend I.A. Berglund has noted that, when entering a hut, the women occupy the left side of the homestead, and the men sit on the right. In every social or ritual custom, the left is female and the right, male, and this form is viewed as a matter of opposites, which compliment each other.[31]

However, in the rites associated with death, the practice of magic, and certain rainmaking rituals, these roles are reversed. The theory being that a reversal of traditional customs heightens the potency of the

Ill. 53. The west-facing, arched sandstone outcrop situated on what was once the bank of the present day Vaal River. The round east-facing "porthole" allows the rays of the morning sun to flood with light the womb-shaped grotto with a round west-facing entrance, to the left of which on the ceiling is the painting of the red man.

Ill. 54. An engraving of an animal-headed, ithyphallic man very similar to the red man painted on the ceiling of the sandstone grotto.

diviner's work, and also, as death is the opposite of life, therefore the customs of the living are temporarily reversed during the funeral rites. According to the Reverend Berglund, the Zulu associate the left-hand side with three things—the shades, evil and the feminine.[32]

Therefore, the deliberate placement of a painting of an ithyphallic male figure to the left of the entrance to the womb-shaped grotto indicates that this grotto was once within a sanctuary area. The orientation of the round east-facing "window", the west-facing egg-shaped entrance, and the curved bridge joining the grotto to an outer buttress, is symbolical of the eternal cycle of birth, life, death, and rebirth.

In Africa red is the colour of fertility, prosperity, fecundity and good harvests. In China and Russia today the colour red equates to beauty, prosperity and fertility, while, in ancient times, particularly in the Middle East, male fertility figures were customarily painted red.[33]

Until serious archaeological research is conducted at this site, it is impossible to guess whether foreign traders and prospectors created the grotto. Or whether this typical image of Seth was the work of indigenous peoples influenced by worshippers of fertility deities who, during the course of their mining activities crossed paths with the indigenous peoples of Southern Africa. Seth was a "red man", so too was Adam.

Diamonds, sacred to the Moon Goddess Adamos Adamas Adamant Adamastos, the Unconquerable, the Inexorable.

How strange it is that the Spirit of Table Mountain,[34] which prophesied doom to the first European voyagers who rounded the Cape in the 16th century, was known by the name *Adamastor*.

Chapter 5

Tsui//Goab and Heitsi Eibib

In the legends of the Khoi and San of Southern Africa, the mythical character Tsui//Goab is referred to as a Rain God. He is identified with all aspects of rain and storms, thunder and lightning.

Tsui//Goab is thought to be the life source of the pasture for the cattle, and for the edible bulbs, roots, fruit, and other vegetation so necessary for the survival of life, human and non-human. This concept included all the animals; all the creatures of the air; all reptiles; all the water creatures; every insect, and plant; and also the minerals of earth. And, as with the Baals, it was believed that Tsui/Goab required regular placatory rituals to ensure his continued good offices. They described his home as a beautiful heaven of light and sunshine, and said that his other name was *Red Dawn*. The stories tell how he died several times, but always returned to life, and that his reappearance was the occasion for great rejoicing and feasting among his people.[1]

The Naman of Namibia call themselves "Red Men", and relate legends about *Toosip*, the Old Man of the Water.[2] They claimed Toosip had the power to do good, or to cause people harm, and he was particularly placated with gifts by those employed in digging for water in desert wastes.[3] The Naman devoutly believed they would die unless they made an offering to Toosip before drinking from the Kuiseb River. Toosip of the Naman is described as being a Great Red Man, with white hair—a description that likens him to the gift-bringing Father Christmas who, parents say, leaves presents only for good children. Their legendary Toosip was a rather lonely and un-warlike deity, having neither bow, nor assegai, nor wife.[4] But he may have had a family connection in the north, for the Mesopotamians and the Hittites had a similar deity, a cattle-owning Weather-Sun-god, with an almost identical name—*Tešup* or *Teshub*.[5]

The Koranna, who are now virtually extinct as a race, had a shared legend. Their ancestral hero was known as Tsui//Goab who, they believed, lived in a Red Heaven or Red Sky.[6] They associated another mythical character with Tsui//Goab, namely *Exia/Kha//Nabiseb*, whom they addressed as *"The All Father, Thou who paintest Thyself with red ochre"*. He was described as "the Man whose body has a brass-coloured backbone". If this description has indeed been handed down, unchanged, over many generations, then the story must have originated way beyond the central Southern African homeland of the Koranna. For, as far as is today known about the Khoi and Koranna, they worked with copper, and traded with the Nguni for iron goods, but had no knowledge of brass.[7]

Before his final battle against *Gaunab*, Tsui//Goab's early name was *U-tixo*. In addition to his other qualities, it was said that U-tixo was a renowned sorcerer of great skill, a prophet, and also that he performed many miracles. His traditional adversary was a wicked chief/evil spirit named Gaunab, against whom he fought, and lost, many times. (The Naron and Kung San identify the same deity as *Hishe*, and know his adversary as *Huwe*.)[8] With each victory Gaunab gained strength, until their final encounter when U-tixo struck Gaunab a mortal blow behind the ear. The dying Gaunab slashed at U-tixo's knee, and the wound crippled him permanently. This fight earned U-tixo the name of Tsui//Goab, or *Wounded Knee*.

In *The Khoisan Peoples of South Africa* I. Schapera makes the very relevant observation that one form of the myth describing the battles between U-tixo and Gaunab recounts the contest as an annual event.[9]

Gaunab is better known as *Heitsi Eibib*, and in the stories of the Kung, he is known as *Heiseb the Magician*, the one who is identified with the black of night. Generally, Heitsi Eibib is described as a deity with the characteristics of a tribal hero/magician who was able to assume the shape of any creature, and he gave each animal its character by "cursing it".

In *The Myths and Legends of Southern Africa*, Penny Miller gives the meaning of his name as "destroyer".[10] Schapera offers the generally accepted meaning of Heitsi Ebib, Heigeib, Heiseb, or Kabib, as "prophet" or "foreteller". He adds that Haun interprets the name as "the One with the appearance of a tree", and notes that yet another name for Heitsi Eibib is Heigeib, meaning "Great Tree".[11]

The Naman describe Gaunab/Heitsi Eibib (Exia/Kha/Nabiseb) as their Great-Great-Grandfather, a mighty and powerful chief who lived originally in the East, and who had plenty of cattle and sheep. He is also described as "the man whose body has a brass-coloured backbone". Heroic tales are told of how he killed various evil monsters, and conquered great lions[12]—a description, which could also be translated as "great kings".

Other legends recount that the mother of Heitsi Eibib was a cow, or a virgin, who was impregnated by eating a herb, and say he committed incest with her.[13]

Gaunab, alias Heitsi Eibib, is also revered for his ability to return to his people after every death and burial. To this day stone cairns throughout Southern Africa are honoured as the many graves of Heitsi Eibib, and passing travellers add stones to the heaps.[14]

One of the most important details in the legend is the disclosure that the recurring contest between Tsui//Goab and Heitsi Eibib was an annual event. The stories about the combat between Tsui//Goab and Heitsi Eibib, and their repetitive reincarnations, describe exactly the annual sacrificial death of the "Old King" and his adversary the Tanist, or Spirit of the New Year, in the Northern Hemisphere. Traditionally the ceremonies took place in midwinter, at the end of their three-season year.

Yet another similarity between this African legend and the known inauguration rites of the freshly crippled "New King" of the ancient Hellenes, the Tuatha dé Danaan, and others, whose way of life was determined by the matriarchs of old is that their year was divided into three seasons. A three-season year of spring, summer, and winter was also recognized by the O!Kung, the north-west Naron,[15] and to the majority of the Nguni peoples of Southern Africa who named the seasons; *intwasa hlobo* (the initiation of summer); *ikwindla* (the autumn); *ubusika* (winter). From earliest times the Egyptians divided their year of 360 days into three seasons, which they called: inundation, winter, summer. And very possibly the Israelites also used a three-season year, because the Bible says, "and on the new moons, and on the solemn feasts, three times in the year" (11 Chronicles 8:13).

It is said that in the matriarchal society of the Northern Hemisphere the sacrificial death of the "Old King" began at sunset. It was then that the High Priestess cut off his long, golden, sunray locks, specifically to destroy the solar powers that were thought to reside in his hair. To onlookers at a distance, who would never have had the opportunity to see the sacred king at close quarters, the long golden hair must surely have given him the appearance of a man with a brass-coloured backbone. Thereafter, the "Old King" was subjected to a succession of ingenious tortures, which lasted throughout the long winter night, and were carefully carried out to ensure he did not actually die until his final battle against the Tanist. Then, shortly before daybreak, the High Priestess, or his adversary, the Tanist, gave the coup de grâce.

The Koranna, who believed Tsui//Goab lived in a Red Heaven, or Red Sky, and the Khoisan who believed he lived in a beautiful heaven of light and sunshine, and that his other name is *Red Dawn*, only confirm the connection between the legendary battles between their heroes, and the inauguration trials of the death and rebirth of the sacred kings of old. For, following the daybreak sacrificial death of the "Old King", as the red light of dawn spread across the sky to turn the heavens crimson, the "New King" of the New Year, alias the "Old King" reborn, emerged to greet his people. And at his appearance the whole community rejoiced and gave thanks—"The king is dead, long live the king!"

In Celtic lore, the "New King" was deliberately crippled, if not in the battle against the "Old King", then at the hands of the priestesses immediately following the coup de grâce. In some instances the tradition was to permanently dislocate his hip, to ensure his leg withered, so he would forever walk with a hobbling gate—that is, when he was permitted to walk at all.[16] The Sacred Kings of the old order in Europe, and in Africa too, were only allowed to touch the ground with their feet during certain prescribed rituals. For it was feared that an uncontrolled release of the solar powers contained within his sacred person would damage the crops, and disrupt the harmony of Earth Energies.[17] However, no logical reasons for the curious custom of laming the otherwise physically perfect sacred king have been put forward—at least I have not been able to find any. Other than an explanation offered by a doctor, who said the crippling of a man's leg diverts the blood flow, and gives him tremendous virility. Well, virility and fertility were the most important assets of the early sacred kings, so the deliberate maiming of an otherwise perfect male, in the prime of life, may well have been introduced to effectively increase his potency.

The Sacred Kings of the Old Order were not political leaders or secular monarchs. Each was the focal point for the distribution of the

Ill. 55. *Pitted surfaces on the otherwise smoothly polished surfaces are a feature of the polished rocks at engraving sites. This dumpy polished rock, situated in the centre of encircling engraved stones, shows a pitted surface and a pockmarked apex. It is said that in pagan times the rocks were beaten "to force the Earth Mother to give us what we ask".*

harmonious Earth Energies. His every action was controlled by disciplined rituals, designed to raise the quality of life throughout the realm, and to protect his people from the ravages of drought and disease. In the beginning, Sacred Kings were seasonal Beings. Theirs was an annual appointment, and their ultimate purpose was to be sacrificed at the end of their reign—a sacrifice of purification. They died that they might take with them all the darkness, disease and sin of the old year. By their bloody and painful martyr's death, they cleansed and absolved their people in order that the new season might be fruitful.

The ancient Libyan, Greek, Celtic, and Middle Eastern rituals have been well researched and documented. What may surprise many classical scholars is Sanusi Credo Mutwa's description of the selection and death of the Divine African kings of antiquity, differs only slightly from the known ceremonies once practised in the Northern Hemisphere.

During one of our discussions in Soweto in the late 1970s, I showed Sanusi Credo Mutwa a photograph I had taken of a smallish, curiously dumpy, polished stone encircled by other dolerite rocks. Some are engraved; others have cup-and-groove markings of the kind Charlotte McGowan identifies as yonic/phallic symbols[18] (Ill. 55, 56).

He studied my photograph, and exclaimed, 'But Mam, it represents God's Testicle! The Sun-god has got only one testicle.'

It was not until years later, while I was researching further about a possible connection between the Lemba and the Falashas, who claim Jewish descent, and the colony of Idumean Jews from the Red Sea, who peopled the Comoro Islands in the days when the fleets of King

Ill. 56. A yonic groove deliberately cut into one of the encircling rocks of the boulder Sanusi Credo Mutwa described as "the testicle of the sun god". According to the farmer, vandals—"collectors"—broke this rock to remove the engraving that was originally part of the whole.

Solomon and Hiram of Tyre traded with the Comoro Islands and Madagascar, that I recognized the global significance of Sanusi Mutwa's statement. This curious mutilation was once common practice among the largely Semitic Beja, on the Red Sea. It was their custom to remove the right testicle from male children. And according to Schapera's translation of Rhyne's account of the Cape, written in 1685, all the Khoi males that were born were immediately, at birth, deprived of one testicle. That the occurrence of this form of mutilation is found among Semites from the Red Sea, *and the Khoi*, cannot be mere coincidence. Historically, the Khoi were eased away from the East African coastal trading territory of Sofala by the southward movement of the migrating Nguni, who attributed god-like qualities to the people of the multinational settlements of the territory who had been trading with the interior for millennia. Commercial trading ventures in any age carry more than mere trade goods. The traders carry with them their hopes and fears, culture, and religious practices, and leave tokens of their presence behind, such as an interaction of religious customs or an interchange of technology with those with whom they come in contact—and children born of local women. In ancient times the trading caravans would certainly have included scribes, and holy men or women who, for the well-being of trade and the traders, would have located by divination places along the trade routes where earth energies were most powerful, and there have created sanctuaries. Places where they reverently engraved and polished rocks, but which in time fell into disuse, their original purpose forgotten to all but a few shamans who carry the race memories and legends of their people as a religious duty to the unborn of future generations.

Sanusi Mutwa's explanation of the rock, and our subsequent conversation, as may be seen from the transcript of the tape, led somewhat abruptly to the subject of Africa's God-kings:-

> **Mutwa**: This stone is twenty times more important than anything in its vicinity. This thing, Mam, is called "God's Testicle", and the Sun-god has got only one testicle. One ear, one testicle, and one leg.
> **Sullivan**: One leg? The single footprint engravings I have recorded? And footprints with six, and four toes (Ill. 57)?
> **Mutwa**: Exactly Mam. The big six-toed foot is the foot of the Sun-god. The engravings mark the place where the man who was elected Sun-god used to put his foot and say, "I take possession. I have arrived." Then his foot was engraved on the rock, and was distorted to include six, not five, toes.
> **Sullivan**: Five toes, plus the testicle?
> **Mutwa**: Yes! You see this foot (photographs of engraving) with the six toes? The engraving shows where that man, that Sun-god,

Ill. 57. Notations on the rocks on the hillock of the Wonderstone Mine, Ottosdal, include three different sets of footprints, one clearly showing a human foot with four toes. The dots, lower right, number 28, one moon cycle.

breathed his last, because he was killed ritually. They were usually very big men, and they put the right foot only because they had only one leg, and the engravings of six toes were deliberately distorted. The foot was distorted to have no shape. This compensated for the missing foot. (In appearance these engravings could indeed be either of a left or a right foot.) Now here stood the God-Man, and here his blood fell, and for as long as people shall live, his footprint is engraved and then when the next Sun-God-Man comes, he will put his foot sometimes over this one. So you find sometimes the footprints are overlapping.

Sullivan: Now, you say, "when the next one comes". Where does he come from?

Mutwa: He was *bred*, Mam. Specially bred. Or he was captured. For example, here we are a tribe, and we breed a man by virgin birth. Or if not, because sometimes the birth might produce a woman, or a miscarriage, we capture the most beautiful youth of our people.

Sullivan: Your custom was to breed a God-king by virgin birth? How was this done?

Mutwa: Mam, to do this we selected a young girl, and kept her secluded from everybody in a hut, until her time was right. Then the priest inseminated her, and to do this he used a feather. Yes, Mam! A feather! But if this virgin birth did not produce the Sun-god we wanted, then we would capture the youth. When last such things were practised, about a hundred years ago, during the time of my grandfather's grandfather, these people were carefully chosen. You see, Mam, you sometimes see Africans with reddish hair.

Sullivan: Do you mean the ones we call albinos?

Mutwa: Exactly Mam. These were the people who were sacrificed. They were the kings who lived for a year, and sometimes for six months. But before his death the Sun-king was brought up in luxury. He was given everything—even twelve wives; twelve wives for each of the twelve months. He went around healing people; a God-like charisma was built around him. Usually, Mam, a man was caught by his dream. Should a man, a young man—not one captured to serve as God-king—dream of the sun rising in the morning, then he was elected. Then he was given everything. Then he became so indoctrinated by religion, for the priests picked on these people and would even use drugs to make him believe he was really a god. And some of these Sun-gods, if they were warrior inclined, they used to go on what we call a "no-win war". He was armed with an assegai, but this assegai had an ostrich feather instead of a metal spear point. And he was supposed to stab to death a warrior who was armed with a real, real weapon. Now this warrior stabs him—*zucch!*—finished!

Sullivan: Then he was sacrificed at the end of his term?

Mutwa: It is a voluntary sacrifice. A no-win war is a ritual war where the victim does not win. Now, where he has stood declaring his authority, his identification with the Father, his footprint is engraved for all time. And all the sick people when they come there, they put their hands on the paint, and paint on the stone at this place, like this (here Credo Mutwa demonstrated by putting his hand print on the wall). So you see, Mam, the paintings of handprints, and footprints, are all the sick people who came to pray at the Place of the Foot. But the Sun-god had one major footprint, and the God-kings were deliberately crippled to have only one leg—because then the Snake of Darkness would not devour them. Occasionally you will find two major footprints. This is an indication that here there were two kings ruling as one.

Sullivan: Do you mean a "twin-rule"?

Mutwa: Yes Mam, a twin-rule. Two kings ruling as one.

Here we have a Sanusi's rendering of ancient African practices relating to God-kings who, like their northern counterparts, were deliberately maimed in the leg, and ritually sacrificed.

The description of the placing of the foot of the king on the rock to claim possession was also once practised in Scotland. According to *The Secret Country* by Janet and Colin Bord, a "swearing stone" was used at the inauguration of Celtic kings.[19] The Bords explain how Celtic and Saxon kings were installed standing or sitting on a sacred stone which was used only for this purpose. They suggest the kings absorbed energy from the stone during the ceremony. They also list the "Stone of Inauguration" or "Stone of the Footmarks" by Loch Finlaggan. It is described as being seven-feet-square, and had footprints cut into it. At the swearing-in of the chief of Clan Donald, as King of the Isles, he stood barefoot on the imprints in the stone, and was proclaimed "Macdonald, high prince of the Seed of Conn" (Ill. 58).

Apart from the few engraving sites, which are dominated by footprints only, engravings of human footprints together with animal

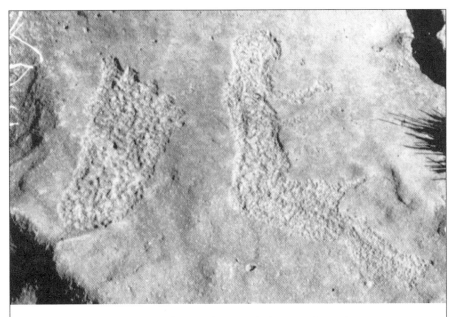

Ill. 58. Male figure together with a single human footprint.

hoof prints are found at the some of the larger sites. Human, horseshoe, or antelope, they are usually depicted singly, and I have never found human prints together as left and right feet. Some are tiny footprints of children, or maybe apes. Others have six, or four toes (Ill. 59).

As described above, Sanusi Credo Mutwa gave an African explanation for engravings of six toes, and earlier I had book-wormed my way through legends relating to archaic six-toed giants—who really did once exist.[20] So there are two logical explanations for the engravings of a human foot with six toes.

But I had also seen an engraving of a human footprint with only four toes and this really puzzled me (Ill. 60). With only four toes a human being cannot walk properly without the aid of a crutch, and although the legs of the God-kings were maimed, there is nowhere any mention of amputations. Researching further, I came across a Biblical reference to the very unpleasant general custom of cutting off the big toes, and thumbs, of captured kings:-

And Judah went up; and the Lord delivered the Canaanites and the Perizzites into their hands and they slew of them in Bezek ten thousand men.
And they found Adoni-bezek in Bezek: and they fought against him, and they slew the Canaanites and the Perizzites. But Adoni-bezek fled;

Ill. 59. Human footprint together with an eland.

Ill. 60. A grouping of human footprints showing one with six toes and one with four toes.

and they pursued after him, and caught him, and cut off his thumbs and his great toes. And Adoni-bezek said, threescore and ten kings, having their thumbs and their great toes cut off, gathered their meat under my table: as I have done, so God hath requited me. And they brought him to Jerusalem, and there he died (Judges 1: 4 – 7).

From this record it would appear that the fate of any captured king, of this period in history, was to have his thumbs and big toes hacked off. Such an amputation would certainly deprive him of his balance, and hamper his ability to walk, or even to hold a crutch. It is no wonder they died shortly thereafter. As so many of the customs and stories of Africa are reflected in the practices of the Biblical pagans, can it be possible that the rock engravings showing human footprints with only four toes are historical records of events as described above? As yet the question remains unanswered.

Also, Sanusi Mutwa's mention of red- (or golden-) haired albinos being sought out for the sacrificial role has a parallel with the Egyptians. In honour of Seth, the Red-headed One, Egyptian devotees are said to have customarily sacrificed red-headed people. People with naturally red hair were rare in Egypt, but common among the Hellenes, and others, from farther north.[21] So, according to Robert Graves, there was an Egyptian practice of capturing red- (or golden-) headed visitors to Egypt, as sacrificial offerings to Seth, who was originally a twin ruler along with Osiris.

As in Africa, so among the Sacred Kings of the Northern Hemisphere. It would appear that, generally speaking, in antiquity the postulant for the role of Sacred King was either the son of the High Priestess—in which event the boy had been trained to the position from birth—or a devotee who voluntarily offered to serve his people in this manner. As far as the boy-aspirant was concerned, it is probably more accurate to say he was conditioned to the role from birth. The Sacred King was not a political leader or state figurehead. He was the focal point for the distribution of the harmonious Earth Forces. His every action was controlled by disciplined rituals designed to raise the quality of life throughout the realm, and to protect his people and flocks from drought and disease.[22]

It is interesting to note that in South Africa this archaic concept is very much alive, even today. The Zulu king, as the Child of the Lord of the Sky, controlled the seasons. In *Zulu Thought Patterns and Symbolism*, the Reverend Berglund states that modern Zulus have been known to attribute drought to the fact that the king no longer functions ritually, as of old. They complain he now sits in an office all day, dressed in western clothes, "and wastes his time writing letters".[23]

U-tixo, the old name for Tsui//Goab, deserves closer attention. The Reverend Henry Callaway, who ministered to the Zulu in the 1830s, was very critical of his contemporaries when they adopted U-tixo (or Utikxo) as the Xhosa, and Khoi, name for God. He insisted that U-tixo was a non-African word, and as such should never have been inserted into the Xhosa or Khoi languages, for whatever reason.[24]

He was most probably correct in his belief that it was a non-African word. A very similar word is used, internationally, as a name for the Sun-god. The Peruvian Sun-god is known as *Tikki Viracocha*. The Polynesian Man-god is *Tici* or *Tiki*. The Scandinavians have a legendary trio of evil spirits, *Lempo*, *Paha* and *Hiisi* who successfully directed an axe into the knee of the aged hero, *Väinämöinen*. So the legend of Heitsi Eibib and Tsui//Goab is certainly not unique to Khoisan culture. There is even a possible link between the name Tsui/Goab and the Celtic Divine Smith, *Goibhniu the Lame*. He was the leader of the triad, Trí dé Dana, whose other members were *Creidhne* and *Luchta*. *Goibhniu* (in Wales he was known as *Gofannon*) was also a healer, a giver of immortality, and particularly noted for the magic brew in his great cauldron and his skill in making invincible weapons.

Another link between the legends of Tsui//Goab, Heitsi Eibib, and the Moon-worshipping/Earth Mother cults of antiquity is to be found in the story about Heitsi Eibib's mother.

The legend describes the mother of Heitsi Eibib as a herb-eating virgin, or a cow, with which he had an incestuous relationship. In early Greek, Phoenician and Egyptian theology the Moon Goddess was often portrayed as a cow, as with Baalat-Gebal and Hathor. The shared biological link of a ten-moon gestation period for both cattle and humans enhanced this empathy, so at one time Moon priestesses and cows were interchangeable—cows were acknowledged to be Moon priestesses, and Moon priestesses, cows.[25] The value of herbs for healing; help in childbirth; increase of potency; virility; fertility; and also for contraception, has been known for millennia. However, the specific mention that Heitsi Eibib was born of a herb-eating virgin, is more likely to be an oblique reference to the hallucinogenic drugs which were the stock-in-trade of the prophetic priestesses, who were also known as Pythonesses. Incidentally, the term "pythoness" not only refers to archaic prophetic Moon priestesses for, even today, female Diviners in South Africa are also known as "pythonesess".[26]

All Moon priestesses were technically virgins. It is said that the conception of their children was achieved by magical means, during visits from the celestial mate of the Goddess. As Sanusi Credo Mutwa explained, in Old Africa chosen virgins were artificially inseminated with a feather. This is in accord with the ancient belief—and it is even today an African belief—that a woman cannot conceive unless a waiting soul is willing to be re-born through her womb.[27] Even so, the human species cannot reproduce unless the female ovum has been fertilized by male semen. And this may well have been why the Sacred King was required to have ritual intercourse with his mother in her role of High Priestess/Rainmaker.

As surrogate Goddess, the High Priestess represented the androgynous primeval creative force—male and female in one. And therefore, she was beholden to no man for procreation. But an important part of archaic rainmaking rites was an enactment of the fertilization of Mother Earth by the Sky God, and necessitated ritual intercourse between the "androgynous" surrogate goddess—herself as the female, and herself as the male.[28] A physical impossibility when the representative of the androgynous primeval creative energy of the Moon Goddess/Earth Mother was a mere human. Therefore concessions to nature were necessary. And this, I believe, is the logic behind the theology that required the technically androgynous High Priestess/Rainmaker to commit ritual incest. For, by coupling with her own son, who was a by-product of her own body, a High Priestess was having intercourse with her own flesh—thereby proving that she was both male and female in one. My theory is supported by the fact that the ritual frenzies of sodomy and masturbation were introduced after the patriarchal Sun/Sky cults had usurped the Matriarchal Great Mother religion, with the males doing their best to be androgynous too.

Sanusi Mutwa told me the Zulu name for the son of the Creative aspect of the Great Mother, or surrogate Queen Mother/High Priestess is *Insizwa*, "He-who-must-be-helped", from the verb *siza* – to help, and *sizwa* – to be helped, in other words, a sexually inexperienced youth. In addition to Ill. 7 (Chapter 1), I have recorded an engraving of a group of people and animals. Central to these images is a bearded circumcised male about to have intercourse with an apparently headless female figure. Sanusi Credo Mutwa's explanation of this cameo is that God the Father had become old and indifferent to sex, but the Earth Mother was very concerned because the population of Earth was declining. So she decided to be impregnated by her own son, *Insizwa*, "he-who-

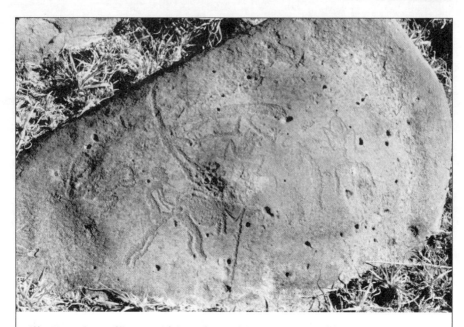

Ill. 61. According to African lore, this panorama of human and animal figures depicts the impregnation of the Earth Mother by her son—Insizwa, he who has to be sexually helped. The story says there were few people on Earth, and God the Father was old and tired, so God the Mother asked her son to impregnate her, to bring more people to life on earth. At first he refused, but she pleaded, and so he finally agreed to her request. But, to hide her pleasure, she turned away her head. Therefore, in this pictograph she appears as a headless creature.

must-be-helped". And in the traditional representation of this story, she is shown with her head turned away, "So that he will not see the pleasure on her face" (Ill. 61).

Artists, worldwide, captured the androgynous quality of the Great Mother. Much of the work of pre-Christian Celtic artists and craftsmen was covertly androgynous. In Celtic lore, antlers were explicitly bi-sexual in character, as was the horned God Cernunnos. In *The Silbury Treasure* Michael Dames says antlers symbolized the body of a woman incorporating the masculinity of a stag. With deer, at least, this is a fact. For, when stags shed their antlers in the winter, to grow a new set in the spring, pregnant does eat the fallen antlers to sustain themselves through the winter months, when food is scarce. Thus does the body of a female incorporate the horned masculinity of the male—and for the purpose of reproduction.

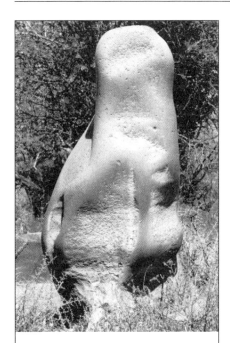

Ill. 62. A classic example of the androgynous qualities of the Great Mother, virile male and fertile female, sculpted in this great rock positioned between a huge yoni and a smoothly polished phallus at an engraving site in the North West Province, South Africa.

The African androgynous theme is not limited to rock engravings. At an engraving site not far from the town of Wolmaransstad in South Africa stands a magnificent androgynous boulder (Ill. 62). But the significance of this smoothly polished, bisexual, rock is that it is aligned halfway between an enormous rock yoni, sited on the western boundary, and a highly polished phallus of about a metre and a half in height, sited on the eastern boundary (Ill. 63, 64). Engraved on the apex of this phallus is the picture of an ostrich, wings outstretched in the mating dance. Below the sand cover that I cleared away at the base, lay hidden the crudely worked engraving of an eland. The great stone yoni mentioned above was the chosen altar for the sacrifice of a white goat by Sanusi Credo Mutwa, in a ceremony to promote peace in the region. Sanusi Credo Mutwa, and the other sangomas who had gathered for the ceremony, identified this yonic rock as a traditional sacrificial altar.

A very curious feature of this yoni, which lies on the western outskirts of the site, is the shadow of the head and shoulders of a bull cast on its western flank at midday, in mid-winter. I visited this site deliberately at midday, on 21st June, (mid-winter in the Southern Hemisphere) during the 1980s, to see whether any unusual occurrence was to be observed on this particular date. Standing to the west of the yoni rock, I first noticed a rather crudely worked engraving of a small human figure, which could have been male or female. Then I perceived that the rock had thrown a shadow onto itself, and that the shadow was clearly in the form of the head and shoulders of a bull within the huge "beak" of a sculptured bird of prey. Birds play a very important

Ill 63. (Left)   The gleaming, smoothly polished, engraved, dolerite phallus situated on the eastern boundary of the engraving site, and aligned, through the androgynous rock, to a large yoni on the western boundary. Ill 63a. (Right)   This engraving of an ostrich doing the male mating dance is worked onto the tip of the highly polished phallus above.

role in mythology and religious beliefs, worldwide, particularly birds of prey. In Greek myths, the Sirens were carved on funeral monuments, pictured as birds of prey, waiting to catch the soul as it left the body. As curious as the shadow of the bull, which was no longer as clearly visible the week before or the week following mid-winter, and the unmistakable head of a bird of prey, is the demonic head and wraith-like figure etched into the surface of the north face (Ill. 65, 66).

Other yoni rocks, some placed close to phallic standing stones, and also flat rocks incised with cupules, or basins, are found at this site. There can be no doubt that these rock formations were deliberately positioned, and the cupules and basins manmade (Ill. 67, 68, 69). It must be equally obvious to any thinking person that this site was a centre, possibly even the greatest centre of the region, for the enactment of fertility rituals and rites. Such practices are said to have been unknown to the San who are the accredited rock artists.

The rocks cannot have gathered there, and polished and engraved themselves, without human assistance. These rocks are dolerite, and

Ill. 64. *The great yoni rock aligned through the androgynous rock, to the polished and engraved phallus beyond.*

dolerite is hard. The academic explanation given for the existence of the smoothly polished surfaces, which are a feature of engraving sites generally, is that they were rubbed to porcelain smoothness by the action of itchy animals. There are, however, several problems with this simplistic explanation.

According to game wardens I have spoken to, it is mainly elephant, buffalo, gnus and warthogs that rub against objects to remove parasites and mud, and they seem to prefer old tree stumps. Many of these rocks are polished from tip to base. In practical terms, it would take untold generations of itchy animals, constantly rubbing away at a rock, to achieve an overall smoothness—with the big animals scratching themselves against the top and sides, and smaller warthogs scrubbing away at the base. Furthermore, I have observed that many of these polished chunks of dolerite carry engravings on the polished surfaces. So, had they been polished to their porcelain-like perfection by animals, and then subsequently engraved by humans, why then are the engravings still clearly visible? How is it that they were not obliterated—simply worn away, in time—by the continued friction of animal hides? If we accept the official explanation, then we have to re-think all that is known about the behaviour patterns of itchy game animals, and admire them as art lovers. For clearly, if the "itchy animal" theory is correct, they ceased to massage themselves against favourite rubbing rocks once the rocks had been engraved.

The question then remains: if not the accredited San, then who were the people who created this centre? And where did they come from originally? Could the creators of this and other sites have been the

Ill. 65.   The shadow of the head and shoulders of a bull are thrown across the open, curved beak of a great bird of prey by the mid-winter sun, at midday.

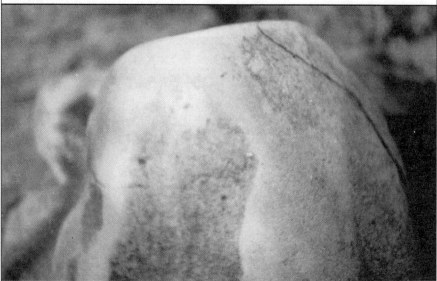

Ill. 66.   On the western face of the great yoni rock, the eyes set into a demonic face stare into the mid-winter setting sun, the traditional time of death and sacrifice.

Ill. 67. Cupules set in the rock beside a perfectly circular basin cut into the dolerite surface. This is but one of several rocks with deliberately worked cupules or basins.

Peoples of the Early Race spoken of by the San? Did the concept of a local fertility deity and his consort, represented by a phallus and a yoni respectively, originate here in Southern Africa? To be later carried northwards by traders and miners from elsewhere? Does this site hold the key to all the unanswered questions, and unknown factors, concerning the pre-history of South Africa?

The worship of fertility deities linked to fixed locations, and represented by the yoni and phallus, was widely practised throughout the Middle East and the Far East—and Africa. Even today in African households a small shrine, enclosing a space for a yoni and phallus, is sited close to the homestead. Sometimes one sees what appears to be only an old food tin with a stick propped up inside, but it is nevertheless a shrine, holy ground, where daily offerings of food are religiously, and reverently, placed by the chief wife.[29]

The early Hebrews, worshipping *Asherah*, erected a wooden pillar (to represent the sacred tree) as an altar; then later a stone pillar, called *Mazzebah*, was added. This stood beside the altar and represented the Baal, the male deity. The upright pillar was the original form of an altar in honour of Asherah, and in nomadic times the blood of the sacrificial

Ill. 68. Dolerite rocks with cupules, runnels and a deep central yonic trough. When first I saw these rocks, the horizontal yoni was completely covered by sand. Acting on an inspired hunch, I cleared away the debris of the ages, and exposed this classic yoni. A runnel leading from the rock on the right has been cut to allow fluids to run into a collection groove on the surface of the yoni, below. While clearing away the dirt, I discovered a small, flat, narrow stone formed in the shape of a "B", with the upper curve of the letter smaller than the lower, placed exactly under the point where liquid from the runnel of the rock on the right would flow into the groove of the horizontal yoni. As this small carved stone had the appearance of a pregnant female, I carefully replaced it in exactly the same position as when found.

victim was poured down beside it. But later, for a more convenient mode of offering the burnt sacrifices, the altar—representing the female aspect—was placed horizontally, but the phallic stone pillar continued to be set upright beside it. Both the Asherah and the Mazzebah underwent development, becoming in course of time carved idols.[30]

The androgynous character of Creative Energy is clearly evident in the engraving at the apex of the hillock where steatite is being mined, at Ottosdal. The anthropomorphic bird-like shape is crowned by a strung bow, another ancient and international symbol for fertility. And the androgynous theme is easily recognized in African rites of puberty, rainmaking and divination. In times of drought it was the custom for

Ill. 69. Cupules are a feature of certain engraving sites in the North West Province. The region has a low annual rainfall, and as these rocks do not lie under an overhang from which rainwater could drip, these perfectly circular cupules cannot be attributed to weathering. This triangular-shaped rock has a total of seven cupules on its flat upper surface—seven, being a prime moon number, is recognized internationally as a ritual/ sacred/good-luck number.

boys to dress in their mother's clothes, to prayerfully intercede with the Queen of Heaven for desperately needed rain. And for Zulu and Swazi girls to dress in their brother's clothes, and do the work of herdboys, to emulate the androgynous spirit of the Great Mother, and thereby draw forth much needed rain. To attract the powerful creative forces of nature, a male Tsonga sangoma wears the fully beaded hair of a woman under his own ochred wig, and underneath his outer garments he ties women's clothes around his waist. Male Shangane diviners also wear a woman's skirt as part of their essential ensemble.[31]

Androgynous rulers were a feature of African life in the past. The joint ruler of the Lozi kingdom in the Zambezi basin was known as the Queen of the South, but when she entered the council chamber she announced, 'I am transformed into a man.' The given reason for this tradition is that an ancestress usurped the patriarchal throne. The Egyptian Queen Hatshepsut, who sent expeditions to the Land of

Punt, indicated her own androgynous status by coating her body with both gold and silver dust after the fashion of West African kings and queens—in Ashanti, gold dust (metal of the sun) was the body covering of kings, and silver dust (sacred to the lady moon) the body decoration of queens.

In addition to their role as the centre of universal harmony throughout their kingdom, and their accredited powers of prophecy and magic, the Sacred Kings of antiquity were also associated with sacred trees—one example being the many stories of a legendary divine king, Hercules, and his tree, the oak. All things of the oak tree were sacred to Hercules—his oaken club, acorns, the parasite mistletoe and doves.[32] Mythographers have placed Hercules' origin in the region of Andalusia, around 3450 BCE, and he may well have arrived there about that time. But, in *The White Goddess*, Robert Graves gives Hercules a Libyan origin, as a Palaeolithic pastoral sacred king from the region of the Atlas Mountains. This makes him an African, and may explain why, to this day, a variety of oak, known as *Iroko*, is propitiated throughout West and Central Africa as a sacred tree.[33]

The description of the legendary Heitsi Eibib as "the One with the appearance of a tree"—sourced to water, the tribal link between heaven and earth, providing food (edible acorns), strong, tall, giving protective shade—most probably does connect him with the Oak cults of northern Africa. But, the phrase that he had "the appearance of a tree", could also be an indication that Heitsi Eibib was a race memory of a real person who had knowledge of the written "tree alphabet" known as Ogam.[34]

Ogam is a most ancient form of alphabetic symbols which are said to have been inspired by the twigs and branches of the oak. Ogam, named after the Celtic God of Learning, *Ogmios*, is better known as the Irish script of the later Druids. Pelasgians and Bronze Age Britons used Ogam, but there is growing evidence that this form of communication was in use long before the advent of the Druids.

Originally a secret language, it became common knowledge after the decline of Druidism. It may even be an offshoot of the archaic script of the ancient Berber tribe, the Garamantes, who were the hereditary guardians of the Oracular Oak sanctuary at Ammon, on the shores of Lake Tritonis (now a salt marsh) in Libya, and whose ancestral hero was Hercules.[35] To the uninitiated, Ogam symbols look like nothing more than simple, twig-like squiggles.

Celtic scholars with knowledge of Ogam will find other evidence of this tree-inspired alphabet in African art, and even engraved on the

Ill. 70. *The sacred slate of Sanusi Credo Mutwa, showing the symbols and script known to the Guardians of tribal lore, and described by Professor Barry Fell as a complete guide to the Ogam alphabet, written in ancient hieroglyphs and Kufic Arabic. The inscription, or the original from which it may have been copied, must date from the first millenium AD, at the latest, and apparently replaces the Book of Ballymote as the oldest account of this widely distributed writing system.*

rocks of South Africa, as did epigraphist Professor Barry Fell. And I have recorded other examples of Ogam, as yet untranslated, engraved on South African rocks (see Ill. 18).

In Africa Ogam is by no means a dead and forgotten form of communication. "Finger Ogam", once known in Europe as "the tic-tac hand language of witches"[36]—is still used today by shamans of higher grade, to relay confidential information to each other—especially amongst the Sanusi, for the order of Sanusi cuts across all tribal and national barriers. Sanusi Credo Mutwa showed me the Sacred Slate of the Law that was given to him at the end of his period of trials and initiation into this elitist order. The symbols on his slate incorporate Egyptian hieroglyphics and Archaic Arabic, as well as the full Ogam alphabet (Ill. 70).

Unfortunately, Professor Barry Fell was unable to meet with Sanusi Credo Mutwa, but he did send me a pre-print of his translation of the photograph I had sent him of the sacred slate given to Credo Mutwa when he was initiated as Sanusi in Zambia. Professor Fell wrote that he was "astonished" to find that on the sacred slate was inscribed a complete guide to the Ogam alphabet, written in ancient Egyptian hieroglyphs and Kufic Arabic. His detailed examination of this slate stated that this slate tablet apparently replaces the *Book of Ballymote* as the oldest account of this widely distributed writing system, adding, "*The inscription, or the original form from which it may have been copied, must date from the first millenium AD at the latest."*[37]

Further proof that Ogam is known to modern African shamans comes with the translation of Ogam script discovered in the USA, and read correctly by Sanusi Credo Mutwa. During my visit to the USA in 1978, to meet with members of the Epigraphic Society, they very kindly took me to several ancient sites, where I was able to photograph Ogam on American rocks. I met with Sanusi Credo Mutwa after my return to South Africa, and showed him my photographs. He immediately read the symbols correctly, and wrote his translation on the back of each photograph (Ill. 71, 72).

But what was to me even more surprising was his translation of the inscription in the pre-Cyrillic alphabet on a fireclay vase from the Alekanovo village near Ryazan, southeast of Moscow on the Oka River in Russia.[38] The original translation, published in the Occasional Papers of the Epigraphic Society in 1979 reads: *"I the man eat this millet grain."*

When I showed Sanusi Credo Mutwa the Russian text, without the translation, his response was, 'Madam Brenda, any sanusi worth his salt can read that! It says, *"the man is eating the green corn!"'* Thus proving beyond doubt that Ogam and the Rune-like Alekanovo script are as indigenous to Africa as the *Iroko* and the African elephant.

The legend of Tsui//Goab and his adversary Heitsi Eibib states that Tsui//Goab raised First Man and First Woman from rocks and stones. Past civilizations, which revered rocks as the Bones of the Earth Mother, raised Earth Energies by simulating copulation with phallic stones, and practised frenzied fertility ceremonies around phallic- and yoni-shaped sacred rocks, also told stories of how First Man and First Woman had been raised through the medium of rocks.

In these legends there is an echo of the Biblical prophet Jeremiah who railed against his flock:-

> *Saying to a stock, Thou art my father; and to a stone, Thou hast brought me forth.*
> *And it came to pass through the lightness of her whoredom, that she* (Judah) *defiled the land and committed adultery with stones and with sticks* (Jeremiah 2: 27/ 3: 9).

As usual, Jeremiah was railing against the followers of the Moon Goddess Astarte/Asherat/Isis/Aphrodite. And it is interesting to note that Haun identified both Tsui//Goab and Heitsi Eibib with the moon, although he did not identify them as king and tanist of the moon cults.

Ill. 71. Ogam inscription inscribed on an American rock, and correctly translated by Sanusi Credo Mutwa.

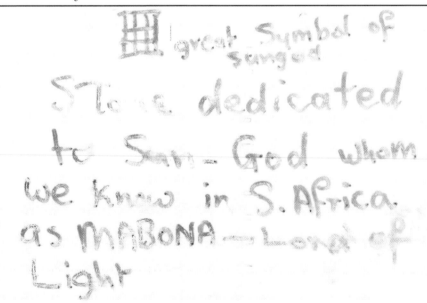

Ill. 72. Ogam inscription from America, correctly translated by Sanusi Credo Mutwa.

To the Koranna, Heitsi Eibib was "the Man whose body has a brass-coloured backbone" whom they addressed as "The All Father, Thou who paintest Thyself with red ochre".

The early sacred kings, folk heroes, or Creator Gods of many peoples were known as "Red Men", or "Red Earth Men". Or, like the red-bearded Thor, they had some aspect, which was specifically referred to as being red. Red is one of the three sacred colours of Africa; it represents the full moon, promising prosperity, virility, fecundity.

The Reverend Callaway recorded the story told to him by Uthlangabeza, one of Ukukulela's people. Uthlangabeza said that all things came out of a mountain in the north, the mountain of Ingome. And that Uthlabati was the founder of his tribe. Uthlabati "broke off" from Uthlanga (who begat the ancestors) and founded his own dynasty. The name Uthlabati is given as meaning "Earth Man", "Earthy", or "Red Earth".[39] The Herero of Namibia say the ancestor of their nation was made by God, and that he was red. According to their beliefs, this Red Man is still alive in the land of God, which is a country of the dead in the north, or over the sea, in the place of the Tree of Life. In the theology of the Herero the serpent belongs to the Underworld, and their serpent is coloured red. It is believed to play a part in the function of priests and doctors, implying a connection with rainmaking, fertility and childbirth.[40]

Adam of the Biblical Garden of Eden has a name that means "red man", and Seth, the sexually powerful Egyptian god of Fertility, Black Magic, and Storms, who finally fell from grace and was demoted to a mere representative of turmoil and storms, was known as "The Red One". Seth of the Egyptians, *Tešup* of the Mesopotamians, and Tsui//Goab of South Africa share many characteristics. All are weather deities associated with fertility. Seth and Tsui//Goab are both Red Men and Seth, the Spirit of the waning year, is renowned for his sunray hair, a detail which could help explain why Heitsi Eibib was described as having a "brass-coloured backbone". Long golden hair was said to be the seat of royal solar power. It was the golden locks of the disposable king, which were shorn by the High Priestess shortly before he was sacrificed, at the end of his term of office, to take away the sins of his people—only to be replaced by the Tanist/New King with another head of golden hair.

Differing styles of rock paintings and engravings depicting figures with sunray hair have been recorded in many places in the world. But I have recorded two almost identical pictographs, one on the banks of the Vaal River in South Africa, the other atop a tumulus San Michael, at

Carnac, in Brittany. Close to the Christian chapel, this ancient engraved phallus has suffered the fate of many pagan relics, for it has been almost hidden from view behind an enclosing wall. I was only able to photograph it with great difficulty. The Free State image is also on the summit of a hillock, and faces the sunrise. At first glance these engravings resemble a human figure with sunray hair, but they are also covertly phallic (Ill. 73,74). A closer look at the South African engraving reveals two sperm-like jets issuing from the "head" of the phallus shaped figure—a spilling of seed on the ground.

The Khoi honoured stone cairns as the graves of Heitsi Eibib. Many of these heaps are ancient, their origin long forgotten, but travellers still prayerfully address them. The Naman place pieces of their clothing or skins, or the dung of zebra, twigs of shrubs and branches of trees, as well as stones on the cairns raised in memory of Heitsi Eibib, with prayers for good fortune, safety and good hunting. Sometimes offerings of honey and honey beer are left at the cairns by the Naman, saying that when he returns in the evening from his walks in the veld, he is glad to see they thus honour him. And it must be remembered that

Ill. 73. Sun-ray figures have been found at many places throughout the world, but this particular South African engraving is certainly overtly phallic. Rays of power flowing outwards on either side from beneath two forceful jets emerging from the "head".

Ill. 74. In Brittany the Tumulus San Michael is crowned by a phallic stone engraved with a "sun-ray" figure, which is almost identical to the South African image, above. Unfortunately a protective concrete wall encloses the stone atop Tumulus San Michael, and this engraving is visible only when the sun strikes the rock through a narrow opening, at certain times of the day. I was fortunate to be on hand at the right time, and by sheer chance noticed the figure.

in African theology, every one of these offerings has a deeply symbolic meaning. The offering of zebra dung is particularly significant, for the eating of zebra meat is taboo to the Naman peoples, as is ostrich meat—another good reason for not assuming that the many engravings of zebra and ostrich were merely "hunting magic".[41]

Among the Pondo it is the custom to pray at the heaps of stones, which are most numerous along the paths and winding trails throughout their mountainous country. The traveller, John Campbell, mentioned the existence of curious cairns in his diary of 1820. He reported that every traveller added a stone to each pile of stones as they passed—"This was done, so they said, in memory of the king of some forgotten race, whose head and hands were buried there." He noted that occasionally, instead of stones, small rings of plaited grass were placed on a boulder at the edge of a path—a logical offering, for grass is the fundamental food of all earth's creatures. The Pondo name these heaps of stone *isivavane*. Traditionally, whenever a Pondo entered the territory of another tribe, or the domain of a clan different to his own, the traveller lifted a pebble with the toes of his left foot, transferred it to his hand, spat on the stone and finally placed it on the heap with a fervent prayer to U-tixo, for a safe journey—*"Sivivane saokoko, ngi ti ketsheketshe ukuhamba kalula"*, which means "Isivivane of our ancestors, may I live without care."[42]

Sometimes the Xhosa salute the isivavane, saying, *"Sa ku bona, bantwana bakasivivane"*, which translates as "Good day, children of Isivavane."[43]

A similar custom was noted among the Namaquas. In 1870 the Reverend Callaway recorded the mention of this custom by Sir James Alexander:-

In the country of the Namaquas there are occasionally found large heaps of stones on which have been thrown a few bushes; and if the Namaquas are asked what they are, they say that Heitsi Eibib, their Great Father, is below the heap. They do not know what he is like, or what he does; they only imagine that he also came from the East, and had plenty of sheep and goats and when they add a stone or branch to the heap, they mutter 'Give us plenty of cattle.'

The Reverend Callaway further relates that among the Khoi he noted many such heaps, which they told him were the graves of *Heitsi Kabip*.[44]

The earliest recorded archaeological excavation in South Africa was of one of these stone mounds, which was situated near Cookhouse, on the Great Fish River. Sparrman, a Swedish naturalist who had been attracted to the many cairns in the area, made this excavation on the 22nd January 1776. He described the cairns as being from one, to one and a half, metres in height, with the bases measuring 1.8 metres by 2.4 metres, and 3 metres in circumference. He reported that these cairns lay in varying distances of each other—10, 20, 50, 200 paces—but that they stood consistently between two particular points of the compass, in rows, which always ran parallel to each other. He said these parallel lines of stone heaps extended over a considerable area, and described the distance as being several days' journey from his starting point. Sparrman was greatly ridiculed for suggesting, in his subsequent report, that these monuments were "irrefragable proofs" that this tract of the country was formerly inhabited by a race of people "who were more powerful and numerous than either the Hottentots, or the Caffres".[45]

Can it be that his critics were all in the thrall of Asura, the demon of Ignorance?

Although Haun did not identify Tsui/Goab and Heitsi Eibib as king and tanist, he drew attention to the fact that all aspects of Khoi life were orientated towards the East. Huts were built so that the doors faced the rising sun, and the dead were placed in graves in such a way that they faced to the east. Even those who owned wagons parked them with the entrance towards the rising sun.[46]

It is to the East we will now travel, following a cairn-lined path, and stopping now and then to respectfully add a stone with the invocation: "Isvivane of our ancestors; may the darkness of Asura never again cloud our intelligence."

For, apart from the legends linking the Koranna and Khoi to their remote ancestors from the East, a visible, physical link between South Africa and the trading stations of antiquity in the Persian Gulf actually exists. The link is rock-hard, a rock engraving link of identical symbols, which I have recorded in South Africa, and in the United Arab Emirates.

Evidence that at some, as yet unknown age, people with shared knowledge and concepts engraved identical symbols on the rocks of South Africa and on the rocks of the United Arab Emirates.

The revered Collective Unconscious at work again?

No, I think not. There are too many similarities in these manifestations for them all to have been spontaneous inspirations of the Collective Unconscious. Ideas can be transmitted across space, but identical, meaningful figures and symbols engraved on rocks say, "Kilroy was here! And here! And here!"

Chapter 6

Isivavane International

Stone cairns and untidy heaps of stones, as well as rambling stone walls, are found throughout the world. And, like the cairns in memory of Heitsi Eibib, these cairns internationally appear to have no known history.

Even Nimrod, the mighty Assyrian king and renowned hunter (of the Ur III period, 2000–3000 BCE), is recorded on the tablets of his day to have "collected great stones: he piled up great stones".[1] Yet there is no hint in these records of the reason for his efforts, nor of the function the heaps of stones served. Most likely, in those days, the royal raising of stone cairns was normal practice, and the scribes felt no need to elaborate further.

Manmade heaps of stones, very similar to those in South Africa, have been found in Tibet and Tartary. A report in the Anthropological Institute Journal of 1877, by M.J. Walthouse describes how travelling Lama Tartars built up long walls of loose stones in the African way. He remarked that many of these ancient and rambling rock piles were about two metres thick, and a metre and a half in length. Every Lama Tartar passed these walls on the right side only, and added to the heap. Walthouse reported that nobody appeared to know how this custom began, nor why it continued. It was always so. He said he occasionally saw flags; scraps of paper with writing; the horns of an ibex, wild sheep, or goat, decorating the cairns, and that round boulders inscribed with Buddhist prayers written in a circle, were often added.[2] The name of these Asian heaps is *Mani*, a name not unlike the Xhosa *isivavane*.

In the south of India, tumuli abound on the Travancor hills, and in Korea similar piles of stones are found in the mountain passes.[3] The researchers who studied the Indian and Korean stone heaps were unable to give any explanation for their presence, but William Corliss notes that at the Korean mounds it is the custom to spit while passing:[4] the creative, or expelling, act of spitting only, not spitting on a stone before adding it to a heap as is the Pondo or Zulu custom. It is recorded that the Zulu king Shaka, while leading his army, stopped at a cairn, picked up a stone with his toes, spat on it, and placed it on the heap. Each warrior repeated his action.[5]

In ancient Egypt, spitting was a symbol of creation through the Divine Word, or entry of the breath of life. Between the Old and Middle Kingdoms, the god Shu was upgraded to become the "Eternal One", Life Itself, and the mediator between the One and all other creatures:-

Shu—"I am Eternity, the creator of the millions, who repeats the spitting of Atum—that which came from his mouth."[6]

A prayer to *Ticci Viracocha*, the Inca name for the Peruvian Sun-god (although, according to Thor Heyerdahl, before the time of the Incas the name was *Kon-tiki*, and came from the Tuamotu Islands of the Pacific) hailed him as:-

"Lord of the Universe! Whether male or female, Commander of heat and reproduction, being one who, even with his spittle, can work sorcery..."[7]

In the olden times, when the kingdoms were annually cleansed in preparation for the new seasons, Celtic and African sacred kings ritually spat a protection towards the four cardinal points of their land, a practice which is still annually repeated during the sacred Swazi rite of Incwala.[8] The Zulu spit to expel evil and anger, and the custom of spitting at funerals—specifically onto a piece of earth, then throwing it into the open grave—is the way of taking farewell, without bitterness.[9] The Zulu also spit on the ground during an electrical storm, to avert a lightning bolt.[10] In Africa, spitting over the left shoulder is to express anger, or to send a curse.[11]

Berglund records the case of a man who held back from spitting ritually on a stone cairn, saying he could not, because at the time he was filled with anger.[12] In other words, he believed the anger within him would be transmitted through his spittle, and so pollute the beneficial energies of the cairn.

Spitting as a means of transmitting virtue, ritually, is known in Islamic North Africa as the passing of *baraka*. Seligman has recorded that one of the most effective methods of transmitting baraka is for the holy man to spit into the mouth of the person he wishes to greatly benefit. The doctrine of baraka is common to both the Arabs and the Berbers. Literally the word means *blessing*.[13] From Islamic North Africa we learn that the meaning encompasses the concept of a mysterious force, or virtue, from God, such as the holiness possessed by the Prophet, who passed a share of baraka to the *shurifa*, his descendants in the male line through his daughter Fatima.[14] In *Races of Africa* Seligman explains that baraka can also be bestowed on heroes who died while fighting a *jihad*, or holy war, and also on particularly spiritual men who are gifted with the ability to perform miracles. A passing of baraka can also be accomplished when the holy man pronounces the traditional formulized blessing at the end of a shared sacramental meal.[15]

A similar philosophy is understood by the Zulu who recognise *amandla* as the neutral power within material substances such as people, plants, soil and stones.[16] Amandla can be passed from a holy man or woman to another through the communion of a shared meal. Elsewhere in Africa this mysterious force is known as *nyama*, the power that inspires people, and enables them to endure and achieve goals far beyond their expectations.[17]

In Morocco there is the dual baraka of the Sultan. One baraka is bestowed upon him, as head of the family of *shereefs*. The other is the baraka of his sultanship, bestowed on him as God's representative on earth—and which is perpetually renewed by the 40 saints who pass over his head every morning. It is believed that the welfare of Morocco depends on the baraka of the Sultan. When it is strong, the crops and livestock thrive, and the women give birth to healthy children.[18]

A solution to the question of why the stone cairns were raised in the first place, may lie in the Muslim doctrine of baraka, as practised in North Africa. Muslim shrines which often, but not necessarily, contain graves, are respected as sanctuaries where life is protected, and where manifestations of baraka are strongest.[19]

In earlier times there were sacred centres throughout Africa where it was forbidden to kill or harm any living thing, and animals or fugitives who reached these places were spared the death thrust of their pursuer's weapon. In addition to the natural shrines at sacred trees, rocks, rivers, wells, springs, caves and mountains of Africa, the graves of kings were traditionally havens for animals and man.[20] At these sacrosanct places, prayers and offerings to the shades of royalty are ritually conducted, to ensure the fertility and health of the community.

Seligman stresses the sensitivity of baraka and makes the point that it can easily be polluted, or lessened, by contact with inharmonious external influences. A similar warning could be heeded about the energies emanating from the ancient standing stones, and herms, elsewhere in the world.[21]

A natural development arising from this ancient reverence for sacred places is the Christian tradition of the sanctity of churches as places of refuge. This tradition doubtless had its roots in paganism, because, after experiencing centuries of stiff resistance to Christianity, the Church under the rule of Pope Gregory VI instructed priests to abandon the practice of murdering pagans. Instead, the Christians were to build churches over the ancient pagan holy places.[22]

Alas for the sanctity of ancient shrines. Today, in a world where rapacious, power-hungry men and women defile all in their obscene striving to emulate God, few sanctuaries remain unpolluted. Fewer still have been tended, and seasonally renewed, to retain and reinforce their primeval, protective energies.

Describing a baraka sanctuary, the shrine of a saint, Seligman made particular mention of the cairns erected on places within sight of the shrine. He emphasized that not only the holy ground within the enclosing wall of the shrine is revered, but that the protection offered by the saint's mosque extends to the cairns, and gives sanctuary to all who come within sight of the shrine. In effect, the powerful influence of baraka radiates outwards, to a series of cairns erected at high vantage points in the surrounding areas. Therefore, travellers or fugitives within sight of the shrine came under the protection of the baraka of the sanctuary, and were then safe from any form of persecution.[23]

Seligman's description of the extended protection offered by the cairns linked to the shrines of Muslim saints, could well be the reason why the isivavane are so often found on mountainous ground, and on borders dividing territories.

In ancient times, the palace/temple complex housing the Divine King was situated over the most powerful beneficial earth energy point in the kingdom. This being the case, let us assume that, originally, the baraka radiating outwards from the central sanctuary was caught, and held, within an enclosure of stone cairns encircling the kingdom. Let us assume that the builders of the original cairns were careful to select only stones with a high quartz content—dolerite, quartzite, granite, etc. Quartz has many natural properties. As well as being a conductor of the natural electromagnetic energies of earth, quartz can be programmed to hold thoughts, blessings—and curses.[24] Therefore, a ring of energized cairns would enclose the kingdom in a veritable force-field of protection. Then, when travellers reached the outlying cairns, they automatically came within range of the beneficial energies emanating from the sacred person of the king. If this was indeed the original function of the cairns, their purpose could well have been twofold. Beneficial within the kingdom but, when necessary, negative energies could be invoked to induce drought, storms, and calamities of all kinds on whoever approached the kingdom with less than friendly motives, in the manner of Mujaji, the Rain Queen of the Lovedu.[25]

If, as I have suggested, this was the reason for cairns in the first place, then it is no wonder that the custom of prayerfully addressing the stones and laying another stone, or suitable offering, on the pile, has continued to this day. Albeit as a forgotten memory of the time when the prayers were of thanksgiving for having passed safely through the dangers every traveller faced, before reaching the security of home ground, unharmed. Well might every traveller, merchant, or fugitive have added a prayer stone, or symbolic gift, to increase the strength of the energies imbued within the cairn, with the fervent invocation *"Sivivane saokoko, ngi ti ketsheketshe ukuhamba kalula."*

The Khoi say that the cairns in South Africa were the graves of Heitsi Eibib—or that they were places where "the heads and hands of some forgotten king" were buried. Their version of the legend is most likely the retelling of an almost forgotten snippet of oral history relating to the ancient practice of burying the oracular skull of a sacred king at the approaches to the city.[26]

Great faith was placed in the oracular powers issuing from the skulls of departed kings and chieftains. The reasoning behind this concept lay in the belief that the head was the centre of spiritual power.[27] And so, after death, if the heirs were in possession of the skull, or head, the spirit of the departed could be called upon in times of need, to give wise counsel to those still living, more particularly because of the experience, and useful information, garnered "on the other side". The Celts were obsessed with obtaining prophecies from the skulls of the mighty, and preserved the oracular heads of their chieftains in cedarwood oil. Some took the cult further, and used the gold-trimmed skulls of their respected enemies as drinking cups, to imbibe inspiration along with intoxication.[28]

Early Hebrews appear to have shared this belief. According to Richard Bovet's *Pandaemonium*, some authorities think the Biblical *teraphim*, which Laban's daughter Rachel stole from his house, were the mummified heads of the firstborn.[29] Their custom was no less lurid than the Celts'. The people of Laban's time used to cut off the head of the firstborn—a child, or maybe the head of the family, after death. No clear definition of "firstborn" is given. This they salted, and embalmed then, after writing incantations on a piece of gold, and placing the inscribed gold under the tongue of the "firstborn", the mummified head was settled in a niche in the wall of the house, as the resident oracle.[30] Laban himself is said to have bowed down to such an image, and to have received oracular messages.[31]

The skulls of royalty were particularly treasured, for, in addition to its oracular power, the decapitated head was valued as a clan talisman. To protect the citizens against invasions and privations, certain tribes buried it in the market place, or at the approaches to the city, which means under a cairn situated on the perimeter of the kingdom, or city-state. Such a custom was most probably practised by people who raised the first cairns in South Africa, giving rise to the Khoisan story about the "heads and hands of some forgotten king" lying beneath the heaps of stone.[32]

On Bahrain, in the Persian Gulf, cairns are found in great numbers. The greatest concentrations of tumuli are on high ground, near the central basin. The main island is thought to have broken away from the Arabian mainland sometime around 6000 BCE, and became known as a Holy Island in the mythology of Sumeria. The Sumerians grew out of an earlier (4th millennium BCE) people, the *Ubaid* culture. Archaeological finds in Bahrain show that the Ubaids were in contact with the island, and that these contacts continued after the founding of Dilmun (Early Bronze Age—around 3200 BC). Thanks to its strategic position on the great trade routes of antiquity, its good harbours and abundant water, Dilmun has been a trading centre between west and east for thousands of years.[33] In its early centuries, Dilmun had strong trading links with the powerful Sumerian city of Eridu (near modern Basra), and was well-known to the Babylonian king Ur-Nanshe of the city of Lagash (about 2520 BCE). In his paper *The Dilmun Civilization, Its Seals and Sun-God Symbols*, Ali-Akbar H Bushiri (of Bahrain) identifies Dilmun as the holy island of the Sumarians:-

> *Dilmun occupied a very special position in the religion of Mesopotamia and it was a holy place in the eyes of the Sumarians, that is not a matter of speculation. Dilmun was repeatedly mentioned in the Sumarian, Babylonian, and Assyrian inscriptions as an important port of call in the Persian Gulf in the sea trade between Mesopotamia and India (Indus Valley). It was described as a place which had many vessels in its harbour, and whose merchants traded in woollens, copper, gold, ivory, rare woods and rare stones. There is one Summarian text, which refers to Dilmun as the land where the oil ships come from. Dilmun has also been chronicled in the mythology of Mesopotamia as the land of Immortality, a favourite meeting place of the gods, which was visited by the hero Gilgamesh in his search for everlasting life. Inscriptions indicate that the ancestors of the Sumarians came from here, and it was here they learned their knowledge of writing. A Sumarian hymn from around 2000 BC claims: 'The land of Dilmun is Holy, the land of Dilmun is pure, the land of Dilmun is clean, the land of Dilmun is Holy.'* [34]

Mesopotamians are known to have sailed 1,000 kilometres, or more, in ore-powered ships.[35] And in the trading centre of Dilmun we find a definite link between a great number of stone cairns, sacred kings, a most holy centre, and lucrative trade routes reaching at least as far as southern India, where cairns were raised on the Travancore Hills.

The many cairns on the island of Bahrain, and the many cairns found elsewhere in the world could be proof that the sailors and traders of Dilmun, who travelled extensively, carried with them the practice of piling up stones to mark their territories. Their trading empire could well have spread, directly or indirectly, as far north as Tibet and Tartary, and as far south as the Drakensberg Mountains of South Africa. After all, why not?

The Khoisan themselves claimed their ancestors, and Tsui//Goab–Heitsi Eibib, came from the East. The sheep tooth found near Kimberley in South Africa and dated 11 – 10 centuries BCE had to have come from somewhere. The fat-tailed sheep of the Khoi, and their steatopyga, are Arabian, some say Somalian, in origin (Ill 75, 76). And their original hunting dogs have been described as very similar in appearance to ancient Egyptian breeds. In addition, there is the very significant but rarely mentioned fact that, unlike the Nguni who fought with spears and the San who were deadly with bows and arrows, the Khoi fought with slings. The report on the death of D'Almeida, in c. 1509, at Saldanha Bay states the Khoi "were armed with many slings, with which their aim is most accurate"—as was the

Ill. 75. Steatopyga. Photograph of a woman of the Northern Cape whose mother was San and whose father was of Koranna descent. Note particularly her small hands and feet, which are characteristic of the San. Conversely, the human figures engraved on the rocks of South Africa are usually portrayed with large hands and feet.

aim of the famous Biblical Semite, David, who with his sling killed Goliath.[36]

Dilmun may have been the first trading centre in the Persian Gulf, but others were established shortly thereafter, and there must surely have been trade and other links between the coastal towns of the Persian Gulf. Flints and potsherds found near the Khatt Hot Springs indicate that Ras Al-Khaimah (situated north of Dubai, in the UAE) has been inhabited since the 3rd millennium BC. For much of its history the region's main town was Julfar, a few kilometres north of the modern city of Ras Al-Khaimah.

By the 7th century AD, Julfar was an important port, and a pearling centre by the 12th century AD. Pottery and other finds from this era indicate that Julfar had significant trade links with both China and India.[37] And, making a direct link to the colonization of the Cape of Good Hope by the Dutch, in the 15th century Julfar was the birthplace of Ahmed Bin Majid, the great Arabian sailor whose books on navigation are still studied, and who was hired by the Portuguese explorer Vasco da Gama to guide him to India in 1498.

Bahrain, with the greatest number of stone cairns, and a history of thousands of years as an international trading centre, and Julfar, another old trading port on the Persian Gulf, could between them provide answers to the riddle of the cairns of South Africa. The key to unlocking the mystery, I believe, is to be found at the rock engraving sites in the UAE, and in South Africa. At the Dubai museum I saw, and

Ill. 76. Portrait of the Queen of Punt, from the Punt Colonnade at the temple of Queen Hatshepsut, Deir el- Bahri. Photo: Ida-Jane Gallagher.

photographed, rock engravings from the region surrounding Ras Al-Khaimah. To my astonishment I realized that some of the rocks were engraved with images and symbols identical to those on the rocks of South Africa. After speaking with the Director of the Dubai Museum, Dr. Hussain Sulaiman Qandil, he very kindly made copies for me of some of the illustrations from Dr. Muhammed Abdul Nayeem's book on the Pre-history and Proto History of the Arabian Peninsula (with a foreword by Professor Abdul Rahman T. Al-Ansary), which included illustrations of engravings from As Sha'm, Wadi al Bih, Wadi Ishi, Wadi Hatta, Khatma Mileha and Sarjah.[38]

It is beyond the realms of probability that these identical figures and symbols were duplicated by chance, for they even appear to have been crafted by the same scribe, or at least by an apt pupil (Ill. 77, 78, 79, 80, 81, 82, 83).

Surely these engravings alone show without doubt that in antiquity there was indeed a link between merchants from the Persian Gulf, and maritime traders and/or miners who, on the trail of early Egyptians, prospected, and exploited the mineral wealth of central South Africa at a very early date.

Unfortunately for historical records, the engraving sites of South Africa have never been given the respect they deserve. No archaeological excavations, or in-depth studies, have ever been carried out on or around these historically valuable sites.

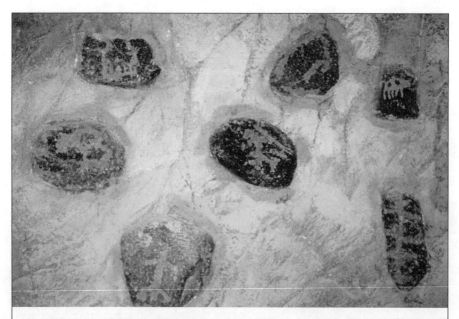

Ill. 77. Rock engraving of a Seth-like figure displayed in the Dubai museum, Arab Gulf States.

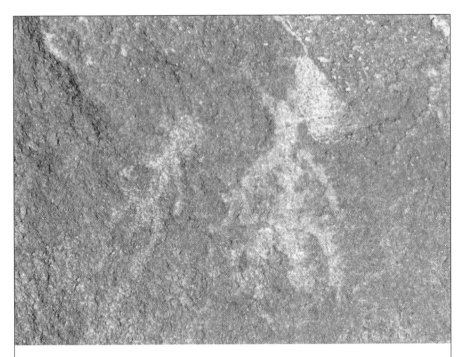

Ill. 78. Seth-like figure engraved on a South African rock.

Ill. 79. "Dancing figures", which most probably did not symbolize dancing—and slashed rock, from the Wonderstone Mine, Ottosdal.

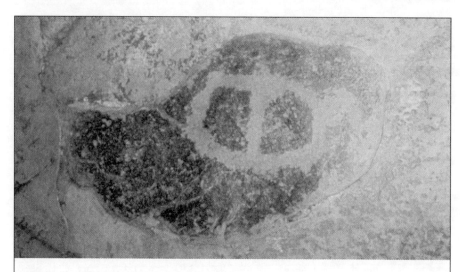

Ill. 80. Engraving displayed in the Dubai museum, Arab Gulf States. In ancient time animals, which parted the hoof, such as cattle, were self-dedicated to the Moon Goddess as their hoof prints resembled two half moons, and a symbol for the goddess was two half moons, or two facing symbols similar to the letter "c". The ancient Greeks marked the flanks of their sacred cows with two facing half-moon figures.

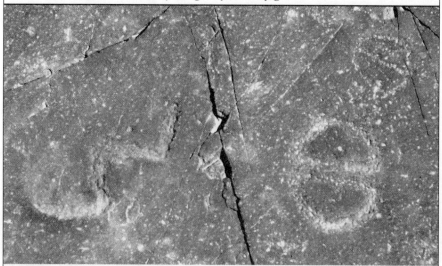

Ill. 81. Almost identical to the engraving from Arab Gulf States is this South African engraving of two almost touching half circles, divided like the hoof prints of cattle. And to enhance the representation of the Moon Goddess, alongside this engraving is the classic zigzag symbol for water/rain.

Isivavane International

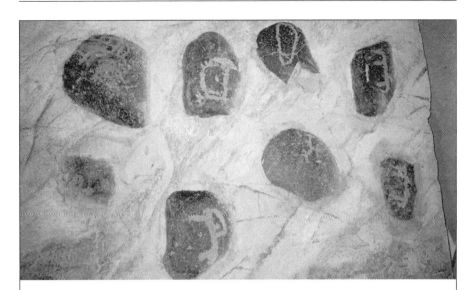

Ill. 82. From the Dubai museum, Arab Gulf States (top right in the grouping of engraved stones), a "stick figure of a man on a horse"—although it surely did not have that meaning to the holy ones who inscribed the rocks.

Ill. 83. From an engraving site near Schweizer Reneke (South Africa), where many enigmatic signs and fertility symbols have been carefully engraved on rocks, another "stick figure of a man on a horse", almost identical to the symbol displayed in the Dubai museum.

Chapter 7

Incwala, the ancient Swazi mid-Summer Festival of Regeneration

As Lion of the People, and co-ruler with the Queen Mother, the Swazi king is still very much a Divine Being of the Old Order. On their death, the sacred Swazi kings are buried in a secret grave on Mount Mdimbza, which has been guarded for many generations by the Gama clan, as a hereditary trust.[1]

Many ancient peoples in the Northern Hemisphere practised the custom of secret royal burials.[2] Greek royalty were once buried in concealed graves on the Isthmus of Corinth. Moses, too, was buried in an undisclosed place in the Land of Moab (Deuteronomy 34:6), and the pharaohs of Egypt were secretly laid to rest in the mountain-ringed Valley of the Kings.[3]

The Swazi Queen Mother is revered as the Lady Elephant. She is the custodian of the Rainmaking hereditaments and, as is to be expected, she occupies a strong position in the government of the country, until the death of her son.[4] In keeping with the tradition of the ancient pagan Moon-worshipping, Earth-venerating Matriarchal societies, there is no automatic succession of the heir. The Swazi Queen Mother and her Council decide who is to become the new Lion. If the new Lion is not one of her own sons, she retires after entrusting the position of Lady Elephant to the newly elected matriarch.[5]

Swazi society is centred on the annual mid-summer First Fruits ceremony of renewal and regeneration, known as *Incwala*. In many ways the rituals of Incwala reflect the cultures of other, earlier matriarchal societies of the Northern Hemisphere. During Incwala the King, as Lion of the people, leads the rituals designed to renew his own vitality and virility that, through his vigour, his people and all life in his kingdom are energized for the year ahead.

For non-Africans to understand the significance of this annual ritual of regeneration and renewal to the Swazi nation, such details of Incwala as are known to outsiders must be viewed with respect for pagan traditions. To comprehend the importance of ancient African fertility rites, it is essential for non-Africans to empathetically "think pagan", and not decry the ceremonies with hands upraised in pious horror.

Incwala is a most sacred ceremony. It is a time of self-control, a period of abstinence, sex taboos, "doctorings", special regalia, taboo songs, and sacred dances.[6] There is also a nationwide prohibition on the eating of the first fruits of the new season's harvest, before the final day of the ceremonial Throwing of the Gourd of the North by the king.

The festival of Incwala is divided into two parts. The Lesser Incwala lasts two days, and takes place at the dark of the moon, before the full moon immediately preceding the summer solstice. At the Lesser Incwala the king "stabs the land with protection" by spitting mouthfuls of powerful medicine to the four cardinal points—north, south, east and west. The rite is followed by ritual dances, and the chanting of songs, which are taboo at any other time. These songs are paeans of hatred and rejection, directed at the king with all the vocal strength and gestures of contempt the people can effect.[7]

The second part, the Great Incwala, starts with the full moon, and lasts six days.[8]

On the first day, a regiment of youths is sent to gather branches with fresh green leaves from the sacred Swazi tree, which is a species of acacia. Immense care is taken to protect the leaves from damage, for the tree is credited with prophetic powers. Should any of the leaves be wilted on arrival at the royal kraal, when the king examines them, this is a sign that the man who carried them is an adulterer. And he is declared to be unworthy of taking part in the Great Incwala ceremony.

The branch-bearing youths arrive at the outskirts of Lobomba at sunrise, to the welcome of drums, bugles, whistles, the blowing of kudu horns, and the acclaim of the crowd. After the king's inspection of the leaves and branches, youths collect branches of "mbondro", which are then placed protectively around the sanctuary where the king will be housed for the duration of Incwala.[9]

On the third day, the Day of the Bull, certain select warriors, and the same youths who collected the acacia branches, must undergo the ordeal of capturing, unarmed—and bloodlessly subduing—a large black ox. This ox is the national symbol of strength. Traditionally it was pummelled almost to death in a prolonged and highly dangerous battle between the youths and the animal. But due to pressure from horrified Europeans, the full archaic ritual is no longer permitted. At the end of this contest, when the animal has been overpowered and slaughtered, parts of the body are immediately removed for medicines to strengthen the king, and the remainder of the flesh is later ritually offered to the ancestors.[10]

After the ceremony is over, another black ox is led into the enclosure, and forced to its knees. It is no ordinary animal, but one from the royal herd, consecrated, and revered for the role it must play annually during Incwala. This part of the ceremony is always screened from foreign eyes, but all reports agree that the king discards his clothing and ornaments, and is washed down with a frothy herbal potion by his two senior blood brothers. Then, naked and imbued with the power of the herbs, he straddles the prostrate animal in an age-old coronation ritual of identification, and rises magnificently potent as the Bull of the People, the living symbol of the fertility and strength of the Swazi nation.[11]

The second last day of Incwala is called the Day of Seclusion, and is most holy. The Lion and the Lady Elephant are secluded in their quarters, and may not be approached or disturbed in any way. Their subjects are banned from washing themselves, and from sexual intercourse.[12]

All of the more important Incwala proceedings are closed to non-Swazi people, and Europeans are not readily given explanations, even of the ceremonies they are allowed to view.

At one ritual from which strangers are excluded, the king hurls a sacred green gourd, called "the Gourd of the North", at the shield of an age-mate. This act is a signal to his people that the old year is officially dead. By the act of the Swazi king, the throwing of the "Gourd of the North", the king and his people pass from a state of death, decay, and disasters, into the new season of life-giving rains and growth. Incwala ends with a great feasting of the First Fruits, and general rejoicing throughout the land.[13]

So much for what is common knowledge about the annual rite of Incwala. What is not well documented are the similarities between this annual Swazi celebration, and the practices of pagans of the Northern

Hemisphere, in ancient times. The reason the similarities between this ancient annual Swazi ceremony, and those of peoples in the Northern Hemisphere in ancient times, are of importance to the world at large is because of our shared heritage.

The living, annual fertility and regenerating rituals of the Swazi nation parallels, in nearly every respect, the well-documented archaic seasonal fertility rituals of the ancestors of the majority of today's Europeans with Celtic roots, and those of peoples living around the eastern regions of the Mediterranean Sea. Even the date of Incwala corresponds to the Elian New Year, which was counted from the full moon nearest the winter solstice, and a second New Year, which began in mid-summer. The winter solstice in the Northern Hemisphere is mid-summer in Natal, the time of Incwala.[14]

According to Swazi history, Incwala is based on the custom of the ruling clan, which lived near the sea far farther north of present-day Swaziland. Many, many generations ago the Queen Mother of the clan fled southwards, taking with her the sacred rainmaking hereditaments, and her young son. The ceremony of "the Green Gourd of the North" is said to symbolize the link between modern Swazi people, and the ancestral spirits who remained behind when the Queen Mother fled her homeland. Therefore it is not unreasonable to guess that the "sacred gourd" is an inherited teraphim, perhaps even an ancestral skull. In the matriarchal societies of antiquity it was not unknown for a royal princess to leave home and start a new dynasty. Nor was the theft of the sacred tribal rainmaking and oracular hereditaments in such circumstances uncommon, for even Rachel, the beloved of Jacob, stole Laban's teraphim when she left her father's house (Genesis 31:19).

In many parts of Africa the ritual filling of the mouth with specially treated water, and spitting in the direction of rain, is customary during rainmaking ceremonies.[15] In Kenya the Akamba, and the Tiv of Nigeria, believe that rain is God's saliva.[16] The act of ritual spitting is one of the most ancient creative actions. But as spitting is equated with male semen, women do not do ritual spitting. The Egyptians viewed saliva, and spitting, with inner knowledge, as the Great Creative Force.[17]

African herbalists, diviners and healers customarily spit medicines over their patients.[18] In Africa, spitting is also done to expel evil and anger. While spitting at a confessional sacrifice is associated with cleansing from anger, spitting over the left shoulder in anger is done deliberately, to invoke a curse. There is an African belief in an association between licking and spittle, and both are connected with fertility. Zulu diviners believe pythons, the great serpents of rain, and procreation, fertilize with their spittle. And so diviners use python spittle in medicines to cure barrenness and infertility.[19] In addition to filling the mouth with water and spitting to invoke rain, protection from evil in general and from enemies in particular is conjured up by spitting powerful medicines in the direction of the looming misfortunes.

Spitting is also an African way of attracting the attention and love of a desired maiden, provided that the correct mixture of herbs are chewed.[20] Perhaps the custom of "saying it with flowers" evolved when men tired of chewing and spewing, and just handed the girl the bunch of herbage instead.

An equally ancient purification and New Year ritual conducted by the Sacred King of antiquity was the rite of spitting to the four cardinal points of the kingdom. From earliest times it was believed that the world was divided into four sections, and even the bronze oxen holding the molten sea created by King Solomon, with the help of Hiram of Tyre, faced the four cardinal points:-

> "It stood upon twelve oxen, three looking toward the northland, three looking toward the west, and three looking toward the south, and three looking toward the east: and the sea was set above upon them, and all their hinder parts were inward" (2 Chron.4:4).

Some sources say the rite was devised to ensure the harmonious progression of the seasons by honouring equally wind, water, earth and fire. But the fact the Egyptians related the numeral 4 to Earth[21], suggests hidden knowledge concerning the importance of numeral 4 to the well being of the planet Earth, and the survival of every form of life on Earth.

In *Spirit of the Rocks* I put forward the suggestion that the Biblical Garden of Eden was in fact planet Earth, the whole planet, and not simply some prized piece of real estate where a garden had been laid out.[22] And that the Rivers of Eden, of which it is written in the Bible: "*And a river went out of Eden to water the garden; and from thence it was parted and became into four heads*" (Genesis 2:10–14), refers not to known rivers flowing on the planet's surface, but to the four great subterranean fault lines, which rise from a single head at the Antarctic. These four major fault lines which flow northwards, effectively divide the Earth four ways, and in truth control the future of this very unstable planet. The existence of these four, primary, highly unstable, subterranean fault lines of planet earth is a truth, which the scientists who test nuclear devices in remote corners of the world apparently fail to take into consideration. Perhaps, instead of spitting at each other in anger, modern rulers should all have more regard for the future of this planet, and expend their energies propitiating Earth and caring for Earth. Before, as the direct result of their current greedy and egotistical activities, we are all blown to perdition by violent volcanic action. If, however, that is to be our fate we cannot cry "unfair" for, steeped as the majority of us are in Western traditions, we are all equally guilty of not respecting the ground underneath our feet, and the unseen, latent, seething energies under our planet's oceans.

An ancient, sacred, universal symbol—as well known to African shamans as it was to early mystics—the five-fold bond, better known internationally as the Celtic cross, is one of the symbols engraved on the rocks of South Africa (Ill. 84). The symbol of the four-armed cross within a circle has many names and many shapes, including the ancient benevolent sign of the swastika. Whatever the shape, and the "mystery explanation", in every case this sign represents the Tree of

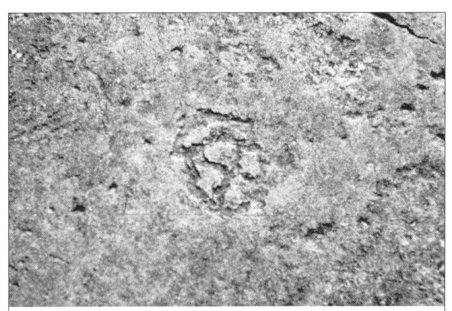

Ill. 84. An international symbol, known by many names—the "Celtic cross", the "five-fold bond", etc—this cross within a circle is as African as it is Celtic. Some years ago I was presented with a brass "Celtic cross" from the staff of a diviner in Soweto, and in ancient times this symbol was engraved on South African rocks.

Life, the Dragon's Pearl—which, if it falls out of the mouth of the dragon, will cause the end of the world.

Focus on this symbolism for a moment. Then take a thoughtful look at the head of the great "river" rising at the South Pole, and the four "heads" which part from it, and mindfully see them as the "rivers" of the Garden of Eden. Reflect on them as the four "heads", the "rivers" of fault lines, quartering the globe. This, I believe, is the truth hidden in the simple symbol of the "Celtic cross", and the inspiration for the Chinese legend of the Dragon's Pearl.

For whatever acknowledged reason, by spitting to the four points of the compass the Swazi king is raising a protection of beneficial Earth forces and creative energies over his entire kingdom.

The Swazi singing of taboo songs of hate and rejection is paralleled by the ancient custom of cursing and insulting divine kings from a nearby hill, to ward off Divine jealousy. Roman generals were thoroughly insulted at their triumphs, while they temporarily impersonated the War God, Mars.[23] A similar protection was placed on seeds, which were forcefully cursed by sowers during planting time, to ensure a bumper harvest.

Robert Graves has noted the archaic custom of eating a victory ox, and pelting the sacred kings with green leaves. He suggests the origin is Pelasgain.[24] The Swazi ceremony, where the king is presented with boughs of freshly picked acacia leaves at the beginning of Incwala, could be a Swazi adaptation of this ritual.

The use of acacia branches in the annual Swazi ceremony has great esoteric significance. The acacia—and there are many varieties—has ritual links that go back in time to the very early Hebrews, and maybe even earlier. One variety of acacia, with golden flowers and sharp thorns, was the Biblical *shittim* wood.[25] It was from the waterproof wood of these trees that the Ark of the Covenant is said to have been built (Exodus 30:1–7; 38: 1). The legendary Ark in which the Egyptian goddess Isis sailed to search for the remains of Osiris was made from the wood of the acacia. And the Arks of other Sun-heroes such as Noah and the Armenian Xisuthros, were also made of acacia wood, as was the death barge of the Egyptian god Osiris, god of fertility and agriculture, husband and brother of the goddess Isis.[26]

The acacia was the sacred tree of Astarte/Aphrodite, the Sea, Fertility and Mining Goddess of the Phoenicians, and later Canaanites, to whom diamonds were sacred.[27] Although its popularity was due to the sea-worthiness of the timber, there may have been another reason why acacia was sacred to Aphrodite/Astarte/Isis. The Egyptians, Phoenicians, and Canaanites were excellent sailors, but in addition to commanding the oceans and tides, their goddesses held sway over mining and love/fertility. There can be no doubt that the main interests of Egyptians, Phoenicians, Mesopotamians, and Canaanites were trade and mining. In *The God Kings and the Titans* Jim Bailey discusses the highly organized gold-mining operations of antiquity. In particular he mentions that the Sudanese word *carat*, the unit by which gold was measured, was taken from the seeds of a particular acacia tree. Twelve carats of gold being the equivalent of twelve seeds.[28] Hence the importance of this tree to the Goddess of Mining, who was also responsible for the increase of minerals in the Womb of the Earth Mother, and for the safety of treasure-laden ships on their journeys between the mines and the home ports.

So important was the acacia to the Egyptians, that the royal ladies wore girdles, which incorporated facsimiles of acacia seeds, carved from green feldspar and carnelian, strung with gold. These jewel seeds were interspersed with large beads in the form of gold cowrie shells, and the cowrie shell is everywhere recognized as an ancient fertility symbol, representing the yoni of the Great Mother. The queen of Tutmosis III (of the 18th Dynasty, which lasted from 1575–1308 BCE) wore a belt comprised of seven rows of acacia seed beads made from carnelian, turquoise, faience, glass, and gold.[29]

A seven-string girdle of carved stones crafted to represent the seeds of the sacred, and useful, acacia must surely have been intended as an invocation to the Goddess in her fertility aspect—if only to increase the fertility of the mines. What must never be overlooked is that the queens of ancient Egypt, like the Swazi Queen Mother, were an integral part of the temple/governing hierarchy, and therefore their jewellery and accessories were of spiritual, and not temporal, importance.

The carnelian was the stone dedicated to the Sun and to the goddess Venus, another form of Hathor/Astarte/Aphrodite, and it was thought to be particularly efficacious against all evil and envy.[30] The turquoise was sacred to Hathor, the Egyptian goddess of fertility and mining.[31] And according to George Kunz it was an Egyptian practice to engrave special chapters of the Book of the Dead, among those referring to the heart, on particular stones. Thus, for instance, the 27th chapter was engraved on feldspar, and the 29th on carnelian so it was not by chance, or personal preference, that Egyptian queens wore a seven-strand belt of carved carnelian, turquoise or feldspar.[32]

By wearing jewelled facsimiles of acacia seeds, and gold cowrie shells, the queens of Egypt emphasized the fertility attributes of the acacia—or perhaps they were advertising the duality of the goddess—life and death. The flip side of fertility is infertility, or induced infertility such as contraception. And in ancient times Egyptian women used the sap from the thorns of acacia branches as a contraceptive. The gummy sap contained in green acacia thorns destroys sperm, and Egyptian women who did not wish to fall pregnant used a contraceptive jelly made of honey, mixed with finely pounded dates and acacia spikes, which they smeared on a wad of fibres and inserted into the vagina.[33]

Perhaps this knowledge lies behind the Incwala identification of the men who carried wilting acacia leaves, as adulterers. Clearly, the sacred trees were only accessible to ordinary people once a year, on the first day of the Great Incwala. So, the pre-dawn ceremony of gathering the branches was the only opportunity an adulterer had of obtaining the material he needed to prevent his lover from falling pregnant. The specially chosen men surely watched each other closely, so it would have been very difficult for one of them to strip off a supply of thorns from the trees, without being noticed. The only way would be to remove such thorns as were on the branch he himself carried, and a branch stripped of spikes would surely wilt, and give away his guilty secret.

The lactic acid in acacia thorns is the same lactic acid used in many modern contraceptive jellies. No wonder the ubiquitous acacia is still the sacred tree of the Arabian Desert, and credited with powers of life and death. There is an enduring belief that anyone found quilty of breaking off a branch, or twig, will be cursed by the tree, and the culprit is expected to die within the year.[34]

In Swazi lore, the acacia is credited with oracular powers. This belief is not unique to the Swazi, for the acacia was the prime oracular tree of Canaan. Robert Graves even suggests that the "burning bush", from which Moses heard the Word of the Lord, was an acacia covered with the red-berried parasitical *iroanthus*, which gave the bush the appearance of "burning". This is an interesting detail, because certain species of acacia in South Africa are very often infested with a red-berried plant very similar in appearance to the *iroanthus*[35] (Ill. 85).

North of Africa, the month dedicated to the acacia was Uath, the time of the Hebron Fair. In Roman times, Uath ended on the Ides of June (the middle of the month, usually the 15th). Almost universally Uath was a time of mid-summer purification of the temples, and ceremonies were held in Greece, Italy, and the Near East.

In addition to rites of purification, Uath was a most holy period. All self-beautification and all sexual congress were taboo, as is the custom during the Swazi Day of Seclusion.[36]

Incwala, the ancient Swazi mid-Summer Festival of Regeneration 157

Ill. 85. The parasitical bush Loranthus, *said to have been the "burning bush" of Moses, is commonly found in the Northern Province (South Africa).*

The Swazi king, whose Incwala sanctuary is ringed by acacia branches, lives in the style of the Essenes. They too surrounded their dwellings with a protective hedge of acacia.[37]

In Southern Africa, acacia branches are also used in the purification ceremonies of Naman Khoisan widows. The specific purpose of these rituals is to exorcise their husband's ghost, and to ensure that he does not return.[38]

For millennia, throughout the Middle East, and in many places of Africa, the acacia has been identified with sacred rituals. The protective powers attributed to acacias encompass even the floundering of ships, and a good riddance to unwanted ghosts—including contraception and the closing of doors to the spirits of unborn children. Therefore it is most unlikely that the incorporation of acacia branches into the Incwala ceremony is a mere coincidence of convenience.

The traditional Incwala practice of pummelling a black ox to death is said to have been a lengthy and very dangerous discipline. A comparison may be made with the known circumcision rituals of the Akamba of Kenya.

On the second day of their period of circumcision and instruction, the candidates are required to fight, and destroy, a frightening monster known as *mbusya*, or rhinoceros. It is said this challenge does not necessarily require a physical battle, as in the case of the Swazi, but is often devised to teach the youths spiritual prowess.[39] Equally, great qualities of faith, inspired courage, and the practical application of esoteric knowledge are required of the Swazi youths who take part in the ceremony known as "the Day of the Bull". The once widely practised methods of sorting out the men from the boys by trials and ordeals continue in the sphere of bullfighting in Portugal. Modern Portuguese bullfights end with the subjugation of the wounded, and very dangerously angry, bull by a group of young men who, so they say, volunteer for the sport, to prove their manhood. Sometimes the bull wins, and with a toss of horns one of the youths at least loses his manhood.

Many of the rituals, which make up the annual celebration of Incwala are accompanied by vigorous drumming, and high-leaping dancing. Again, this practice hearkens back to ancient fertility rituals beyond the borders of Swaziland. The traditional Scottish folk dances, such as the sword dance and the highland fling, originated as seasonal fertility and rainmaking rituals.[40] High-leaping dancing was of the greatest importance to early Greek and Celtic fertility ceremonies, for by imitating, and urging the *woivre*, the powerful, throbbing, invisible energies of earth, to flow strongly, pulsatingly, and harmoniously through the land, it was believed rain would fall in season, and all would prosper.

An invocation to the rainmaking qualities of the Moon Goddess is concealed in the preference given to black animals during Incwala. On the Day of the Bull, a black ox is pummelled bloodlessly to death, and the king straddles a sanctified black ox to rise again as "the Bull of the People". In Greek lore, black was one of the three colours most sacred to the Moon Goddess, and in African theology, black is a most sacred colour. Black is associated with the ancestral shades, and when diviners communicate with their spirit guides they wear the "black cloth of the shades".

Offerings of black animals are associated with purity and sacredness, and throughout South Africa the sacrifice of a black animal is witness of a *request offering* to the Ancestors. Among the Zulu the gift of rain is requested with the sacrifice of black oxen, specifically to invoke the darkest of rain-clouds. Rainmakers sometimes lie on black river rocks when invoking dark, water-laden rain clouds and black stones are used in many rainmaking rituals.[41] Therefore it is not by chance that only perfectly formed, pure black oxen are chosen for the most sacred ceremony of Incwala.

The written material describing the bloodless death of the ox does not mention why this occasion should not permit the letting of blood. The Xhosa place a similar taboo on the bloodletting of the sacrificial animal during their *Umkhosi* ceremony.[42] Umkhosi and Incwala are both very sacred rituals, every action has purpose, and hidden meaning. Therefore, as information on these African ceremonies is not readily forthcoming, the answer may lie in the wealth of ancient Greek and Celtic lore concerning the blood of sacrificed animals in general, and of bull's blood in particular.

Sacrificial blood was usually poured directly onto the ground, or onto the yoni altar, so that the soul, or life-power, in the blood could be re-absorbed by Mother Earth, and return from whence it came (Ill. 86). There was a general belief among all ancient peoples that bull's blood was imbued with extraordinary potency, power—and poison.[43] And the eating and drinking of bull's blood was forbidden to the common people. So only Moon Priestesses, as surrogates of Mother Earth (or, in later times, the High Priest) could drink the blood of bulls with safety.[44] Perhaps there is a good medical reason for this taboo. Perhaps Mad Cow disease has been around longer than we think

In Celtic lore, the blood of the sacrificed bull was used in divination—with particular regard to the selection of the new king. The High Priest gorged on meat and blood, and then fell into a stupor, to dream of the future heir to the throne, for Celtic kings, like their Swazi counterparts, did not automatically inherit the throne of their father.[45]

An absolute taboo on the eating of blood was enforced on the Hebrews by the laws of Moses:-

Moreover ye shall eat no manner of blood, whether it be of fowl or of beast, in any of your dwellings. Whatsoever soul it be that eateth any manner of blood, even that soul shall be cut off from his people (Leviticus 7:26,27).

And whosoever man there be of the house of Israel, or of the strangers that sojourn among you, that eateth any manner of blood; I will cut him off from among his people.

For the life of the flesh is in the blood: and I have given it to you upon the altar to make atonement for the soul.

Therefore I say unto the children of Israel, or of the strangers that sojourn among you, which hunteth and catcheth any beast or fowl that

may be eaten, he shall even pour out the blood thereof and cover it with dust.

For it is the life of all flesh: the blood of it is for the life thereof: therefore I say unto the children of Israel, ye shall eat the blood of no manner of flesh: for the life of all flesh is the blood thereof: whosoever eateth it shall be cut off (Leviticus 17: 10–14).

Ill. 86. *An offering to the Great Mother. The liver and blood of the sacrificial goat is here prayerfully laid on the flank of the great yoni rock. Before the sacrifice, a fire was ritually ignited in the depths of the yoni rock, and after the blood was sprinkled on the yoni altar, portions of the liver were placed on the hot stone, and ritually eaten when it was cooked. The African tradition of sprinkling sacrificial blood on the altar was common to all our pagan ancestors. In the theology of Old Africa, the blood contained the soul and the life force. An offering of sacrificial blood was a most holy covenant between man and God. Sacred objects, too, were sprinkled with the blood of sacrificial victims, to honour the ancestors—and the victims. The ancestral spirits were thought to drink the soul of the blood, the inner force/life force, and be strengthened. Ancient Greeks held the same beliefs. And the Biblical Moses ritually purified his people by sprinkling them with the blood of his sacrificial offerings* (Exodus 24: 6–8). *In the Book of Leviticus the Israelites were given very explicit instructions about the disposal of sacrificial blood:* "And the priest shall sprinkle the blood upon the altar of the Lord at the door of the tabernacle of the congregation, and burn the fat for a sweet savour unto the Lord" (Leviticus 4: 1–6; 16: 14, 19).

Incwala, the ancient Swazi mid-Summer Festival of Regeneration 161

In traditional African religion, too, the blood is believed to contain the soul of the sacrifice. According to Professor John Mbiti, the theology of Africa encompasses the concept that when the blood is shed in making a sacrifice, it means human or animal life is being given back to God, the origin of all life.[46]

Therefore the esoteric purpose of the Incwala sacrifice, when the ox is bloodlessly killed, can only be to ensure that the power resident in the soul-charged blood of the animal does not escape the body after death. This theory is strengthened by the knowledge that certain portions of the carcass are removed immediately, and used in medicines for doctoring the king. In other words, the life-force/power/soul of this animal is not offered directly to God, but *indirectly*, through the medium of the medicines administered to the king in his role as the earthly personification of God.

The straddling of the prostrate sacred ox by the naked Swazi king is one of the oldest inauguration rituals of this kind. Celtic kings were rendered incarnate by copulating with a bull or a horse, which represented the Mare-goddess, Demeter. The Irish kings symbolically simulated re-birth from a white mare, and there was a taboo on eating horseflesh. The horse was a sacred animal to the ancient Britains, the Saxons, and the Danes.[47] In Celtic lore horses, and the wild asses (zebras) of Egypt and Libya, were sacred animals, self-dedicated to the Moon Goddess by virtue of their new moon-shaped hoof prints. For wherever they walked they left imprints of the sacred new moon on the earth. Cattle, with the hoof print of a double half-moon, were equally sainted.[48]

The Libyan "goat marriage" required the ritual mating of the Sacred King with a goat.[49] And the pagan queens of India ritually mated with, or simulated copulation with, horses. In addition to being an inauguration ritual for kings, bestiality is a most ancient shamanistic practice, and associated with sorcery.[50] An English chronicle of the 12th century states the wife of King Edgar was accused of witchcraft because a bishop saw her "running and leaping hither and thither with the horses, and showing herself shamelessly to them". Reports on the magical tradition of transformation into an animal survived for some time in witch cults of the Northern Hemisphere. During witch trials in c.1673 Ann Armstrong, the Northumbrian witch, confessed to having been temporarily transformed into a horse by her mistress, who threw a bridle over her head and rode her to a meeting of five witch covens. Human male copulation with a female animal was part of a shamanistic identification among the Tuatha de Danaan. And bestiality was also part of the oath-binding ceremonies of the Mau-Mau of Kenya.[51]

The Queen Mother of Swaziland, honoured as the Lady Elephant, is the guardian of the nation's rainmaking hereditaments, and in Africa rainmaking ceremonies include the use of a specially consecrated rain-spear.[52] Engravings of elephant are found at most engraving sites, but one depicts an elephant surmounted by a yoni groove, which is clearly an invocation for rain, and another very beautiful image shows an elephant holding up a spear with its trunk. A specially consecrated rain-spear is used in rainmaking ceremonies, so clearly pagan rainmaking rituals were once conducted at this site (Ill. 87, 88). And not only in antiquity, for Christianized black people living in the area told me that, in times of severe drought, their priest leads them in prayerful dance around these same rocks, to call on God to send the rain. When the rain comes, there is great rejoicing.

Every Incwala festival ends with rejoicing. The people feast and celebrate the start of a New Year of plenty, secure in the knowledge that the ancient rituals have been correctly performed, and the seasonal rains will fall as God wills it. Secure, too, in their belief that all the special qualities inherent in their king have been renewed against the rigours of the coming year.

Prophecy was one of the qualities attributed to all the Sacred Kings of antiquity, and the long-standing independence of the Swazi nation is said to be due to a prophetic dream of King Sobhuza, which foretold of the coming of invaders from lands across the ocean.[53]

In the dream he saw people the colour of red porridge, with hair like the tails of cattle. Their houses were built on platforms, which were pulled by oxen. But the most distressing aspect was that they spoke barbarous languages, and they were shown to be completely ignorant of human courtesies. In short, to the Swazi way of thinking these future invaders of their land were godless heathen barbarians, with no redeeming features whatsoever. Nevertheless, the ancestors also warned of the terrible might of the weapons these approaching hordes carried. The priests were consulted, and the dream was interpreted to mean that King Sobhuza must never attempt to fight the foreigners. When the foreigners arrived, as the dream had predicted, the king heeded the advice of the interpreters of his dream, and diplomacy prevailed.

Thereafter, the Swazi looked upon the invaders as useful allies, and put themselves under the protection of Queen Victoria, whom they visualized as the Lady Elephant of the uncultured, porridge-coloured foreigners.

Incwala, the ancient Swazi mid-Summer Festival of Regeneration 163

Ill. 87. Traditionally the Zulu and Swazi queen mother, keeper of the rainmaking hereditaments and co-ruler with the king, her son, was most respectfully hailed as the "Lady Elephant". Here a wonderful engraving portraying an elephant below a classic yoni on the apex of the rock.

Ill. 88. A rainmaking spear was an essential item of "rain-making magic". In Africa the majestic elephant—the herd always led by a matriarch, the tusks referred to as "wisdom sticks"—symbolized the true leader of the people, the Queen Mother, as portrayed by this noble engraving of an elephant proudly bearing a spear.

Chapter 8

In honour of Khulu-Khulwané

*U*njan, what do you say about that Unkulunkulu, of whom the black men used to talk?
The ancients said that it was Unkulunkulu who gave origin to men, and everything else besides, both cattle and wild animals. They said it was an ancient man who gave origin to these things, of whom it is now said that ancient man is lord; it is said, he is the Lord, which is above. We have now heard from you that the Lord, which is in heaven, is he who made everything. The old men said that Unkulunkulu was an ancestor and nothing more, an ancient man who begat men, and gave origin to all things.[1]

So spoke Chief Unjan of the Abambo, in answer to the question put to him by the Reverend Henry Callaway, the Scottish missionary who settled among the AmaZulu in Natal, around 1830, and meticulously recorded their traditions and beliefs. The Reverend Henry Callaway was exceptional because he not only strove to understand the beliefs and customs of the AmaZulu, but he closely questioned chiefs and elders on their history and traditions, and he wrote down every word, verbatim, in Zulu, and translated it into English.

There should no longer be any doubt that the region of Southern Africa was visited over millennia by waves of traders, miners, seamen, and even missionaries in the service of Isis. The traces they left behind are today limited to unexplained ruins, artefacts, race memories, legends, and rock engravings. Yet, before the misconceptions largely propagated by Christians of the 19th century, who came to Africa imbued with missionary zeal, and steeped in centuries of prejudice against the slave races—"the children of Ham"—the indigenous people themselves had tales of First Man.

The San said their ancestors arrived in baskets from the east. The Zulu, and others, relate a tribal history of First Man who arrived with a wife, companions, cattle, a dog, the knowledge of cooking with fire, who introduced circumcision, and who commanded his followers to take wives of the indigenous peoples and start new tribes. Before the interaction of Christian missionaries this Older than Old ancestor was known as *Khulu-Khulwané*, or more commonly *Unkulunkulu*, Lord. He was an ancestor, and nothing else.

In modern English/Zulu dictionaries the word for God is listed as *uNkulunkulu*. But in Africa traditionally the Godhead, God the Father, was only spoken of obliquely as *The Giver of Things; Alone the Great One; He is Surprised by Nothing; Maker of Children; The Great One in the Sky; The Owner of All Things,* and so on. The Zulu also revered other aspects of the Most High, God the Mother as *Nomkhumbulwana* or *Nomcubulwana* the Earth Mother; God the Son as *Mvelinqangi,* who was also the Sun God; and God the Tree of Life, known to the Zulu as the *Simikade* tree.

Untutored in African theology, and unaware of the African manner of respectfully speaking indirectly of the Godhead, Christian missionaries from Europe assumed that pagan Africans had no knowledge of God.

The strict traditional training of African youths, during their period of circumcision, prevented them from betraying tribal secrets regarding the secret, sacred things of their people throughout their entire lives. In West Africa, traditionally, the period of circumcision was also the time when the youths were instructed in the lore and the laws of their people, the rules and regulations governing life as a responsible adult. Often, during this educational period, rites were concluded by taking the youths to a shrine, and showing them certain sacred symbols. In *Races of Africa* Seligman describes how the Jukun novices were led blindfold to a shrine, and as the bandage was suddenly removed the initiates were asked what they could see. The correct answer was "Nothing at all." If, however, a boy lost his self-possession, and named any one of the sacred objects before him, he was immediately put to death as one who could not be trusted with tribal secrets.

There is a case on record of Christian missionaries to the Herero in Namibia who wrote that, prior to their arrival, the Herero had no concept of God. This is but one example of how greatly missionaries misconstrued traditional African religious beliefs, for the Tswana and Herero were forbidden to mention God's name at all. It was thirty years before this communication barrier was breached, and the misunderstanding resolved. By which time the idea that the Herero were nothing but "Godless heathen" was firmly entrenched in the minds of good Christians everywhere.[2]

In Africa God lives, and is in and of every living creation—be they people, animals, plants, rivers, or rocks. Pagan, the indigenous Africans may have been, but Godless? Never!

The main reason for the secrecy, and the unwillingness on the part of African peoples to utter God's name directly, was because to them the power of God was ineffable. Therefore, only a High Priest, or Sacred King, dared invoke the Presence by name directly, and then only during certain solemn ceremonies.

Strange as this pagan African tenet may seem to modern Christians, the concept was by no means limited to the indigenous peoples of Africa. The Celts, early Greeks, Romans, and for that matter the Hebrews too, hid the name of their God under dark cloaks of sworn secrecy.[3] There is on record a Sabine, Quintus Valerius Soranus, who was put to death for divulging the name of his God.[4] The reason for the enforced secrecy, and even for the fact that the basic group of classical gods and goddesses were honoured by a variety of names, was the ever-present fear that if the local or tribal name of a protective deity became known to an enemy, it would be within the enemy's power to invoke the deity and reverse its "loyalties".[5]

A concept not to be scoffed at too quickly. Words, and even thoughts, carry great power if used with intent—which is why prayers, and curses, are so often "answered".

The Romans not only specialized in learning the names of enemy gods, they even conducted a magical ceremony, *elicio*, by which they summoned the deities of their foes. And elicited (drew out) from the deities everything the Emperor and his generals needed to know about the strengths and weaknesses of their opponents.[6] Having gleaned all the relevant information, the Romans then carried their para-psychological warfare a step further, and performed a ceremony of destructive magic against their enemies. They drew the power from the enemy god, and directed it as a flow of negative energies towards the people they intended attacking.[7] The formulae used by the Romans to summon the Juno of Veii to Rome is mentioned in the writings of Livy. So threatening was this practice that the Tyrians used to bind their holy statues in chains as a precaution.

In *The White Goddess* Robert Graves describes a magic ceremony of this kind, which was carried out in Jerusalem, in the 2nd century BCE, on the orders of King Alexander Jannaeus the Maccabee. The god summoned was the Edomite Ass-god of Dora, near Hebron.

These ancient pagan beliefs, and practices, suffered a severe setback with the arrival of Christian missionaries who fearlessly preached a religion which proclaimed God's holy name loudly, and in public, at every possible opportunity. In South Africa, not only did Christian missionaries, of whatever denomination, laud God loudly and clearly, they fervently exhorted their converts to do the same. Faced with shaking heads, and blank stares, the missionaries assumed that the indigenous peoples had no knowledge of God and, undaunted, set about finding a suitable African word in the local dialect on which to hang the story of Jesus of Nazareth.

In 1837, a zealous missionary named Captain Allen Gardiner adopted the name *Unkulunkulu*. A contemporary of Allen Gardiner, the Reverend Henry Callaway, stated very precisely how this occurred:-

> *"Mr Hully, a missionary for some years connected with the Wesleyans, went up to the Zulu country as interpreter to Mr Owen, in 1837. He says the word Unkulunkulu was not then in use among the natives; but that Captain Gardiner introduced it to express the Greatest, or the Maker of all men. Mr Hully refused to use it in this sense. He allowed that the word 'kulu' meant great, but denied that which Captain Gardiner wished. But he persisted in using it through a young man named Verity."*[8]

The Reverend Callaway was particularly interested in the story of Creation, as it existed among the AmaZulu and neighbouring tribes. Drawn by a sincere desire to understand the customs and beliefs of the indigenous peoples of Natal, he sought out knowledgeable elders, asking them to tell him what they knew of the story of Unkulunkulu—the word adopted by Captain Gardiner to convey the meaning of "God"—and meticulously recorded every word of his detailed research, verbatim, with the English translation alongside. The elders he interviewed were emphatic that Unkulunkulu was a man, a human being who died, calling him First Ancestor—the old, old, old one—the Most Ancient Man. They stressed that Unkulunkulu was most certainly never worshipped. Nor was he to be confused with

Umvelinqangi, the Primal Source of Being, for it was Umvelinqangi who gave origin to Unkulunkulu. As may be seen from the following excerpt taken from the Reverend Henry Callaway's book *The Religious System of the AmaZulu*, they were equally adamant that Unkulunkulu was not to be confused with the Lord of Heaven:-

> Unbebe, who related the following, was a very old man, belonging to the Amatanja tribe. He had seen much. His people were scattered by the armies of Utshaka and he showed four wounds, received at different times: 'The Chief (meaning Callaway) enquires then what our forefathers believed. The primitive faith of our fathers was this, they said, 'There is Unkulunkulu, who is a man (indoda, that is a male) who is of this earth.' And they used to say, 'There is a lord in heaven.'[9]

The informants said that although Unkulunkulu had existed in the beginning, the Earth, created by the king of heaven, was in existence long before Unkulunkulu. Where the expression "in the beginning" was used, the Reverend Callaway was careful to stress that this referred to "the beginning of the present order of things", and not "from all eternity", which is quite a different concept.

There was a great deal of mistrust, mayhem, ivory poaching, land grabbing, and dastardly political manoeuvring going on in Natal during the mid 19th century, at the same time as missionaries were making their inroads into the interior. As stated above, it was Captain Gardiner who lifted the name Unkulunkulu, from the traditional folklore about First Man, known to the Zulu as Khul-Khulwané, or Unkulunkulu the older than old ancestor. An act which thoroughly confused his converts, and successfully buried forevermore the memory of the tribal histories passed down from generation to generation of the coming of the strangers, Khulu-Khulwané.

No doubt it was out of politeness, an unwillingness to make the missionaries appear ignorant that caused the converts to accept Unkulunkulu as the Christian word for God. Whatever the reason the tribal elders, or the interpreters, had for speaking of Khulu-Kulwané as Unkulunkulu, the story of the legendary Khulu-Khulwané is worth looking at more closely, for his arrival completely changed the lives of the people he encountered. He introduced new blood, in the form of companions whom he commanded to take wives and start new tribes, cattle, fire, the preparation of cooked food and circumcision.[10]

The Unkulunkulu researched by the Reverend Henry Callaway is said to have "broken off", or "peeled off" in the beginning—*wa dabuka ekukgaleni*—and to have sprung from a bed of reeds. The word used by the people to express "break off" was *dabuka*, which literally means to separate by fissure or division, not to snap or fracture. The same word is used when a living area becomes overcrowded, and the eldest son of the chief, or the princess/priestess, "breaks off", or "peels away" from the home kraal to start a new centre with chosen followers.[11]

Not only do these legends tell how the first ancestor sprang from the reed bed, but that a woman followed him and, "after her sprang all the primitive men". When asked how they themselves were created, the people told the Reverend Callaway they did not know if the primitive men were begotten, for they emerged from the reed bed as they were.[12]

Our first ancestor, they said, came out as he was. Perfectly formed and fully grown. So they said he was the First Chief, he who begot men:-

> *Some say that Unkulunkulu was many colours, they say he was white on one side and on the other side black, and on another side he was covered with bush. So we said perhaps they spoke of the hairiness of his body, and so called it a bush. And people say he too gave them existence in begetting them.*[13]

Their first ancestor was not the only one of the group to procreate, for legends tell how his companions also took wives, and begat offspring. Usithlanu, an old Zulu soldier who had fought in Utshaka's army said:-

> *The first man is called Unkulunkulu. He came out with a wife; and the other men came out of the bed of reeds after him, all the primitive men. He the first was chief indeed, he who begot men. We say 'They were begotten by him who came out first.' We do not know that the primitive men were begotten. They came out as they were, out of the bed of reeds; and Unkulunkulu came out as he was. We do not see him, and hear only of Uthlanga (the place from which Unkulunkulu and all other things came). So we say he was first; he made the earth and the mountains, the water, corn, food, cattle, and everything. All things came out of the water, dogs and cattle. We say they were made by him, for when we came into being they were already in existence. Unkulunkulu came out of Uthlanga with a wife; she as well as he, is called Unkulunkulu. Whether it is a man or woman we say Unkulunkulu, both of the female and of the male.'* [14]

The Reverent Callaway asked Unsukuzonke Memela to collect information on his behalf, and he contributed the information that, after springing out of the reed bed, the most ancient man said:-

'Unkulunkulu are the offspring of Umvelinqangi; he begat us with a reed, it being in the water.' At his origin he said, 'We will fight and stab each other with spears, that the strongest may be manifest who overcomes the other; and he who overcomes the other shall be a great king; and he who is overcome shall be dependent. And all people shall wait upon him who is the king who overcomes the other.' [15]

From other sources the Reverend Callaway collected the information that their first ancestor introduced cattle, and told the people to eat the flesh and drink the milk:-

Unkulunkulu said, 'These are cattle. Be ye broken off and see the cattle; and let them be your food; eat their flesh and their milk.' And the grass was created by Unkulunkulu and he told the cattle to eat. He said, 'Let firewood be fetched that a fire may be kindled, and food be dressed.' Unkulunkulu looked at the fire and said, 'Kindle it, and cook and warm yourselves and eat meat which has been dressed by the fire.' [16] *Unkulunkulu said, 'Let there be men, and let them cultivate food and eat.'* [17] *Unkulunkulu said, 'Let there be marriage among men that there be those who can intermarry, that children be born and men increase on earth.'*

At this point there is a footnote by the Reverend Callaway: "Literally, let children be begotten or born with one another. An allusion to a supposed period in which if blood relations did not marry there could be no marriage. The meaning really is, let brothers and sisters marry, that in the progress of time there may arise those who are sufficiently removed from close relationship, that there may be *abalanda* i.e. persons who may lawfully intermarry."[18]

Yet another command he gave was:-

"Let there be black chiefs; and the chief be known by his people, and it be said, 'That is the chief, assemble all of you and go to your chief.'[18] *Unkulunkulu said, 'Let men circumcise, that they may not be boys.' And Unkulunkulu also circumcised, for he commanded us to circumcise.' Unkulunkulu gave men Amatongo; he gave them doctors for treating diseases, and diviners; he gave them medicines to treat diseases occasioned by the Itongo.'* (an Itongo is the spirit of the dead, a disembodied spirit, usually appearing in dreams or in the form of a snake).[19] *It is said that at his death he prophesied the future of his children, telling them by what conduct, good or bad, they would be*

characterized. Thus the phrase is often used to express perfection of goodness and to express also utter wickedness. He died uttering his last word, and this has now become an idiom to express merely the last word on any matter."

Unlike many a legendary figure, this first ancestor—Unkulunkulu, alias Khulu-Khulwané—did not go up to heaven in a golden cloud, a mystical ladder, or a fiery chariot. He was human, and mortal. He simply died. Yet during his lifetime among the indigenous Africans he introduced cattle; agriculture; at least one dog; a wife; fire, and the cooking of food; spears, and companions willing to fight, physically, to claim the title "Champion of Champions", and circumcision. On his deathbed he gathered his children together, and told them what their future held.

With the passing of time, the praise-name of Khulu-Khulwané was forgotten. Other names were taken up, each house having its own *isibongo*, or praise-names for their tribal ancestor.

Until, eventually, there was no one who said, *"For my part, I am of the house of Khulu-Khulwané."*

Chapter 9

Olulu, Olulu

The last task of Khulu-Khulwané when, at his death, "he prophesied the future of his children" is paralleled by the dying Moses and Jacob: *"And Jacob called to his sons, and said, Gather yourselves together, that I may tell you that which shall befall you in the last days"* (Deut. 33 & Genesis 49: 1 – 33). And in no uncertain way did Jacob detail their faults and failings, with many a cautionary word about the hard days ahead.

The legend of Khulu-Khulwané is an African legend. Therefore, it is important to keep in mind the fact that, before the advent of the first pioneering Moravian mission at Genadendal in the Cape, in 1737, the craft of recording events in writing, or with cryptic Ogam symbols, was unknown to all but the highest grade of shaman, the Sanusi.

In Old Africa, the telling, retelling, and memorising of ancient history, as handed down from generation to generation over the ages, was held to be a sacred trust for the enlightenment of future generations. Therefore, it did not matter whether the storyteller, or his audience, understood the meaning of the words and phrases used. What did matter was that the tales were to be remembered, and passed orally from generation to generation, without editing or censorship.

Throughout his research the Reverend Callaway emphasized that, although the people he interviewed described how their first ancestor, his wife, and companions, together with cattle, a dog, spears and implements, *"sprung from a bed of reeds"*, and that they all agreed the bed of reeds was *"in the sea"*, *"in water"*, or *"at a river bank"*, he commented that they did not appear to understand what the phrase actually meant. In other words, he believed that the oft-repeated phrase *"bed of reeds"*, although important to the story, was meaningless to the Zulu living in Natal during the early 19th century.

To a European, the-oft repeated statement that the newcomers *"sprang from a bed of reeds"* conjures a picture of people appearing, as if by magic, out of a clump of reeds growing in a marsh, or on the banks of a river. As the legend was only of passing interest to the newly arrived colonists in Natal, they assumed that these reeds were growing quite normally in a marsh, or along a riverbank. And therefore, there was no need for anyone to take the matter further. Possibly, for this reason, the accounts, which place the reed bed in the sea, were disregarded as a misinterpretation, because Europeans know that reeds do not grow in the sea. So no one bothered to query, or search for, the historical truths concealed in this curious tale.

Now, traditionally, the Nguni-speaking peoples did not use the phrase *"a bed of"* to denote a clump of plants growing together. To a non-Westernized African, the English expression *"a bed of roses"* or *"a rose bed"* would be taken to mean quite literally a bed, or sleeping mat on the floor, made of roses. So let us look more closely at the details in this story, starting with the arrival of Khulu-Khulwané.

The subjects examined by the Reverend Callaway said the strangers *"sprang"* out of a bed of reeds. To spring out of a marshy patch of reeds is difficult, if not impossible. A person can only escape from this kind of tangled vegetation and thick mud by splashing, squelching, and often sinking waist-deep into unexpected hollows while struggling towards dry land. There is no grace or poetry of movement in this action, no "springing out" of the morass.

On the other hand, the best way to disembark from a beached vessel is to place one hand on the bulwark, and spring ashore. In other words, the legendary *"reed bed"* of Khulu-Khulwané and his party was most probably one of the many reed, or papyrus, ships which sailed the oceans of the world in ancient times, ships known to the peoples of Africa as *umKhumbi*.

Bulrushes, papyrus, and reeds, were in general use in the Middle East, Arabia, and Egypt as the basic materials for sandals, mats, baskets, rope, houses—and ships. Reeds and papyrus were most commonly used for the building of ships. Primitive reed rafts and boats were plying the Nile, and other great rivers, from the time mankind first learned to catch fish, or cross a waterway without wading or swimming. Seaworthy ships, designed for long-distance ocean travel and made from bundles of papyrus lashed, or sewn, together, are known to have been built in Egypt from the early Dynastic period, which was around 3000 BCE.[1]

Not only the Egyptians were engaged in sailing and shipbuilding. The Mediterranean Sea was buzzing with Sumerian, Hamyarite (of Southern Arabia), Mesopotamian and Cretan traders, some of whom are known to have ventured far across the Indian Ocean and down the East African Coast, even to Madagascar, in ships of papyrus or reeds. All the traders, miners, prospectors, slaves, goods, and necessities of life, which had to be transported along the rivers, or across oceans, were carried in ships constructed from bundles of reed or papyrus. Later vessels were constructed from wooden planks sewn together with papyrus ropes in the same way as the "basket" ships of reed bundles had been constructed.

Even the Hebrew prophet Isaiah, who started his ministry around the year 740 BCE, was well informed on the subject of seaworthy ships. Foretelling:-

> *Woe to the land shadowing with wings, which is beyond the rivers of Ethiopia: That sendeth ambassadors by the sea, even in vessels of bulrushes upon the waters, saying 'Go ye swift messengers to a nation scattered and peeled; to a people terrible from their beginning hitherto; a nation meted out and trodden down, whose land the rivers have spoiled'*
> (Isaiah 18: 1–2).

In Biblical times the expression *"rivers of Ethiopia"* was a reference to the White and Blue Nile. The term "Ethiopia", as used by the prophet Isaiah referred to the country to the south of Egypt, Kūsh or Cush, whose kings invaded Egypt during the lifetime of Isaiah, and ruled as Egyptian pharaohs of the XXIV and XXV Dynasties (750–656BCE).[2]

If it can be assumed that the *"bed of reeds"* was in fact a primitive ship floating, not growing, on the sea or in a river, then it is logical to accept that it was one of the many *"vessels of bulrushes upon the water"* as described by Isaiah. And that Khulu-Khulwané arrived from across the sea in a great reed raft, as did the Mayan folk hero *Kukulkan*. I would venture to suggest that the reason this legend has not been taken literally is because fishing, ships, and shipping have never been important to Zulu economy or survival. Nor are the Zulu even a fish-eating nation. Traditionally, among the Zulu, fish is only eaten ritually—a taboo they share with the Ancient Egyptians, Early Britons, and the Khoi.[3]

The traditional disinterest in matters maritime may explain the fact that the Zulu word for a ship, *umKhumbi*, has remained unchanged throughout the ages.

Sanusi Credo Mutwa brought this to my notice during the course of one of our conversations relating to foreign influence on Zulu culture: *'Now you see, Mam, here is something which is very, very, funny.'* ("Funny", in this instance, meaning curious, not humorous.) *'The Zulu people have a name for a ship. See? You know what it is called? umKhumbi! The name does **not** apply to a modern European ship. The name umKhumbi means, literally, a rope spine. It means a huge rope spine! Does this mean anything to you? No?'* He paused. Then, speaking slowly and giving emphasis to every word said, *'Ancient Egyptian ships had a rope spine across them! They had a huge rope, which went from the bow to the stern, and was supported by supports in the middle. Now this rope is what we are referring to when we say umKhumbi.*

'The word umKhumbi we also use, not only to denote a ship, but to denote a very strong-willed man—in other words a man with a spine of rope. Our name for a ship goes back very far, to the first ships we knew. The ships with rope spines.'

Thus, although the Zulu may never have been a seafaring nation, there can be no doubt that long, long ago their ancestors had contact with reed or papyrus ships often enough to coin a descriptive word for this mode of travel.

Where Khulu-khulwané and his party came from, at what point on the African continent they encountered the indigenous inhabitants, or when this meeting took place, can only be surmised. Nevertheless, details in the legend narrow the field of conjecture for, although Khulu-Khuluwané and his group were materially more fortunate than the people they encountered, they were themselves at a stage of development we today refer to as primitive. The possessions they brought ashore were simple and basic. The records mention only that the party included men and at least one woman, cattle, a dog, pottery, seed for sowing, knowledge of how to kindle a fire and the custom of eating cooked food, and spears. There is no mention that First Man and his group practised the art of iron smelting or weaving, nor that they introduced the wheel.

Historically, the smelting and working of iron started in the Near East towards the middle of the 3rd millennium BCE, but early iron objects were rare, precious, and restricted to jewellery and temple ware. Not until the end of the 2nd millennium BCE were weapons forged out of iron. The Hittites took the lead and monopolized this offensive weapon industry, and only after their defeat around 1200 BCE did the knowledge of smelting and casting iron spread to the rest of the world.[4]

Wheeled vehicles, horses, horse-drawn chariots, and new military techniques involving cavalry and war chariots, are said to have been introduced into Egypt, and North Africa, by the Hyskos, who swept in from Asia and occupied Egypt from about 1680–1575 BCE. During their domination the horse, chariot, and new military techniques were implanted onto the Egyptian culture, and spread rapidly across North Africa thereafter.[5]

With these approximate dates in mind, a good guess is that the landing of Khulu-Khulwané, and his pioneering party, probably took place before the wheel was in general use in the Middle East, Egypt and North Africa. The Nguni-speaking tribes are believed to have started their southward migrations from, as has been suggested, somewhere in the Karanga region, around 400–1000 BCE, arriving in South Africa around 270.[6]

The suggested time slot of before 1680 BCE means, either the meeting with Khulu-Khulwané occurred generations before the commencement of the southward migrations, in which case the umKhumbi beached on one of central Africa's great lakes or rivers. Or that it beached on the shores of the Zambezi, the Limpopo, maybe even somewhere along the east coast of Africa. If so, then the Nguni-speaking peoples were already occupying Southern Africa much earlier than historians believe.

The Swazi—who, African historians maintain, were already inhabiting parts of South Africa and living in very primitive conditions when the Nguni-speaking peoples first arrived—know First Man who came out of a reed bed as *Umkhulumncandi*. The Matabele of Zimbabwe honour *Unkulunkulu*; the Thonga of Mozambique, and the Nongi of Malawi speak of *Umkulunquango* or *Umkulu-kakulu*.

The Thonga, who settled eventually in Mozambique, are believed to have migrated southwards down the East Coast, and not via the inland trail followed by the other tribes.[7] Although they differ in many ways from the Nungi, having different traditions and language, they may have brought the legend of the reed-springing founders of their race with them. Or Shonshangane introduced the tradition into Thonga culture.

Sonshangane was one of Zulu King Shaka's warriors. He arrived in Mozambique from the south, and conquered the Thonga, 1820–1821.

In tribal society it was usual for the conquered to adopt the ancestral spirits and folk heroes of the victors so that, in time, people really believed they were descended from the same mythical ancestor, although historically it was not the case.[8]

To assume the landing must have taken place on the shores of the Limpopo River, because the Matabele of Zimbabwe knew their creator-ancestor as Unkulunkulu, is wild guessing. The present-day Matabele of Zimbabwe originally inhabited areas in Natal until their founder, Mzilikazi, fled from the wrath of his king, Shaka of the Zulu, in 1823. By 1830 Mzilikazi had established a powerful chiefdom in the Transvaal, on the site of the modern city of Pretoria. But after a difference of opinion with the Voortrekkers, helped by the Tswana, as recently as 1838, he and his people crossed the Limpopo River to settle at what is today known as Bulawayo.[9]

Another temptation to be avoided is to pinpoint the place where Khulu-Khulwané disembarked by tying the story down to an origin in or around present-day Malawi, and Lake Malawi, and hail the Nongi as the descendants of an original group from that region. Unfortunately, once again history records that the Nongi are themselves an offshoot group who broke away from the main Nguni of Zululand as recently as the early 1800s. Under Zwangedaba, they too fled northwards from the army of King Shaka, and established the Nongi kingdom near Lake Malawi. Later they moved even farther north, and reached Lake Tanganyika.[10]

However, the last migration of the Nongi may well have been a return to their ancestral home. For many place names to the west of Lake Malawi and Lake Tanganyika point to a connection between Khulu-Khulwané and the Katanga province—which is today regarded as the region the Nguni migrated from originally, around 1000 BCE. The main tributary of the Congo River that passes through the area is called Lualaba. A large town to the French-speaking west is Liluabourg. Other towns and villages around the upper reaches of the Lualaba River are:-

Malemba Nkulu
Mutombo Mukulu
Kayembe Mukulu
Lukula
Mubulula
Kundelungu

Another route into this region of Africa is via the Congo River, and along the Lualaba River to Katanga. But the most significant clue is the island on Lake Victoria, in Uganda, named Lului. Lake Victoria is the source of the Nile River, and was thus accessible to the commercial fleets of the Egyptians and the Cushites, as well as to the sleek and active fleets of the temple hierarchy. Therefore the party of Khulu-Khulwané could have started their journey from an established trading depot, or religious centre, stationed on or near Lului Island.

In his book *The God Kings and the Titans*, Jim Bailey refers to the widespread mining and trading routes of antiquity. And says the name of the island Lului, on Lake Victoria, (Uganda)—where symbols of mariners working the ancient trade routes are to be found engraved on the rocks—may be a corruption of *El, Eloah*, the Semitic name for God.[11]

While this theory is most logical, the origin of the word Eloah may even have evolved from the great shout of invocation of the Libyan Moon priestesses. The Libyan devotees of the Oracular Oak and Black Dove cults, originally centred at Lake Tritonis, honoured their Goddess with loud cries of "Olulu, Olulu". The same intercession was uttered at Thebes. This particular form of adoration travelled to Greece, and was used there to honour the Athena, Goddess of Wisdom—and to the ancients "wisdom" was the term bestowed on persons having occult powers, or knowledge of mysterious things, i.e. wise-woman = witch. Quoting the information he obtained from the Egyptian priests, Herodotus stated that the centres at Ammon and Dodona were established at much the same time. And that the sacred black doves flew from Thebes in Egypt, to Ammon at Lake Tritonis in Libya, and to Dodona in Greece from about the beginning of the 3rd millennium BCE.[12]

Khulu-Khulwané is a strange word. It too sounds like the cooing of doves. "Olulu Olulu". What could the sound mean, other than the accepted Unkulunkulu, "Great, Great One", or "Older than Old"?

Most likely this is exactly what the sounds do mean, and that Unkulunkulu is an echo of the peons of praise uttered by a boatload of weary travellers, or missionaries, to the Deity who brought them safely to land on some remote African shore. A Deity so omnipotent that only an oblique form of address was possible:- *"Great, Great, One", "Older than Old"*. No doubt, with the passing of time the original meaning and purpose of the cries "Olulu, Olulu" blurred into memory, and the arrival of this group was remembered only as first man and woman, the Khulu-Khulwané.

Other traces of an early Nguni contact with Libyan/Greek/Egyptian devotees of the Moon Goddess linger on in Zulu language and traditions. An obvious connection is the small basket, *ilulu*. The Reverend Berglund describes this basket as the place where a diviner keeps divination bones, the special ritual knife, spirit wand, the leaves of the imphepho (the everlasting plant, *Helichrysum miconiaefolium*, used by diviners in rituals, and burnt ritually when addressing the ancestral shades). The ilulu is also used to hold the live snakes caught by novices as part of their training. He further records that the ilulu is found in the cooking, or store hut of dwellings and is then used to hold maize and other cereals.[13] Very significantly, he adds that only the women handle the ilulu in domestic use. And in ancient Greece—at Sparta and Athens—it was the women who carried the special baskets woven for the agricultural orgy known as *Thesmophoria*.[14]

According to Robert Graves, during Thesmophoria the severed genitals of the sacred king, or his surrogate, were placed in specially woven baskets and carried in the procession by priestesses, but, in more civilized times, these offerings were replaced by phallic-shaped loaves and live serpents.[15] For millennia, the women of Greece are known to have carried specially woven small baskets containing seeds, or fertility symbols and phalli moulded from ground wheat, barley, rye, or other cereals, and phallic and religious objects, during fertility rites. The Spartan reliefs show Helen as an orgiastic goddess, carrying a special basket that is thought to have contained certain fertility tokens, and in Greek myths Herse and Oreithyia ritually carried special baskets containing ritual objects associated with fertility rites.[16] In ancient Athens, devotees of the goddess Athena placed tokens in small baskets, as offerings. These baskets were made from rushes and wild asparagus, and were carried in fertility ceremonies.[17] As all these ceremonies were in honour of the Moon Goddess, giver of rain, and as it was the women who sowed the seed, only the priestesses, or tribal matrons, were allowed to touch the precious baskets. Believing that the magical energies bestowed on the basket and its contents, during the processionals, would flow through the stored seed to seed planted in the earth. And, as the women carried the baskets, and sowed the seed, the future crops of the entire community were literally in their hands.

Clearly the Zulu ilulu, used for storing the ritual objects of diviners; live snakes caught by novices; sanctified seed; and which are taboo for a man to handle, must surely be relics of archaic seasonal fertility ceremonies handed down, from generation to generation, as is the legend of Khulu-Khulwané. The party led by Khulu-Khulwané may even have introduced the concept of the ilulu to the indigenous people among whom they settled, along with their other civilizing influences.

For it is obvious from the details of the oral history that the people they met had no knowledge of crop planting; had never seen cattle; nor did they know how to make fire or cook food.

Another deep-seated race memory going back to the time when the peoples of Africa worshipped the Moon Goddess survives in the Zulu name for the pre-rain halo around the moon. To the Zulu this phenomenon is known as *lulu-lulu*, and many diviners and herbalists take the name *Lulu* when they are initiated. Not, as they have been at pains to explain to me, because it is a "nice" English name, but in honour of the inspirations emanating from the moon, and received through the good offices of their ancestors.

A further indication that First Man and First Woman honoured the Moon Goddess, is to be found in the statement that Khulu-Khuluwané did not say, "I am your leader, fall in and follow me!" No, Khulu-Khuluwané ordered the men to fight to choose a king. This argues that a woman of high rank, such as a priestess, may well have led the party.

The records of the Reverend Callaway particularly note that the word "Unkulunkulu" (Khulu-Khuluwané) referred to both First Man and First Woman:- *"Unkulunkulu sprang from a bed of reeds, and a woman* (a wife) *sprang from the bed of reeds after him. They had one name, Unkulunkulu."*

In a note on this particular comment, Callaway says, *"This is very precise. The first man and woman sprang, the man first and then the woman, from the bed of reeds; and both are called by the name Unkulunkulu; that is Great-great-grandparent. According to Moses, the male and female were both called Adam"* (Genesis 5: 3).[18]

Certainly it is clear from the story that the female Khulu-Khuluwané was a person of high rank, for she disembarked immediately behind First Man, and before any of the others in the party. Added to this is the statement that First Man did not mate with any of the indigenous African women. Although he instructed the other men in the group to take wives from the people they had encountered, to "peel off" and form new tribes, each to its own chief, he bred children by First Woman, thus forming his own tribe, independently. This detail in the story makes sense of the order for sister to marry brother (the royal prerogative of high priestess/sister/queen and king in the courts of Egypt) until there were sufficient people for the distance between them to be acceptable for normal ties of marriage.

The command:- *"Let there be black chiefs; and the chief be known to his people, and it be said 'That is the chief: assemble all of you and go to your people'"* may refer to a tribal tradition whereby a new chief "breaks off" or "peels away" from the parent body, and forms a new unit. The important part of the new unit is that it takes on a new appearance, and develops its own typical characteristics, linguistic and physical, as well as ceremonial. Hence the fact that the Zulu, Xhosa, Swazi, Tsonga, and Matabele—all Nguni—have different facial features, tribal dress, and other minor or major differences in language, custom and ritual.

The oral history of the Zulu, recorded by the Reverend Callaway, attest to the presently unfashionable idea that the indigenous peoples of South Africa are the result of at least a certain amount of miscegenation. The ancestors of many African peoples are likely to have included the offspring of the early prospectors, and traders, who were left to grow to adulthood on African soil. Also the abandoned progeny of maritime foreign devils from the north, northeast, and east—the Semitic, Haematic, Indian, Chinese, Polynesian, all of who came to Africa's southern shores. And even the surviving offspring of the small yellow people who are said to have worked as slaves in the ancient mines at Phalaborwa, and who laid their dead to rest, facing east, the direction of whence they had come. If they were not ancestors of the San, then where had they come from originally? If they were San, then did the ancestors of the San also reach the shores of Africa in "baskets", as their legends say?

As long ago as 1978, when I first visited Sanusi Credo Mutwa at the Oppenheimer Centre in Soweto, I tentatively put to him my theory about early diamond miners from Egypt being active in South Africa. The following is from a tape recording of our conversation on the subject of foreign influences lingering on in the bloodlines and traditions of the Nguni peoples, and others, of South Africa:-

> *But it has got to be. Because, look Mam; before people can risk their lives and sail across the Atlantic Ocean, they've **got** to come to Africa. Some scientists say these people came for short visits. I have been reading some of these papers you gave me. Now this is absolutely bloody nonsense. These people founded tribes—right here in Africa!*
>
> *At first these people didn't come here to do mining specifically. They left their homes for other reasons. In those days religion was a new thing. A beautiful, exciting, new thing. It made you... it made you altruistic! The first ones came as missionaries. Later they came in great numbers for the minerals. These people who came to Africa and founded tribes, they did not allow anybody to marry and produce any kind of children. No! The First Chief who started that nation had many children. Then the*

children of these children were carefully examined, and only those who had the face of the founder of the tribe were allowed to breed.

And they graded their women because they wanted strong mothers. The girls with strong hips, full breasts and the features of the tribe were kept separate from the others and cared for, and were allowed to grow fat and beautiful. Only they were permitted to marry and have children. The other girls were sent out into the fields to do the planting and the digging. These ones were not allowed to have any children. This was to keep the face of the nation pure. So that we would always be the people of our first ancestor.

Khulu-Khuluwané was described as being of many colours, white, black, and covered with bush. The crews of the papyrus ships were often made up of just about anybody, from anywhere. Epigraphist Professor Barry Fell has written that the Stele of Kuban, line three, states:- *"Libyans are white, Syrians light brown, Nubians black, and Egyptians a beautiful dark brown."*

The Zulu chiefs and elders told the Reverend Callaway that agriculture, cattle, the custom of eating cooked food, and circumcision were all introduced to their ancestors by Khulu-Khuluwané. But contacts of a less positive nature, in particular the hereditary disease known as scrofula, could well have been implanted by the crews of the umKhumbi or other wanderers.

Dr A.T. Bryant, who arrived in Natal from London in 1883, mentioned the scourge of scrofula among the Zulu. He went so far as to refer to the disease as *"their national physical weakness"*. One of the side effects of this complaint is that it caused impotency.[19] And among the peoples of Africa impotency is more than a social disease, it is rated as a calamity, because sterility, or impotency, blocks the possibility for the return of an ancestral spirit to the tribe.

Scrofula, which so plagued the health of the Zulu nation, was also a scourge among the Celts. As so little was known about the treatment of this disease during the Middle Ages, in Europe one of the favourite remedies was to drag or push the patient through a "holed stone"—such as the Men-an-tol, in Cornwall. Or make them walk around accredited healing stones a specific number of times. Scrofula was also said to be cured by a "king's touch", or the touch of a seventh son.[20]

The Scottish doctor, William Buchan, writing in Edinburgh in 1814, says:- *"There is no malady which parents are so apt to communicate to their offspring as scrofula, for which reason people ought to be aware of marrying into families affected with this disease."*[21]

In other words, the scourge of the Zulu and the Celts is hereditary, and may well have passed from generation to generation, from clan to clan, perhaps even as long ago as the arrival of Khulu-Khulwané, and the party who sprang from a bed of reeds. Or perhaps the disease was introduced around 2,300 years ago, when Celtic mercenaries were serving in Egypt in 274 BCE. This was the period covering the overthrow of the Persian Dynasties, the end of the domination of Egypt under Alexander the Great, and the beginning of the Greek or Ptolemaic period, 341-30 BCE. But there was an earlier time in the history of Egypt when early Celtic peoples, known as the Tuatha dé Danaan—the people of the Earth Goddess Danu—could have migrated down the African continent, or sailed southwards down the east coast of Africa to integrate with the indigenous tribes.

During the course of my research, I discovered that Celts, early Greeks, Egyptians, and the Zulu appear to have identical beliefs about sacred kings, oracular pronouncements, bulls and serpents. I learned that in ancient Egypt the priests sang wordless hymns by uttering the seven vowels in succession, the sound producing a strong musical sound, like a lyre or flute.[22] I also learned that in the southernmost part of the African continent, the traditional national song of the AmaZulu consisted of a number of musical sounds only, without any meaning, and which cannot be committed to writing. Each tribe had its own chief's song; some of these consisted of words more or less intelligible, others of mere musical sounds which have no meaning whatever.[23] Both Egyptian and Zulu royalty were privileged to wear leopard skins, the leopard being an animal sacred to the Goddess. The Zulu shared with the Cretans and the Celts the custom of keeping boys in the women's quarters until puberty.[24] In times of drought, the Zulu danced a shield dance, and sang a rain song, while pre-Hellenic rainmakers beat on huge, tightly stretched ox-hide shields. The explanation here being that the shield was also a thunder instrument.[25]

I felt that all these similarities could not be coincidental. In fact there were too many coincidences for everything to be only by chance, and that somewhere there had to be a mutual link between ancient Egypt, the Tuatha dé Danaan, and African peoples. Apart from the record of the Celtic mercenaries in Egypt, in 274 BCE, when the country was at the mercy of the Persians, Greeks and Romans, there is the Greek, Cadmus, from Byblos. Cadmus conquered Egypt, Crete, and Greece around 1900 BCE (more or less 150 years either way)—during the Middle Kingdom, and is known to have introduced Phoenician shapes to the 26-letter Ogam alphabet.[26] Another possible Afro-Celtic link between the proto-Zulu, early Egyptians, and the Tuatha dé Danaan is that when Cadmus conquered Egypt, Crete and Greece, the Tuatha dé Danaan fled in four directions.[27] The Tuatha dé Danaan were literate, they were craftsmen and miners, and they were experienced sailors and traders. While their migrations have been traced to Ireland, via Greece and Scotland, there is no reason why some of them at least could not either have remained behind in Southern Africa—abandoned by Egyptian mining projects—or emigrated in a hurry, taking a southward direction away from Greece, Egypt and Crete. In addition to these suggested possibilities for an Afro-Celtic connection, there is also the evidence of Irish annals that state Nius, son of Fenius Farsaidh of Scythia, taught his father's alphabet to the Pharaoh of Egypt around 2353 BCE (within 100 years either way), and married the pharaoh's daughter.[28]

Cretans, Celts, early Greeks, and Zulu, appeared to have identical beliefs about sacred kings, oracular pronouncements, bulls, and serpents. Although I have certain unsupported information relating to an early Sotho-Egyptian connection, I chose the Zulu as the African control because I was able to source more information on the Zulu than any other indigenous Southern Africa peoples. When I researched further into this apparent Afro-Celtic connection, I came across fifty further shared traditions. In addition to the Celtic and Zulu hereditary disease known as scrofula, the fifty shared traditional ways of life are as follows:-

1. The importance of oral learning, and the esoteric significance of ears. The common claim by wizards was that their ears had been licked by serpents. Ears of children are pierced that the mind might also hear.
2. Riddles for entertainment, and for stimulating thought, which also contained esoteric mysteries.
3. An obsession with magic, and ritual through blood sacrifices.
4. The ritual sacrifice of children. Also adult human sacrifice.
5. "Beltane-type" sacred fires. The annual purification of the people, livestock, and land, when all the old fires in the kingdom were ritually extinguished, the land cleansed, and the fires ritually relit and carried to the four corners of the kingdom. A time when all the people and livestock were ritually purified by passing between, or around the fires. Nowhere was this ever a gentle gambol through any old smoke—the herbs used in both instances were known to be

natural insecticides, so the people, and livestock, were not only purified spiritually, but all external body parasites were simultaneously fumigated. *umLilo* the Zulu word for "fire": *Imbole* the Celtic purification of ewes: *-dubula* the Zulu verb for fire as when muskets and cannon belched smoke and flame.

6. The annual harvest rituals were *not* a thanksgiving for past blessings already received, but prayers for the protection of future crops, and for trouble-free pregnancies of wives and livestock.
7. *Fled Gobnu*—Celtic feast of beer brewing in honour of the Divine Smith, *Giobhniu*. *Fled*, the Celtic word for "brew". *Phehleka* the Zulu word for "brew", as in beer.
8. The brewing of magical beer for the sustenance of the Deities, and to strengthen them in their battle against the powers of misfortune. This custom was continued down the ages, and the Celts used beer as a sacrament and for inspiration well into historical times. The Celtic word for inspiration is *vates* or *fathi*. The Zulu counterpart is *ukufakwa*.
9. Deities of the land, or territory, to be placated at rivers, trees, rocks, hills, springs, mountains, caves.
10. Tribal and Nature Deities.
11. The shaman/sangoma as the living embodiment of the collective psyche, the link with the ancestral spirit world.
12. Shamans/sangoma needed a summons that came in a dream, ecstasy, trance, or vision.
13. The importance of fasting for spiritual enlightenment.
14. Poets/Sanusi cursing with magical rhymes—"throwing a mad-man's wisp".
15. The co-mingling of Deities with those of other friendly tribes.
16. A terrible fear that the secret, sacred name of oneself, or that of the tribal Deity, would become known to the enemy, and be invoked against the individual or the tribe.
17. A belief that life is an endless cycle of birth, death, and reincarnation.
18. The burying of sacred treasures in the earth, with secrecy.
19. Ogam, the tic-tac secret hand language of the Druids, is to this day practised by African sangomas who have attained the rank of Sanusi.
20. The importance of eloquence, and an admiration of a great orator.

21. The praises of chiefs and kings chanted by high-ranking "praise poets".
22. Youths confined entirely to male society for military training of periods from two to three years.
23. Wealth measured in cattle.
24. Lobola, or "wife purchase", particularly with cattle as the medium of exchange.
25. Plurality of wives permitted, with a single principal wife.
26. Thatched, circular huts, built around a framework of posts.
27. Deep storage pits for corn, or silos sunk into the ground within the homestead, or farm enclosure.
28. Sanctuary, and meeting places for the men a feature of the villages.
29. A great love of battle and ceremonial gear.
30. Ritualistic boasting. Individual warriors challenging each other before a main battle.
31. The champion's challenge, and tumult kept up by the hosts of fighters.
32. High-leaping dancing of warriors before battle, to work themselves into a state of ecstasy.
33. The "doctoring" of warriors before a battle with "magical" potions, salves, and amulets.
34. Weapons had names. The weapons of chiefs had grandiose names.
35. The sling, used skilfully by the Khoisan, was not a weapon of the Celts, nor of the Zulu.
36. Warriors' love of beer and feasting after the battle.
37. The seating at the post-battle feasts was according to rank, and the champion's portion was often bitterly contested.
38. The ritual eating of the shoulder portion of an animal.
39. A well-defined social system.
40. The king was elected within the kin of his predecessor, but he was not necessarily the son.
41. The ritual functions of the king were of great importance to the well-being of the tribe.
42. Marriages contracted outside kin and clan.
43. Very devout, strong belief in the Godhead. After Christianity replaced paganism, a great punishment was to be excommunicated from the Christian church.
44. The land belonged to the tribe. There was no individual ownership of land.

45. Great annual assemblies fulfilled economic and ritual needs, and were held at the residence of the king, and also at a sacred site often associated with the burial place of the dynasty.
46. The virtue resident in the king's foot, so kings were forbidden to touch the ground with their feet.
47. Collecting the heads of enemies—the belief that the soul resides in the skull.
48. The custom of funeral pyres for kings, with the followers burned alive.
49. The board game known in English as "Nine Man's Morris" and played by ancient Greeks, Viking Norsemen; old Romans; Indians; Chinese; Amazonians; was played under the Zulu name of *Umlabalaba*, or *Ra-ba-Ra-ba* long ages before the first Westernized Europeans arrived in South Africa.
50. The houses of Celts and Zulu are universally circular.

(NB: - This data has a reference section all of its own. See Appendix.)

In other words, pagan Zulu social customs, beliefs, rituals and ceremonies were practised by the Celts. Or, if you prefer, the Zulu/Nguni heritage incorporates at least fifty Celtic social customs, beliefs, rituals, and ceremonies. How, or why, the similarities occurred in the first place, and whether all people were once of a kind, or whether First Man, Khulu-Khulwané who introduced his form of civilization to the very primitive peoples his party encountered was of the earliest Celts, known as the Tuatha dé Danaan—the people of the Goddess Danu—I cannot say.

The purpose behind my apparently curious passion to make an Afro-Celtic link was to find a rational explanation for the inescapable fact that the verdite phallus, inherited by Sanusi Credo Mutwa from his grandfather as a sacred trust, is inscribed with both Egyptian and Arabic Ogam. He told me that in the past this phallus was kept attached to a statue, and used ceremonially in fertility rituals. The fact that the phallus was crafted from verdite is in itself significant, for to Africans verdite was revered and used mainly for fertility objects and charms (Ill. 89, 90).

Professor Barry Fell deciphered the inscription of this phallus (Ill. 91). The translation of the Arabic Ogam is:-

"*To incite distension of the penis, which is to increase sexual pleasure.*"[29]

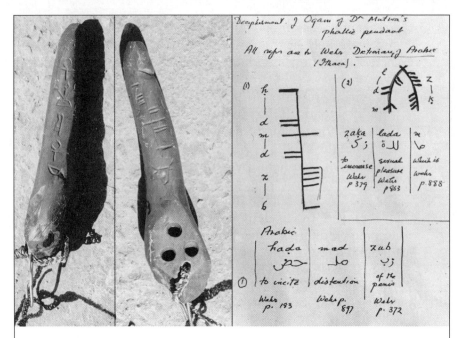

Ill. 89, 90, 91. The sacred verdite phallus of Sanusi Credo Mutwa. In length 32 centimetres, width 20.4 centimetres at base, and 12.2 centimetres at tip, this phallus is engraved on three sides: a "Celtic Cross" and twig ogam; Ogam script below the symbolic head of a bull and three cupules; and Egyptian hieroglyphs. The Arabic Ogam script was translated by Professor Barry Fell: "an amulet—the penis—to cause—to rise up—with joy—for thee". Photo: Warren Dexter.

After receiving this translation, Sanusi Credo Mutwa sent me the following letter, dated 2nd November 1980, and I quote in full:-

Greetings Madam Sullivan,
I was honoured to receive your letter with the decipherment of our Sun-god's Pendant inscription done by Professor Barry Fell. Professor Fell's decipherment of both the Egyptian and Arabic scripts on the pendant match exactly with the FUNCTION of the pendant as my grandfather showed me when he handed it to me for keeping together with many other relics of great antiquity. My grandfather used this sacred pendant, which is part of a copper necklace which has since fallen to pieces, to treat impotent men; he first gave them a drink of a strong aphrodisiac consisting of "BANGALALA" roots powdered and mixed with raw eggs, and then he used the pendant to massage the patient's

penis twice a day. The pendant was first "given life" by being dipped in a virgin's urine boiled in a small clay pot, and the three shallow holes at the back of the pendant were used in oath-taking when a group of medicine men took the Oath of Secrecy in a ritual which consisted of sipping semen from a God-man. The pendant had another, rather strange use; high Priestesses of the Earth Mother who were not allowed to marry or even look at men used to warm this pendant and use it as their "husband". If possible, Madam Sullivan, could you please send Professor Fell my earnest wish that he please visit South Africa before I die? I have much to show him on the day he gets here; I shall also be happy if you could send him a copy of this letter.

With greetings, Madam,
Credo Mutwa.

Unfortunately Professor Fell, who died in 1994, never came out to South Africa during his lifetime. And so he never had an opportunity to examine, and verify the authenticity of the ancient treasures in the possession of Sanusi Credo Mutwa, and others who hold enigmatic objects as a sacred trust. Today the answers to at least some of these enigmas, I believe, lie deeply hidden in the folk legends and the images engraved on the sun-baked rocks.

To eradicate the misrepresentations and misunderstandings nurtured in the dank mists of time, we have only to look at these things of Africa with new eyes.

Chapter 10

Water demons and the dragons of the Drakensberg

A monstrous water demon is believed to inhabit the Victoria Falls. When early European travellers reached these falls, no indigenous people were living within 95 kilometres (60 miles) of the place. The missionaries, who arrived later, reported a common belief in a malevolent and cruel Divinity at the falls, which the natives regularly placated with offerings. This creature is not entirely mythical, as there have been several confirmed sightings by staid government officials of a gigantic black serpent, about thirty feet long, at the foot of the Victoria Falls.[1]

The ancient rite of offering sacrifices, devotions, and devotees, to sacred serpents and monster reptiles was practised by the nomadic Neolithic hunters of Libya and Egypt, and the custom was most enthusiastically perpetuated by the Celts and Early Greeks. The later Egyptian pharaohs, the Ptolemies (2nd century BCE), even went to the length of constructing a great temple to the Crocodile God, at Kom Ombo, where the sacred crocodiles of Sobek regularly received their ritual ration of human flesh.[2] When these monsters died, they were mummified, and interred in special tombs (Ill. 92).

In *The Khoisan Peoples of South Africa* Schapera describes two games played by San children of the Naron, and Auen tribes.[3] In one game, a child takes the part of a "snake" lying in wait at a waterhole, to capture

Water demons and the dragons of the Drakensberg

Ill. 92. The sacred mummified crocodiles at the double temple of the crocodile-headed god Sobek, and the falcon-headed god Haroeris, at Kom Ombo (Egypt). Photo: Warren Dexter.

its prey. In the other, a child pretends to be a water snake at a "magic pool". In this game his companions form a sitting chain, one behind the other, and sidle towards him while they sing a song of such antiquity, that the words are no longer understood. When the chain of sitting children reaches the imaginary pool of water, they break formation, and gather around the pool while making pretence of scooping out water. Their mime lasts until the "water serpent" jumps up and catches one of them—which it then pretends to swallow. The game ends with this mock sacrificial offering. Clearly, folk memories of human sacrificial offerings to the Snake in the Water linger on in the games these children play. In addition, the shamans of the Auen practise the technique of self-inoculation against snakebite.[4] It may be purely coincidental that these people had this knowledge but, in ancient times, this technique was an important part of the "magic" of snake-worshipping cults elsewhere in the world. The description of the Northwest Auen and Naron, as given by Schapera, lifts them out of the usual image of the San as finely boned, golden people of small stature. The Auen and Naron are distinctly taller, and their skin colour is a fairly constant reddish brown or yellowish black, the result of considerable miscegenation throughout the ages.[5]

Other San have legends of a monster rain serpent they call *Koutein Koorou*. Although serpent veneration, as celebrated by devotees of the Old Religion elsewhere in the world, is not known to have been practised by the southern San, yet they continue to observe their traditional Moon rituals, and claimed that the legends of Koutein Koorou were taught to them by those whom they call the People of the Early Race.[6] In other words, this particular legend was not something inherited by the San as being of their own race memories, but something grafted onto their culture by an outside influence—the People of the Early Race.

So, who were these People of the Early Race who inhabited Southern Africa before the ancestors of the San who, according to their own legends, arrived in "baskets" from the east? Osteological remains show that races, other than San and Khoi, have in past ages occupied the areas where engravings are found. Furthermore, it is now fully established that there existed in Southern Africa a number of different stone implement industries, clearly separated in time as well as in character, thus proving that the San were indeed preceded by peoples of earlier races.[7]

My summons to researchers in the field of rock art, to throw away their blinkered misconceptions of the San, and work towards a meaningful explanation of things relating to the pre-history of Southern Africa, is not to decry, or deny, the intelligence, artistry, sensitivity, and spiritual qualities of the San. On the other hand, it is a plea to discourage the fixation that the stories told by the San of the People of the Early Race are simply explanations of the first spirit in mankind. But rather to widen this philosophy to include the probability that, in addition to deeply spiritual meanings, there were on occasion references to actual earlier inhabitants of the land. And to encourage a move towards an empathic understanding of the truths sealed into the legends of all the peoples of Southern Africa. In simple terms, "let's get the record straight!"

Other African tribes who are known to sacrifice to snakes, to make ritual sacrifices to snakes, and who keep sacred serpents, include the Acholi, Alur, Banyoro, Bari, Bemba, Dorobo, Ganda, Gisu, Masai, Nandi, Ndebele, Suk, Turu, Venda and Zala.[8] Being very wary of snakes myself while doing fieldwork, I once asked a sangoma acquaintance how the snake worshipping system worked. Supposing a venerated puffadder had multiplied into a veritable nest of vipers, which, for instance, had taken up abode in a storage bin, or somewhere equally inconvenient to the snake worshipping assemblage. She very gravely assured me that such problems were easily resolved. The tribes that venerate serpents, and those with taboos about the killing of snakes believed to be sacred, have a very practical method of ridding themselves of a sacred serpent, should it inconvenience their lifestyle unduly. For instance, if a sacred puffadder has to be removed, then the puffadder-revering shamans contact another group who venerate any specie of snake other than the puffadder, and request that a team from that tribe dispose of the unwanted intruder. And of course, they are always willing to return the favour, as long as they are not asked to harm or inconvenience a puffadder.

Myths and legends from many lands include tales of monster reptiles, dragons, or great serpents. Serpents were regarded as solar, sexual, funerary, and the manifestation of energy at any level. Serpents, or dragons, were revered as the guardians of the threshold, temples, treasures, esoteric knowledge and all lunar deities.[9] But in the Western world the reptiles are usually portrayed as offensive, and depicted as great snakes or fiery dragons that have to be regularly placated with sacrifices of maidens, children, or livestock, to stave off disasters.

Or, as in Christian theology, they are damned as the Devil.

Sacred snakes, and emblems of serpents, were used symbolically to invoke the natural, powerful, pulsating electro-magnetic energies of earth, the *woivre*, and were painted or engraved on many sacred objects and rocks. Early representations of serpent or dragon energies were symbolized by a spiral—the coiled serpent of the primordial waters, *kundalini*. Or by a zigzag line which represented a serpent in motion; the earth currents; the ripple of flowing water; life itself.[10] Such representations are also found engraved on the rocks of South Africa. In addition to an engraving of a coiled serpent, and another of the dualistic, two-headed serpent, I recorded a most unusual engraving of a cobra-like undulating snake carrying a flower on its back (Ill. 93). Although I was unable to find an African explanation for this form of symbolic snake, there is a Babylonian legend about the serpent that stole the herb of eternal life from Gilgamesh.[11] And in ancient Crete where snake symbolism was prominent, Cretan legends tell of Polyides who saw a serpent carrying an herb that could restore life to the dead.[12]

There is no doubt that this very unusual engraving depicts a serpent carrying a flower or herb on its back. And as it, and the other

Ill. 93. A serpent—identified as a cobra—carrying on its back a flower with four petals. Other symbols were also engraved on this rock slab at the Wonderstone Mine (Ottosdal), including two representations of the "ox-hide"—symbolizing wealth and prosperity.

illustrations of serpents mentioned here, are all from the same hillock of steatite (soapstone) now being destroyed by the owners of the Wonderstone mine, it would certainly appear that the engravings at this site are the work of early miners, or traders. For the style of the engravings on this hillock differs from any I have seen elsewhere in South Africa. The engravings are not the only unusual features at this unique site. An ancient, man-made rockslide is grooved into the west face of the outcrop, and runs vertically from near the apex of the hillock, to the base (Ill. 94). And, although it has nothing to do with serpents, but only to emphasize this point more clearly, I bring to your attention the cover picture which is but one of the very strange images inscribed on either the side of this slide at this site—the engraving of a "pecking bird" created to represent—what??

A most unusual painted serpent, with the head of a man, was recorded in the Citrusdal district in the Cape.[13] The San and the Khoi were confirmed smokers of a very hallucinogenic mixture of wild dagga (Leonotis Leonurus, which in itself is only mildly narcotic) and a species of mesembryanthemaceae but, far from being the freakish

Ill. 94. *The ancient rock slide, reaching from the apex of the hillock—an outcrop of very good quality soapstone of the Wonderstone Mine at Ottosdal, now being mined away—to the bottom. On either side of this slide are many very curiously worked engravings, including the "pecking bird" on the cover of this book.*

inspiration of hashish-inspired addicts, this painting may indicate the presence of the cult of *Erichthonious*. Erichthonious, whose name means "from the land of heather", was the legendary son of the Libyan Goddess Neith/Athena. So he was an African creation, for in antiquity the continent of Africa was known as Libya. His cult could have originated in South Africa where erica (heath/heather) grows as plentifully in the Cape mountains as it does around the northern shores of the Mediterranean. This legenbdary son of the Land of Heather was lauded as the "personification", or oracular ghost of sacred kings. Aided by woivre, he was expected to make known the wishes of the Great Goddess, and in Greek art he was traditionally portrayed as the body of a serpent with the head of a man.[14]

Erichthonius is remembered for having taught his people the use of silver, a metal sacred to the Moon Goddess, and once thought of as more precious than gold because it was more difficult to refine.[15] It is certainly strange that this painting of a man-headed serpent should exist in one of the few areas of South Africa where silver has been mined in the past. He is further remembered as the first king to recognize paternity. In other words, his cult was introduced at the very beginning of the patriarchal overthrow of the Moon Goddess/Earth Mother social order.

Prior to this, in the matriarchal society, the line of descent was through the mother's family, and the identity of the father was unimportant. As an example of how the system worked, in ancient

Spain women were limited to one man a month, but were allowed to change lovers at the new moon. In Malaya, a married woman was permitted to have twelve lovers, in addition to her husband—for thirteen is a prime Moon number. Even in modern times the women of the Ait Hadiddou, a Berber tribe in the Atlas mountains of Morocco, have the freedom to divorce their husbands as they wish, and attend the traditional "marriage market" to select a new husband.

In honour of the prophetic powers of the serpentine Erichthonius, the ancient Athenian royal family wore amulets in the form of golden serpents.[16] On ceremonial occasions, Sanusi Credo Mutwa wears a copper replica of a cobra on his right arm. This amulet is but another of the very ancient objects which were entrusted to his safekeeping by his grandfather (Ill. 95).

In antiquity, legendary serpents were invariably associated with sacred kings, oracles, Earth worship, and the regeneration of all life forms—healing, water and rain. Most particularly were they linked to fertility and water—underground water, springs, rivers and lakes—and to the woivre, the electro-magnetic earth energies generated by

Ill. 95. Sanusi Credo Mutwa leading a discussion on one of the engraved soapstone slabs removed from the Wonderstone Mine (Ottosdal), now exhibited in the Klerksdorp museum. On his right arm he wears the sacred serpent bracelet.

the forceful friction of underground water against strategically placed, quartz-charged, standing stones in sanctuary areas.[17]

The Reverend Callaway, who did his best to convert Zulu pagans to Christianity during the early 19th century, bewailed the fact that his converts continued to placate serpents long after their conversion to Christianity.[18] He particularly lamented their practice of dedicating a bull to a snake, then sacrificing the bull to the ancestors, which were envisaged as having taken the form of serpents. One of his parishioners explained the pagan Zulu belief:-

> *They say a man dies, and when he is dead, he turns into a snake; and they gave that snake the name of Itongo, and they worship it by sacrificing cattle, for they say the cattle, too, belong to it.*[19]

Remembering that in conversation with the Reverend Callaway, the Zulus told him it was First Man, Khulu-Khulwané who gave them the ideology of Itongo, and, mindful of the cultural Afro-Cretan-Egyptian-Celtic link, I turned again to Greek mythology.

In the cult of Dionysus, the Bull King was portrayed as a horned serpent, and his devotees ate him sacramentally by dedicating to him a bull, and eating its flesh. In the same way the Zulu solemnly sacrifice and eat a bull dedicated to an ancestor, one of the Itongo, who is envisaged as á snake.[20]

In Celtic, Greek, and Cretan theology the sacrificed Sacred Kings, in their role as the Bull of the People, were believed to return to their clan in the form of oracular serpents. A concept which will be immediately understood by Africans, because when a snake is seen entering an African homestead, it is regarded as an ancestor returning with messages, or demands.[21] In keeping with this ideology, the early Hebrew believed that snakes who entered a house were disembodied spirits who roamed the world at will.[22] Serpent worship was also a way of life for some of the Children of Israel. Nehushtan, the bronze serpent made by Moses, was worshipped in Jerusalem until Hezekiah destroyed it (c. 728–701 BCE).[23]

The oracular qualities attributed to the serpents/ancestors, and Sacred Kings, stem from the belief that, as free-ranging spirits, they are closer to the hierarchy of more senior spirits leading upwards in rank to the Godhead. Therefore, logically, they are well placed to glean information about future events before they happen. It is assumed they will dutifully relay items of relevant news, or warnings of forthcoming disasters, to the group they left behind, and to whom it is believed they will one day return.[24] It was generally believed that the steady stream of advance information, and warnings, was powered by the undulating, underground, serpentine Earth Energies, the woivre. And because information, in the form of divinations and oracular pronouncements, emanating from the guiding spirits of the departed, were thought to travel along the channels of the woivre, serpents were seen as being the embodiment of Earth Energies. Therefore the oracular powers of Celtic, Greek, Libyan and African Sacred Kings and Diviners were accredited to snakes in general, and associated with pythons in particular.[25]

In Zulu lore the python is revered because, like God, it kills without spilling blood, therefore it is known as the Lord of the Shades.[26] Traditionally, because of their accredited oracular and spiritual qualities, only members of royalty were permitted to destroy pythons.[27] The Zulu have a saying, "Earth is the Mother of the Diviner" and so, to receive inspiration from the Earth Mother, diviners go to caves where pythons live.[28] These caves are called "the caves of divination".

The ancient Greek Moon priestesses who served at oracular centres, such as Delphi were known as *pythonesses*. This tradition has not yet died out in Africa, for modern female African diviners are also known as pythonesse. And as far as I have been able to learn, African diviners today use techniques which may have been ancient when the Greek pythonesses plied the same trade at the shrine of the Delphic oracle.[29]

In much the same way as 7th century Christian missions took over pagan standing-stone sites in the British Isles and Ireland, the priests of the Sun-god wrested the duties from the pythonesses. As the Earth Force is androgynous, no sex change was required. After "killing the python", as the legends describe the historical rape of Delphi and other similar sanctuaries, it was the High Priests of the male-dominated Sun religion who gave ear to the dreams of kings, and read the oracles. Serpents became masculine symbols. Ritual sodomy replaced the mating of the high priestess and her son, and the business of religion continued as usual.[30]

In ancient Greece, one of the ways devised to terminate sacred kings was to throw them into the sea from high cliffs, or have them dropped off into lakes, at the end of their annual reign. It was believed that the spirit of the sacrificed king would then be in a position to impregnate women who bathed in the sea, or sacred lakes, in the hopes of bearing a child.[31] The kings of Sparta were usually wrapped in branches of a sacred tree and drowned as a sacrifice to the water monster, *Eurotas*.[32]

Sparta was the centre for the worship of the female water Being, the Pleiad Taygete, a daughter of the African Atlas. One of the sons of Taygete was Lacedaemon—his name means "lake demon"—and Taygete was known as "the Mother of the Snake in the Water".[33] And here we find a most remarkable Afro-Greek link to the Greek Goddess, Taygete, in the African tale about an ancient people, the BaFiki, Ma-Iti or Ma-Hatu. For, according to this African legend, the Ma-Iti once inhabited the Drakensberg area of Southern Africa and they, too, worshipped a great serpent known as Tegati, Mother of the Snake in the Water.

The African legend about the Ma-Iti, or Ma-Hatu, tells of the time when sacred snakes were kept in a secret shrine in the Drakensberg. It is said that those legendary people revered the diamond as the Stone of the Sun—and that the priests of this serpent cult burned diamonds to their Sun-god, *mBali* (and, as previously mentioned, even today the Zulu word for a writer is *umBhali*).

The legend recalls a time when they ceremoniously dedicated diamonds to the sun, wrapped them in the skin of an eland, and burned the offering in a specially constructed furnace. This furnace is said to have been located in the very heart of the Drakensberg Mountains, and that two concentric circles of power ever protect this most ancient shrine. According to Sanusi Mutwa, the secret, sacred sanctuary still exists, and is guarded and maintained by dedicated priests of the cult—the *AbaTegati*—who continue to serve the female serpent deity known as Tegati, the Mother of the Snake in the Water.

The Xhosa also have a sinister folk story about a monster serpent that was believed to inhabit a gorge in the Drakensberg. The Xhosa say this reptile was adorned with an enormous diamond in the forehead, just above the eyes and that, in ages past, youths and maidens were regularly sacrificed to this monster. And the BaSotho still widely believe that malicious snakes of immense proportions, sometimes with horns but more often with a great light shining from their head, inhabit deep pools and rivers in Lesotho.[34]

A connection of some kind with the Egyptians is also indicated in the story of the legendary Ma-Iti. The scribe in the original landing party is described as belonging to a race "totally different" to the "Strange Ones". His skin is described as being considerably darker, and he was clothed in a green and black striped loincloth. On his shaven pate he wore a tight-fitting green leather cap, and he carried a large leather bag containing rolls of writing material—similar to calfskin; small clay jar containing "coloured medicines"; and many pointed reeds and sticks tufted with animal hair. According to the legend, this odd man escaped and founded the Varozwi tribe who are today known among the black tribes of Africa as the only people to practise the mummification of its chiefs, and the only tribe to practise the art of fortune-telling by gazing at the stars. In the story the subjugation of the Ma-Iti ended when the Nguni slaves revolted and not only killed every Ma-Iti man, woman, and child, and their San and Khoi wives and concubines, but razed the cities and settlements to the ground, stone by stone.[35]

Although the tale of the Ma-Iti, BaFiki, or Ma-Hatu is only an old African legend, yet scattered throughout Southern Africa is the physical evidence of thousands of ancient mines, including the evidence of the prehistoric mining of alluvial diamonds. And the details in the story, together with what is known of the trading and sailing activities of the peoples of *Atika*, and the maritime and mining exploits of the ancient Egyptians, could explain certain archaeological enigmas. To mention but a few:-

1. A vast reservoir of non-Bantu language has left no recognised trace.[36]
2. There is an abrupt change in pottery, which cannot be explained by evolution.[37]
3. Conservative theorists have suggested the first metal-using farmers might have been Negro or Sudanese.[38]
4. The indigenous blacks told early explorers from Europe that the ancient mines were "the work of the devil".[39]
5. The discovery of non-Negroid skeletons at the ancient settlement of Mapungubwe, where many beautifully crafted golden objects, and a not inconsiderable quantity of glass beads were found.[40]

Believing, as I do, that a core of truth is to be found at the heart of every legend, when I heard the story about the AbaTegati, I thought it would probably be relevant to my research to take a closer look at known facts about the Drakensberg massif.

One school of thought claims that the Voortrekkers gave the mountains the name of Drakensberg, because the jagged peaks of the virtually inaccessible mountainous terrain resembled the spiny back of a dragon.[41] Another source maintains that the Voortrekkers reached the region years after the massif was so named by a party of European hunters, or travellers, who were exploring the area early in the 19th century. They heard a tale about a dragon which had its lair somewhere in the southern region of the massif, and from the story they named the mountains "Drakensberg"—"Mountain of the Dragon".[42] But it was not the Europeans who were the first to put the dragons of the Drakensberg on the map. The great massif, which is now almost all contained within the borders of the Kingdom of Lesotho, was known to the tribes inhabiting the region as the "Dragon Mountain" long before the first European colonists "discovered" it.

This raised the question in my mind as to whether the indigenous Africans named the mountain simply because of the legendary dragon lair of the AbaTegati. Or, if there was something else about the region, something more tangible, something highly visible and dragon-like, to have inspired the name?

Researching further, I found that paintings of monster serpents are not uncommon in the Lesotho Drakensberg. I plotted the position of all the paintings of animal-headed, horned, or monster serpents recorded by rock art enthusiasts that I could trace. And I was astonished at what came to light as the result of the hours I spent poring over books on rock paintings. This exercise revealed that the perimeter of the diamond-rich Kingdom of Lesotho is virtually encircled by no less than thirteen (a prime moon number!) representations of mythological reptiles, and that a "tail" of five (another Moon number!) monster snakes dips southwards through the mountainous Eastern Cape. Even more remarkable is the fact that these images are not found in easily accessible shelters on the foothills of the massif, but in the most inaccessible places, and only at high altitudes. The majority of the paintings of monster serpents encircling Lesotho are located at altitudes of between 1,372 and 1,829 land metres (4,500–6,000 feet) above sea level, and a few occur between 1,829 and 2,943 land metres (6,000–9,000 feet) above sea level.[43]

Elsewhere in Southern Africa paintings of monster serpents are not distributed evenly throughout the region, as are pictures of people, eland, and other animals, but are found in only three areas other than the Lesotho mountains and the Drakensberg of the Eastern Cape (Map, Ill. 96):-

1. the Matopos hills of Zimbabwe.[44]
2. Birchenough Bridge in Zimbabwe.[45]
3. the Brandberg of Namibia.[46]

In Celtic lore relating to dragons, it is said that they frequently coiled themselves around hills, which were convenient to their lair, to hold in,

Map of Serpents and Monster Reptiles Encircling the Drakensberg

1. Fouriesberg
2. Rouxville
3. Ladybrand
4. Barkly East
5. Wepener
6. Harrismith
7. Cathcart
8. Queenstown
9. Brakfontein Cave
10. Klein Aasvoël's Kop (lower Caledon)
11. Brandberg
12. Matopo Hills
13. Birchenough Bridge
14. Mahahla's Shelter
15. Bamboo mountain
16. Swartberg
17. Tsoelike River
18. Khomo Patsoa
19. Mount Currie
20. Mzimkuulu River

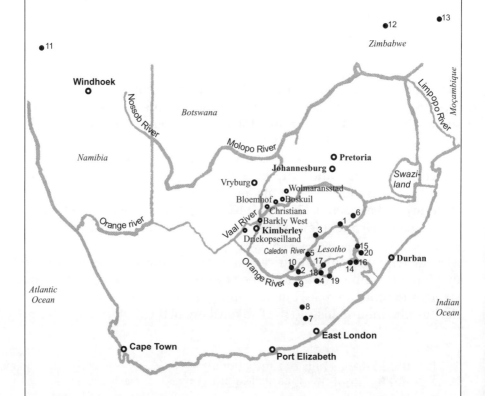

Ill. 96 (Map) Map of the Drakensberg region, showing the locations of the sites depicting monster reptiles, which completely encircle the mountain kingdom of Lesotho.

or contain the Earth Currents, and so prevent the power from escaping.[47]

Regarding the encircling of the Drakensberg by paintings of dragons from an unconventional, Celtic-friendly, angle, it would appear that these depictions of dragons or water monsters were either deliberately executed at specific points with the intention of locking in the Earth Power of this great mountain range, or they were strategically placed as a protective barrier enclosing something treasured or sacred.

The deep interiors of the mountains of Lesotho, which are the heart of the Drakensberg, have never been thoroughly explored by rock painting enthusiasts. There are many places where no white person has ever ventured. Therefore nothing is yet known of the hundreds of paintings, which must exist in unexplored caves and shelters. I have shown that the perimeter of the Drakensberg is encircled by paintings of monster serpents. Future explorations, if permitted by the AbaTegati and the Spirit of the Drakensberg, could well reveal evidence of a second, inner, concentric circle of great mythical snakes, giving truth to the Zulu legend of a shrine dedicated to Tegati in the heart of the Drakensberg, enclosed protectively by two concentric circles.

The apparently ridiculous detail in the story that diamonds were sacrificially burned to a serpent deity, in fact lends credence to the legend of the AbaTegati of the Drakensberg. The custom of offering jewels to the Sun-god was once fairly widespread. The Chinese burned amber to their gods, and the Incas of Peru burned gold and emeralds on their altars, as offerings to the Sun.[48] The Mound Builders of the American Midwest—who also constructed a huge serpent mound—burned pearls in the same way.[49] The theology of these peoples included the concept of Earth Power controlled by underground serpentine energies. And so the fragment of Zulu legend referring to the burning of diamonds by the AbaTegati serving Tegati, Mother of the Snake in the Water, is another pointer to the truths woven into the story, because diamonds are only a very pure form of carbon.

Carbon is an element, not a mineral, and when exposed to great heat a diamond will vaporize. It simply becomes smaller, and smaller, until there is nothing left except the spirit of the stone. A procedure followed by diamond smugglers, who have illegally bought a stone and suspect it is "trap diamond" planted by detectives of the Diamond branch, is to pass the suspect diamond briefly through the flame of a blowtorch. The diamond vaporizes just enough to change its shape, and sometimes also its colour, and makes it unrecognisable for purposes of official police identification. Thus, the smugglers get to keep the stone, and save themselves the inconvenience of a heavy fine, and possible goal sentence.

Therefore there is no reason to doubt the part of the legend that describes how the Ma-Iti burned diamonds to the Sun-god.

Diamonds abound in the mountains of Lesotho, and although on the whole archaeologists maintain they have never found diamonds in association with the San, or any trace of diamonds near rock engraving sites, at least one of their number did discover diamonds at an archaeological site. During a discussion with the late Dr Adrian Boshier, he told me that while excavating caves in Swaziland, he found "piles of pretty coloured stones, including rough diamonds". Unfortunately for science, he never recorded this find, saying no one would have believed him, anyway. Nor would he tell me what he had done with the treasure-trove—a wise decision, in view of the laws governing illicit diamond buying in South Africa! Yet his statement was made in all sincerity.

The ritual burning of a diamond in the skin of an eland is not an unlikely detail either. Eland were revered as Animals of the Sun and the Moon, and sacrificed by the Tswana, at least, during times of drought. So the sacrifice of a diamond within the skin of an eland reads as an offering to both the sun and the moon. But this still leaves open the question why eland were revered, over and above their obvious grace, beauty and fertility. And there is indeed something very important about the eland, which seems to have escaped the attention of rock art researchers, namely the fact that the San particularly valued eland fat.

Now, whenever I learn that something is valued, or sacred, I want to know why it is so. A phone call to a friendly game ranger gave the answer that whereas the fat of all game—antelope, zebra, buffalo etc.—was hard when cold; the fat of the eland remained soft. Another enquiry of a traditional herbalist confirmed what I had guessed, that because eland fat does not harden, it is the perfect base for herbal salves and other remedies.

In other words, the healing quality inherent in eland fat was medicinal, not cosmetic. As such it was an essential link in the cycle of birth, life, death and rebirth, and so the San had a very practical reason to value the eland so highly.

Therefore the ritual burning of the skin of an eland by the AbaTegati was in itself an invocation for health and fertility—which equals prosperity—carried to the Most High by the vaporized Spirit of the diamond.

The term Tegati, or AbaTegati is not only used to describe priests of the legendary Ma-Iti. At an annual general meeting of the Traditional Healers' Association, in Johannesburg, I heard traditional herbalists speak darkly of practitioners of black magic and sorcery as AbaTegati.

And in the Northern Province of South Africa the name Tegati was given to a rogue crocodile. According to the story, an old, and very wily, crocodile plagued a farmer of the Potgietersrust district. It was known to have killed several calves, but when it dragged one of the local children into the river, the farmer hired a hunter to track down the creature, and kill it. The cunning of the crocodile was no match for the patience and experience of the hunter, and eventually it was killed with a shot in the eye as it swam just below the surface of the water. To the amazement of both the farmer and the hunter, instead of expressing joy that the devourer of the child had been destroyed, the farm hands were thrown into a state of utter terror. Loudly lamenting the fact that Tegati had been killed, they packed all their possessions and the entire community moved off the farm. To their way of thinking, because law now forbids the old custom of ritual sacrifice, the ancestors had guided the calves and the child to the crocodile, as sacrifices to Tegati. Therefore, as the deliberate killing of this manifestation of Tegati could, and most probably would, bring down the wrath of all that was terrible on everybody living in the area, they had no alternative but to leave as fast as possible.

The Drakensberg legend of Tegati, Mother of the Snake in the Water, was told to me as an African legend. But in Sanusi Credo Mutwa's book *My People* there is another mention of the BaFiki, Ma-Iti or Ma-Hatu. And it is possible that these legendary people were historically from the land of Atika, and supplied mineral ores to the Greeks during the reign of the Egyptian pharaoh Rameses III.

During the reign of Rameses III Egypt traded with the Greeks for copper, and other ores, from the land of Atika. The goods were transported by sea, in the ships of the Atika and by land, on the "asses" of the people of Atika. In *Peoples of the Sea* Immanuel Velikovsky says the location of Atika is uncertain, but that the known translation of the word used to describe the ore from the mines of Atika is *hmt*. He suggests that *hmt* was a word used to describe hard metals, such as pyrite and chromite, which are plentiful in "Rhodesia"—i.e. Zambia and Zimbabwe.[50] His suggestion makes sense when the facts about the trade between Rameses III and Greece are laid alongside the legend of the Ma-Iti; the expansion of Egyptian maritime achievements during the reign of Rameses III (New

Kingdom XX Dynasty); and the volume of gold and other ores mined in ancient times in Southern Africa.

At the time of Rameses III there was a strong Greek presence in Egypt and, as stated in the paper, *Egyptian Gold Seekers and Exploration in the Pacific*, it was during the reign of Rameses III that the great sea voyages to the East were undertaken. But according to the research of Professor George Carter, it was also during this period that Punt in Africa shifted to Punt in the East Indies. This can be interpreted to mean that the Egyptians had by this time lost their earlier monopoly over Punt in Africa. And that Greeks, or Phoenicians, or Creteans, or the Pereset—or the Atika, who could have been a cross-section of any of them—controlled the mining of ores in Southern Africa. The manpower required by this industry, as stated by Rameses III in the Papyrus Harris, quoted by Immanuel Velikovsky in *Peoples of the Sea*, tallies with the quantities of minerals known to have been mined in Southern Africa in ancient times:-

> *I sent forth my messengers to the country of the Atika. To the great copper mines which are in this place. Their galleys carried them. Others on the land journey were upon their asses. Their mines were found abounding in copper. It was loaded by ten-thousands into their galleys.* [51]

Now cast your mind back to two examples of the Ogam script from Driekops Eiland translated by Professor Barry Fell. The one being a desperate message, "under constant attack we have quit this place to occupy a safe stronghold", and the other inscription beside a zebra, which Fell translated to read, "ambush, hunt and capture of the striped ass". Is it possible that such events could have taken place in this remote part of Southern Africa in prehistoric times? Or that literate people, at some unknown time in the past actually occupied this inhospitable region, and inscribed records of their misfortunes and activities on the rocks?

I have personal experience of this district, and believe me, it is no paradise. From November until March daily temperatures average 38°C, in the shade. The only water for kilometres, is to be had from the seasonal stream flowing through the rocky outcrop. In the scant rainy season, devastating thunderstorms, and occasional flooding, submerge this engraving site entirely, and in the winter temperatures drop well below freezing every night. Therefore one can well ask why people who, one supposes, had the whole of Southern Africa to choose from, would hang on here until forced by violent events to leave? Not only did they leave, but actually took time to inscribe a desperate message on the rocks.

It was Alexander Marshack in *The Roots of Civilisation* who said the human brain has not changed in the last 35,000 years.[52] So we can be fairly certain that love, hate, fear, as well as the seven deadly sins of anger, pride, covetousness, lust, envy, sloth, and gluttony preoccupied these early people, as we today are moved or motivated by our passions. Logically then, when the people occupying this site were forced to flee, they surely did not take time out to painstakingly inscribe a message for some future archaeologist to puzzle over. In such circumstances the scribe would have been ordered to leave a message for other equally literate peoples, possibly traders from afar, with whom they were in regular contact.

The Driekops Eiland site is a massive slab of striated amygdaloidal diabase. The rock is hard—incising the surface takes time, strength, and a writing tool with a point considerably harder than the rock. Perhaps, and because they were in a region rich in alluvial diamonds—Driekops Eiland is only about fifty kilometres from the diamond centre of Kimberley—like the Biblical prophet Jeremiah, they too used a diamond-tipped pen to inscribe their message (Jeremiah 17:1).

Very little archaeological research has been done at this site. Yet taking into account only three facets of the data relating to Driekops Eiland, the message does not stand unsupported. Apart from the deposits of diamonds, and tiger's eye in the area, a very good quality hematite has been found on the hill above the site. In addition to its use as an iron ore, hematite is used as a pigment and as a polishing powder. The name is derived from the Greek word for "blood" and is descriptive of the colour of the powdered mineral. I cannot here digress to elaborate on the importance of hematite in ancient times, sufficient to say that red ochre, revered as the menstrual blood of the Earth Mother, was universally essential for all rituals pertaining to the cycle of birth, life, death, and rebirth.[53] Red ochre was placed reverently in fields at the time of planting; it was essential for burial rites; initiation; protection during a journey; and so much more.[54] And red ochre is iron ore!

Also, at not too great a distance from the hematite deposit are ruined stonewalls, and a "rock gong", or dolman, found by Mrs Miems du Toit.

Then there is the still unresolved mystery of the vanished skeleton. Mentioned by H.C. Woodhouse (Archaeology in Southern Africa), and again by D.N. Lee and H.C. Woodhouse (Art on the Rocks) is the discovery of a skeleton, in 1954, during a visit to Driekops Eiland by members of the Witwatersrand Centre of the South African Archaeological Society.[55]

The body had been buried in a contracted position, and with it was an inverted half ostrich shell, coated with red ochre and containing a film of specularite. Accompanying the skeleton was the skull of a reedbuck, minus its lower jaw. The skeleton was excavated by Dr Revil Mason, Mr B.D. Malan, and Dr Clark Howell of Washington University. According to H.C. Woodhouse, despite a promise by Dr. Mason of a physical report on this very valuable, and telling, discovery, there the matter rested. It would appear that the mysterious skeleton subsequently disappeared.

The second message from Driekops Eiland, translated by Professor Barry Fell, emphasizes the ambush and capture of a zebra, described here as a "striped ass". There is nothing in this translation to suggest people were hunting for food. The zebra were sacred to the Kung San, who tattooed their bodies to represent the adored zebra.[56] A piquant intrusion is that, speaking of the Auen and the Kung (of Namibia) Professor Raymond Dart suggested their "nearest serological relatives" in Africa are the Douiret, a Tunisian Berber tribe, and another Libyan inscription from Ahagger also records the ambush, hunt, and capture of a "striped ass".[57] Now, it was the female shamans of the Berbers who are known to have been rock engravers. Zebras were certainly not in short supply in Africa at any time, so why should anyone bother to go to all the trouble and effort of inscribing details of the hunt and capture of zebra on this particular rocky outcrop, and nowhere else? The only explanation is that zebras were necessary to the existence of the people living there at that time, either as a ritual sacrifice, or to be used as draught animals.

Although the zebra is a wild animal, yet they have been tamed, and even harnessed to draw coaches in recent historical times. The mail coach owner and transport pioneer in South Africa, Roelof Zeederberg, established a mail coach system between Pretoria and Rhodesia during the time of Cecil Rhodes[58] and, because of the tsetse fly problem they tamed and harnessed zebra to draw the coaches. So it is not impossible that the "asses" of Atika were trained zebra, and that the Atika had set up mining stations in Southern Africa, possibly in partnership with the Greeks who then sold to the Egyptians. This suggests that sometime between Queen Hatshepsut and Rameses III—a period of about 400 years—other sea-faring nations wrested the monopoly of the mining and exporting of Southern African ores from the Egyptians. The dates certainly tie up with those given in the paper by Professor George Carter, *Egyptian Gold Seekers and Exploration in the Pacific*, with Punt in Africa becoming Punt in the Far East.

The final question, "Did the people who inscribed the rocks at Driekops Eiland leave any image of themselves on the rocks?" is easily answered in one word—yes! Apart from the quantity and variety of the inscriptions covering this unique site, which to all appearances stresses its potential as a "power point" of Earth Energies, there is one panorama of two humans and a wraith. The man and woman, clothed, are to the left of a serpentine-like wraith leaning through the branches of some tree

Ill. 97. There is an African legend, which says that God created a mountain, and gave it the ability to talk to mankind. Here an expanse of rock, facing the sunrise, is engraved with geometrical signs and, central to this panorama, is a wraith-like figure bending forward and apparently thrusting a checkered rectangle through a tree towards two humans wearing clothing and pointed hats. The "Giving of the Law" perhaps? This grouping of humans together with a spirit form on the opposite side of the "tree" suggests that here was an outlet where Earth Energies could be tapped for divination and oracles—a place where the mountain could talk to those with ears to hear.

"And the Lord God took the man, and put him into the Garden of Eden, to dress it and to keep it."

towards the human figures, and holding out a slab, or slate divided into small blocks. Professor Norman Totten has identified such symbols as representing land division, or territorial apportionments.[59] The group, consisting of the humans and the wraith, is inscribed on the edge of a large slab, facing the rising sun. Below and around them are many symbols, including an apparent representation of a caduceus (Ill. 97).

In addition to many other geometrical symbols, on the flat rock above this grouping is a wheel comprised of three concentric circles divided into two circles of 13 and 28 sections each. Thirteen is the number of lunar months in an annual seasonal cycle, and twenty-eight the number of nights in one lunar cycle.

There is nothing casual about the engravings at this site. They exude energy, a power and knowledge still foreign to modern Westerners. Nor are the engravings at any site in South Africa, or anywhere else in the world, merely mindless doodles. In South Africa they are, as I have stressed throughout this book, the archives, the inscribed pre-history of Southern Africa. A pre-history which must be accepted to include the physical presence of peoples from the northern hemisphere, and serving under many kings and pharaohs, who influenced the physical make-up and theology of the indigenous peoples of Southern Africa. As they themselves were most probably also influenced by their contacts with the indigenous Africans.

The importance of comparisons lies in the fact that, whereas the traditions of the Egyptians, Polynesians, Celts, Hebrews, Cretans, and early Greeks are now only historical memories gleaned from folk tales, and ancient records, among the Zulu and others of Africa, these things continue to play a part in daily life. And so, for a better understanding between all races, far from regarding traditional African customs with disdain, people of the Western world should put prejudice behind them, and look back at their own roots without recoiling in hypocritical horror. For only then will the traditions of African society be regarded with empathy.

Hopefully certain beliefs, such as the sight of a snake entering a homestead, and being accepted as a bringer of tidings from the Ancestors, will remain an integral part of African faith, hope, and trust for generations to come. At least, in my Afro-Celtic soul, I say, "I hope things will remain so."

finis

References

Introduction
1) Marshack, A. *The Roots of Civilization*, McGraw-Hill Book Co., New York 1872 p. 24 – 25, 34
2) Woodhouse, Bert. *The Bushman Art of Southern Africa*, Purnell, Cape Town 1979 p. 20
   Wilman, Maria. *The Rock Engravings of Griqualand & Bechuanaland South Africa*, A.A. Balkema, Cape Town 1968 p. 3
   Bruce H. *The Museum Of South African Rock Art*, Africana Museum, Johannesburg 1976 p. 3
3) Schapera I. *The Khoisan Peoples of South Africa, Bushmen and Hottentot*, Routledge & Kegan Paul Ltd., London 1951 p. 84
4) Inskeep, R.R. *The Peopling of South Africa*, David Philip, Cape Town p. 122
5) Wilman. *The Rock Engravings of Griqualand & Bechuanaland South Africa*, p. 60
   Schapera, I. *The Khoisan Peoples of Southern Africa*, p. 53
6) Ibid. p. 59
7) Ibid. pp. 53 – 59
8) Ibid. p. 87
9) Ibid. p. 44
10) Ibid. p. 27
    Wilman, *The Rock Engravings of Griqualand & Bechuanaland South Africa*, p. 61
11) Gayre of Gayre R. *The Origin of the Zimbabwean Civilization*, Galaxie Press, Salisbury 1972 p.105
    Woodhouse H.C. *Archaeology in Southern Africa*, Purnell, Cape Town 1971 pp. 125 – 126
12) Cameron T. & Spies S.B. *An Illustrated History of South Africa*, Southern Book Publishers, Johannesburg 1988 p. 32
    Rosenthal E. *Encyclopaedia of Southern Africa*, Frederick Warne & Co. Ltd., London 1965 p. 64
13) Mitchison, Naomi. *The Africans*, Granada Publishing Ltd., London 1970 pp. 123, 133
14) Casey, Albert & Downey – Prince, Eleanor. *Odyssey of the Irish Documented by Blood Group and Craniometric Analysis*, The Epigraphic Society Occasional Papers, Vol. 6 Part 2, 1979 pp. 138 – 156

15) Graves R. *The White Goddess,* Faber & Faber Ltd., London 1977 pp. 51, 55, 201, 293
16) Bryant A.T. *Zulu Medicine And Medicine-Men,* C. Struik, Cape Town 1970 pp. 26, 61
17) Tyrrell, Barbara. *Tribal Peoples Of Southern Africa,* T.V. Bulpin, Cape Town 1976 p. 6
    Corliss, William R. *Ancient Man: A Handbook of Puzzling artefacts,* The Sourcebook Project. USA 1978 p. 710
18) Gayre of Gayre R. *The Origin Of The Zimbabwean Civilization* p. 20
    Velikovsky I. *Ages in Chaos* Abacus, London 1977 p. 101
    Carter, George. *Egyptian Gold Seekers and Exploration in the Pacific,* The Epigraphic Society Occasional Publications, Vol. 2. No. 27, February 1975
19) Herm, Gerhard. *The Phoenicians,* Victor Gollancz Ltd., London 1975 p. 142
20) Ibid. p. 142
21) Ibid. p. 142
    Baines J. & Málek J. *Atlas of Ancient Egypt,* Phaidon Press Ltd., 1958 pp. 51, 177, 148
22) Gayre of Gayre R. *The Origin of the Zimbabwean Civilization,* pp. 28, 95 – 96
23) Boland C.M. *They All Discovered America,* Pocket Books, New York 1963 p. 164
24) Herm, Gerhard. *The Phoenicians,* p. 209
25) Stichin, Zecharia. *The 12th Planet,* Stein & Day, New York 1978 pp. 289 ff
    Gayre & Gayre R. *The Origin of the Zimbabwean Civilization,* pp. 27, 194
26) Herm, Gerhard. *The Phoenicians,* p. 206
    Boland C.M. *They All Discovered America,* p. 26
27) Covey, Cyclone. *Calalus,* Vantage Press, New York 1975 p. 23
28) Hapgood, Charles. *Maps of the Ancient Sea Kings,* E.P. Dutton, New York 1979 p. 104
29) Colvin, Ian D. *The Cape Of Adventure,* T.C.& E.C. Jack, Edinburgh 1912 pp. 26 ff
    Chilvers, Hedley A. *The Seven Wonders Of South Africa,* Published by Authority of the Administration of the South African Railways and Harbours, Johannesburg 1929 pp. 3 – 7, 14 – 15
    Bulpin T.V. *To The Banks of the Zambezi,* Books of Africa, 1968 pp. 72 – 75
30) Ibid. pp. 74 – 75
    Robison, Gordon. *Arab Gulf States,* Lonely Planet Publications,

Australia 1993 pp. 277, 329
31) Hapgood, Charles. *Maps Of The Ancient Sea Kings*, p. 190
32) Ibid. p. 191
33) Harden, Donald. *The Phoenicians*, Penguin Books UK, 1971 p. 156
34) Bord, Janet & Colin. *The Secret Country*, Granada Publishing Ltd, UK, 1979. p. 59
35) Hardingham, Evan. *Circles And Standing Stones*, Abacus, London 1978 p. 27
Oppenheim A. Leo. *Ancient Mesopotamia*, University of Chicago Press 1977 pp. 146 – 147

Chapter 1 Through the mists of time

1) Davidson Basil. *Black Mother*, Longman Group Ltd., London 1970 pp. 51 – 52
2) Ibid. p. 53
3) Ibid. pp. 59, 65 – 66
4) Ibid. pp. 60 – 71, 87
5) Murphy, Jefferson. *The Bantu Civilization Of Southern Africa*, Thomas Y. Crowell Co., New York 1974 p. 182
6) Colvin, Ian D. *The Cape Of Adventure*, p. 290
7) Krüger, Bernhard. *The Pear Tree Blossoms*, Moravian Church, Genadendal 1966 pp. 31 – 39
8) Cameron T & Spies S.B. *An Illustrated History of South Africa*, pp. 71 – 72, 105, 107
9) Ibid. p. 71
Shaw E.M. *Man in South Africa the Hottentots*, The South African Museum, Cape Town 1972
Smith A.D. & Pheiffer R.H. *The Khoikhoi at the Cape Of Good Hope*, South African Library, Cape Town 1993 p. 17
10) Willcox A.R. *Rock Paintings Of The Drakensberg*, p. 17
Woodhouse B. *The Bushman Art of Southern Africa*, pp. 28, 47
11) Inskeep R.R. *The Peopling of South Africa*, pp. 87 – 88
12) Johnston, Sir Harry. *Pioneers in South Africa*, Blackie & Son Ltd., London pp. 130 – 132, 156
University of Bophuthatswana, Department of History. *History Course For Bophuthatswana Tour Guides*, August 1990 p. 3
De Bruyn J.T. & Cuthbertson G.C. *History* (Introduction to history of South Africa until 1806 in pre-colonial and colonial perspective), UNISA, Pretoria 1989 pp. 370 – 371
13) Laubscher B.J. *The Pagan Soul*, Howard Timmins, Cape Town 1975 p. 112

Oesterley W.O.E. & Robinson T.H. *Hebrew Religion,* Macmillan, New York 1937 p. 85
14) Woodhouse B. *The Bushman Art of Southern Africa,* p. 20
Wilman M. *The Rock Engravings Of Griqualand and Bechuanaland South Africa,* p. 5
15) Cooke C.K. *Rock Art of Southern Africa,* Books of Africa (Pty) Ltd., Cape Town 1969 p. 3
16) Brentjes, Burchard. *African Rock Art,* J.M. Dent & Sons Ltd., London 1969 pp. 7 – 8
17) Cooke C.K. *Rock Art of Southern Africa,* p. 32
The South African Archaeological Bulletin, Claremont, Cape Town June 1979 Vol. XXXIV No. 129
18) Mbiti, John S. *Introduction to African Religion,* Heinemann, London 1977 p. 33
Graves R. *Greek Myths* 1 38. D
19) Parrinder E.G. *African Traditional Religion,* Sheldon Press, London 1976 pp. 25
Mbiti, John. *South African Religions and Philosophy,* Heinemann. London 1976 pp. 69 – 71
20) Michell, John. *The Earth Spirit,* p. 83
Oesterley W.O.E. & Robinson T.H. *Hebrew Religion,* pp. 10 – 11, 49, 174 – 175
21) Gehman H. & Wright R. *The New Westminster Dictionary of the Bible,* The Westminster Press, Philadelphia, USA p. 82 Baal
Velikovsky I. *Peoples of the Sea,* p. 70
22) Mbiti, John *African Religions and Philosophy,* p. 55
23) Brenthes B. *African Rock Art,* p. 88
24) Mbiti, John. *Introduction to African Religion,* p. 33
Michell, John. *The Earth Spirit,* p. 4
25) Berglund A. *Zulu Thought Patterns and Symbolism,* David Phillips (Pty) Ltd, Cape Town pp. 222 – 223
26) Miller, Penny. *Myths and Legends of Southern Africa,* T.V. Bulpin (Pty) Ltd., Cape Town 1979 p. 248
Woodhouse H.C. *Archaeology in Southern Africa,* p. 128
27) Michell J. *The Earth Spirit,* p. 7
Kunz G.F. *The Curious Lore of Precious Stones,* Dover Publicatons, New York 1971 p. 76
28) Rudner J. & I. *The Hunter and His Art,* p. 32
29) Tyrrell B. & Jurgens P. *African Heritage,* Macmillan South Africa (Pty) Ltd., 1983 p. 225
Willett F. *African Art,* Thames & Hudson, London, 1977 p. 56

30) Marshack A. *The Roots of Civilization*, pp. 22, 26
31) Berglund A. *Zulu Thought Patterns and Symbolism*, p. 339
32) Hadingham E. *Circles and Standing Stones*, p. 156
    Gayre of Gayre R. *The Origin of the Zimbabwean Civilization*, p. 142
33) Schapera I. *The Khoisan Peoples of Southern Africa*, P. 27
    Clarke J. *The Bushman*, Museum of Man and Science, Johannesburg 1975 p. 1
34) Fell, Barry. *Ogam Inscriptions From North And South Africa*, The Epigraphic Society Occasional Papers, Vol. 6. No. 116, January 1979
35) Van der Post, Laurens. *The Lost World of the Kalahari*, Penguin Books, U.K. 1958 p. 20
36) Bruton, Eric. *Diamonds*, NAG Press Ltd., London 1981 pp. 36 – 39
37) Ibid. p. 31
38) Chilvers H. *The Seven Wonders of South Africa*, p. 110
    Cameron T & Spies S. *An Illustrated History of South Africa*, pp. 81 – 85, 129 – 130
39) Ibid. pp. 134, 146, 152
    Rosenthal E. *Encyclopaedia of Southern Africa*, p. 255 "Inboeking" University of Bophuthatswana, Department of History. *History Course For Bophuthatswana Tour Guides*, 1990 p. 6
40) Noble, John. *The Official Handbook History Productions and Resources of the Cape of Good Hope*, Cape Town 1886 pp. 179 – 180
41) Chilvers H. *The Seven Wonders of South Africa*, p. 176
    Kunz F. *The Curious Lore of Precious Stones*, p. 74
    Bruton E. *Diamonds*, p. 36
    Rosenthal E. *Shovel And Sieve*, Howard Timmins, Cape Town p. 24

Chapter 2   Ancient Diamond Miners?
1) Noble, John. *The Official Handbook, History Productions and Resources of the Cape of Good Hope*, 1886 p. 178
2) Wagner P.A. *The Diamond Fields of Southern Africa*, p. 1 ff
    Bruton E. *Diamonds*, pp. 352 – 365
3) Ibid. p. 77
4) Ibid. pp. 77, 357
5) Wagner P.A. *The Diamond Fields of Southern Africa*, p. 90
6) Schapera I. *The Khoisan Peoples of South Africa*, p. 27
7) Gayre of Gayre R. *The Origin of the Zimbabwean Civilization*, pp. 139 – 140
    Mongait A.L. *Archaeology in the USSR*, Penguin Books, U.K. 1961 p. 97
    Duerden D. *African Art An Introduction*, Hamlyn, London 1974 pp. 71, 74

8) Michell, John. *The Earth Spirit*, p. 7
9) Tyrrell B. *African Heritage*, p. 226
10) Woodhouse H.C. *Archaeology In Southern Africa*, p. 123
11) Graves R. *Greek Myths* 1 30 [1]
    Frazer, Sir James. *The Golden Bough*, p. 384
    Oesterley W.O.E. & Robinson T.H. *Hebrew Religion*, p. 43
12) Graves R. *The White Goddess*, p. 161
    Leigh R. & Baigent M. *Black Madonnas Guardians of the Living Earth - The Unexplained*, Vol. 1, Issue 8, London p. 156
    Graves R. *Greek Myths* 1 83 [1]
13) Ibid. 24[15]
    Ibid. 83[1]
14) Ibid. 96 [2]
    Graves R. *The White Goddess*, pp. 67, 384
15) Powell C. *The Meaning of Flowers*, Jupiter Books Ltd., London 1977 p. 118
16) Ibid. 118
17) Aldred, Cyril. *Jewels of the Pharaohs*, Ballantine Books, New York p. 18
    Graves R. *Greek Myths* 1 70 [8]
18) Oesterley W. & Robinson T. *Hebrew Religion*, pp. 174 – 175, 162
19) Michell, John. *The Earth Spirit*, p. 5
    Oesterley W.O.E. & Robinson T.H. *Hebrew Religion*, pp. 198 – 200
20) Frazer, Sir James. *The Golden Bough*, p. 157
    Green, Lawrence. *There's A Secret Hid Away*, Howard Timmins, Cape Town 1956 p. 48
21) Wilman M. *The Rock Engravings Of Griqualand and Bechuanaland South Africa*, pp. 27 – 41
22) Ibid. p. 52
23) Sullivan, Brenda. *Ancient Diamond Miners In South Africa*, The Epigraphic Society, Occasional Papers, Vol. 7, No. 154, April 1979
24) Bruton E. *Diamonds*, pp. 16, 23, 364
25) Ibid. pp. 9 – 10
26) Holbeche, Soozi. *The Power of Gems and Crystals*, Judy Piatkus Ltd., London 1989 p. 36
    Bruton E. *Diamonds*, pp. 9 – 10
27) Kunz G.F. *The Curious Lore of Precious Stones*, pp. 154, 156
28) Bruton E. *Diamonds*, p. 10
    Holbreche, Soozi. *The Power of Gems And Crystals*, p. 36
29) Bruton E. *Diamonds*, p. 3
    Mongait A.L. *Archaeology in the USSR*, Pelican Books, UK 1961 p. 258

References

30) Ivimy, John. *The Sphinx and the Megaliths*, Abacus, London 1974 p. 84
Corliss W. *Ancient Man A Handbook of Puzzling artefacts*, p. 11
Holbreche, Soozi. *The Power of Gems and Crystals*, p. 49
Hancock, Graham. *Fingerprints of the Gods*, Heinemann, London 1995 pp. 330 – 333

Chapter 3   Old Gold
1) Chilvers H. *The Seven Wonders of Southern Africa*, pp. 26 – 29
2) Graves R. *Greek Myths* 1 78 [1]
Velikovsky I. *Ages In Chaos*, Abacus Sphere Books, London 1977 p. 126
3) Ibid. p. 126
4) Ibid. p. 128
Málek J. & Baines J. *Atlas of Ancient Egypt*, p. 43
5) Aldred, Cyril. *Jewels of the Pharaohs*, p. 15 – 16
Velikovsky I. *Ages in Chaos*, p. 119
6) Mitchison N. *The Africans*, Granada Publishing Ltd., London 1971 p. 63
7) Velikovsky I. *Ages In Chaos*, p. 101
8) Gayre of Gayre R. *The Origin of the Zimbabwean Civilization*, p. 105
9) Nabarro J. *SA Archaeological Bulletin June 1973*, Letter to the Editor, p. 61
10) Rosenthal E. *Shovel and Sieve*, pp. 138 – 141
11) Rudner J. *The Use of Stone Artefacts and Pottery Among the Khoisan Peoples in Historic and Prehistoric Times*, The SA Archaeological Bulletin, Vol. XXXIV No. 129, p. 15
Hromnik C. *Indo-Africa*, p. 115
Gayre of Gayre R. *The Origin of the Zimbabwean Civilization*, p. 111
12) Location of wild camels in Southern Angola from private notes by Harry Sullivan: Cahinde (near the Coroca River; Va. Arriaga; north-west of Impulo)
13) Málek J. & Baines J. *Atlas Of Ancient Egypt*, p. 51
14) Ibid Map pp. 48 – 49
15) Velikovsky I. *Peoples of the Sea*, pp. 4, 6, 8 – 9, 29 – 34
16) Waters, Frenk. *Book of the Hopi*, Ballantine Books, New York 1974 pp. 60, 62, 129
Dewdney S. & Kidd K. *Indian Rock Paintings Of The Great Lakes*, University of Toronto Press, Toronto 1967 pp. 70, 115, 161
Fell Barry. *The Polynesian Discovery Of America 231 BC*, The Epigraphic Society, Occasional Publications, Vol. 1 No. 21, Dec. 1974 p. 6
Robinson A. *The Story of Writing*, Thames & Hudson, London 1995 p. 184

Tyrrell B. *Tribal Peoples of Southern Africa*, p. 86
Diringer. *The Alphabet Vol. 2*, Funk, New York 1964 p. 174
17) Gayre of Gayre R. *The Origin of the Zimbabwean Civilization*, p. 173
Catalogue for Cairo Museum Exhibition, published in 1976 by the Metropolitan Museum of Art, pp. 104 – 105
18) Ibid. pp. 104 – 105
19) Graves R. *Greek Myths* 1 90^3
Hancock, Graham. *The Mars Mystery*, Michael Joseph, London 1998 p. 124
20) Ibid. pp. 124 – 125
21) Graves R. *Greek Myths* 1 33^7
22) Bailey, Jim. *Sailing To Paradise*, Simon & Schuster, New York 1994 p. 162
23) Graves R. *The White Goddess*, p. 324
Frazer, Sir James. *The Golden Bough*, pp. 331, 336
Graves R. *Greek Myths* 1 23^1, 96^1
24) Graves R. *Greek Myths* 2 148^{14}
25) Lane E.W. *The Manners and Customs of the Modern Egyptians*, J.M. Dent & Co., New York pp. 86, 211
26) *History Course for Bophuthatswana Tour Guides*, University of Bophuthatswana Department of History 1990 p. 2
27) Tyrrell B. *Tribal Peoples of Southern Africa*, Introduction
28) Parrinder G. *Africa's Three Religions*, Sheldon Press, London 1969 pp. 52 – 53
Parrinder E. *African Traditional Religion*, Sheldon Press, London 1962 p. 69
29) Mitchison, Naomi. *The Africans*, pp. 23 – 24
Egypt Tour Guide, Lehnert & Landrock, Cairo 1976 p. 31
30) Seligman C.G. *Races Of Africa*, Oxford University Press, Oxford 1978 p. 30
31) Mitchison, Naomi. *The Africans*, pp. 23 – 24
32) Ibid. p. 24
33) Tyrrell B. & Jurgens P. *African Heritage*, p. 133
Egypt Tour Guide, Lehnert & Lasndrock, Cairo1976
34) Seligman C.G. *Races Of Africa*, p. 70
35) Pfeiffer, Charles. *Ras Shamra and the Bible*, Baker Book House, Michigan, USA pp. 46 – 47, 52
36) Kunz G.F. *The Curious Lore of Precious Stones*, p. 225 ff
Steiger, Brad. *Worlds Before Our Own*, Allen, London, 1980 p. 73, Chapter 5 ff.
Aldred, Cyril. *Jewels of the Pharaohs*, pp. 20 – 21

References

37) Zaehner R.C. *Living Faiths*, Hawthorne Books, New York 1959 p. 71
    Graves, Tom. *Needles Of Stone*, p. 153
38) Graves R. *The White Goddess*, pp. 170, 220, 229 – 230, 303, 379
    Graves R. *Greek Myths* 1 96 [24]
39) Ibid. 23 [1]
    Graves R. *The White Goddess*, p. 379
    Aldred, Cyril. *Jewels Of The Pharaohs*, pp. 19 – 20
40) Küsel, Udo. *"Primitive" Iron Smelting in the Transvaal*, National History Museum, Pretoria 1974 pp. 5, 13
41) Ibid. pp. 5, 13
42) Schwantes, Siegfried. *A Short History of the Ancient Near East*, Baker Book House Michigan 1981 pp. 47, 161
    Peiffer C. *Ras Shamra and the Bible*, pp. 46 – 47, 52
43) Mitchison N. *The Africans*, p.24
44) Seligman C.G. *Races Of Africa*, p. 26
45) Ki-Zerbo. *General History of Africa 1 – Methodology and African Prehistory*, David Philip Publishers, Cape Town p. 109
46) Wagner P.A. *The Diamond Fields of Southern Africa*, p. 289
47) Ibid. pp. 282, 283
48) Bailey, Jim. *Sailing To Paradise*, p. 172
    Bailey, Jim. *The God-Kings and the Titans*, p. 183
49) Ibid. p. 193
    Inskeep R.R. *The Peopling of Southern Africa*
50) Gayre of Gayre R. *The Origin of the Zimbabwean Civilization*, p. 51
51) Ibid. pp. 50 – 51, p. 177ff,
    Mitchison N. *The Africans* p. 90
    Bailey, James. *The God-Kings and The Titans*, p. 194
52) Hromnik, Cyril. *Indo-Africa*, Juta & Co., Cape Town 1981 p. 116
53) Gayre of Gayre R. *The Origin Of The Zimbabwean Civilization*, p. 206
54) Carter George F. *Egyptian Gold Seekers And Exploration In The Pacific*, Epigraphic Society Occasional Publications, Vol. 2 No. 27, February 1975
55) Seligman C.G. *Races of Africa*, pp. 69, 70
56) Bailey, James. *The God-Kings and The Titans*, p. 184
57) McGowan, Charlotte. *Female Fertility Themes In Rock Art*, Journal of New World Archaeology, May 1976 pp 15 – 27
    Friede P. *The Classical Engravings of South Africa*. Rock Art Studies in South Africa, SA Archaeological Society, Witwatersrand Centre, Occasional Paper, 1975 p. 64
    Bruce, Hilary. *The Museum of SA Rock Art, A Descriptive Guide*, Johannesburg Africana Museum, 1976 p. 9

Oesterley W.O.E. & Robinson T. *Hebrew Religion*, p. 73
58) Hadingham, Evan. *Circles and Standing Stones*, Abacus, U.K. 1978 p. 156
59) Cooke C.K. *Rock Art Of Southern Africa*, pp. 10 – 11
Brenthes, Burchard. *African Rock Art*, pp. 24 – 25, Map p. 3, p. 38, Ill. 18
Bruton E. *Diamonds*, pp. 157 – 158
60) Wagner P.A. *The Diamond Fields of Southern Africa*, pp. 100, 103, 288 – 289
Cooke C.K. *Rock Art of Southern Africa*, p. 17
Wilman, Maria. *The Rock Engravings of Griqualand and Bechuanaland South Africa*, pp. 16 – 17
Rudner J. & I. *The Hunter and His Art*, pp. 230, 232
61) Wagner P.A. *The Diamond Fields of Southern Africa*, p. 3 Fig. 2
Gayre of Gayre R. *The Origin of the Zimbabwean Civilization*, pp. 156 – 157
Cooke C.K. *Rock Art of Southern Africa*, pp.43 – 45
62) Rudner J. *Rock Art In South West Africa And The Neighbouring Areas Of Angola, Western Botswana And The North West Cape*, Rock Art Studies in South Africa, SA Archaeological Society, Witwatersrand Centre, Occasional Paper, 1975 p. 40 ff
Rudner J. & I *The Hunter and His Art*, pp. 10 – 16
Wagner P.A. *The Diamond Fields of Southern Africa*, p. 2
63) Ibid. p. 2
Fock G. *An Analysis of the Petroglyphs At Bushman's Fountain and Comments on some other sites in the Cape Province*, Rock Art Studies in South Africa, SA Archaeological Society, Occasional Paper, 1975 pp. 86 – 87
64) Walker N.J. *Later Stone Age Research In The Matopos*, National Museums and Monuments of Zimbabwe, Bulawayo, South African Archaeological Bulletin Vol. XXXV, June 1980, No.131 p. 22
65) Hromnik, Cyril. *Indo-Africa* p. 104

Chapter 4   Diamonds, Sacred to the Moon Goddess
1) Kunz G. *The Curious Lore of Precious Stones*, pp. 281 – 282
2) Ibid. pp. 28ff, 276 – 281
3) Ibid. pp. 121 – 122
4) Hamilton W.R., Woolley A.R., Bishop A.C. *The Hamlyn Guide To Minerals, Rocks And Fossils*, Hamlyn Publishing Group Ltd., London 1979 p. 10
Hancock, Graham. *Fingerprints of the Gods*, pp. 330 – 334

References

           Hutchinson R.W. *Prehistoric Crete*, Penguin Books UK, 1962 p. 135
5)   Ibid. p. 135
           Kunz G. *The Curious Lore of Precious Stones*, pp. 278 – 279
6)   Ibid. p. 280 ff
           Gehman H.S. & Wright R. *The New Westminster Dictionary of the Bible*, p. 392
7)   Holbreche, Soozi. *The Power of Gems and Crystals*
           Bruton E. *Diamonds*, pp. 3 – 4, 6
8)   Ibid. Appendix 1, pp. 145 – 146
           Wagner P.A. *The Diamond Fields of Southern Africa*, pp. 145 – 146
9)   Noble, John. *Official Handbook History, Productions, and Resources of the Cape of Good Hope*, 1886 p. 179
10) Marshack, Alexander. *The Roots of Civilization*, pp. 22, 26
11) Wagner P.A. *The Diamond Fields of Southern Africa*, pp. 147 – 148
           Noble, John. *Official Handbook History, Productions, and Resources of the Cape of Good Hope*, 1886
           Bruton, Eric. *Diamonds*, pp. 3, 6, 451 – 452
12) Bailey, James. *The God Kings and The Titans*, pp. 150, 214 – 217
13) Oesterley W.O. & Robinson T. *Hebrew Religion*, pp. 151 – 156
           Bright, John. *A History of Israel*, The Westminster Press, UK, 1980 p. 127
14) Kunz G.F. *The Curious Lore of Precious Stones*, pp. 289 ff.
           Gehman H.S. & Wright R. *The New Westminster Dictionary of the Bible*, p. 392
15) Ibid. p. 272
16) Graves R. *The White Goddess*, p. 64
           Ivimy, John. *The Sphinx and the Megaliths*, pp. 36 – 39
           Callaway H. *The Religious System of the Amazulu*, p. 99
17) Kunz G.F. *The Curious Lore of Precious Stones*, p. 244
18) English/Zulu Dictionary – diamond
19) Kunz G.F. *The Curious Lore of Precious Stones*, p. 321
           Gehman H.S. & Wright R *The New Westminster Dictionary of the Bible*, pp. 93, 633
20) Kunz G.F. *The Curious Lore of Precious Stones*, pp. 70 – 71
21) Gehman H.S. & Wright R. *The New Westminster Dictionary*, p. 1013
22) Gayre of Gayre R. *The Origin of the Zimbabwean Civilization*, pp. 95 – 96, 128
23) Velikovsky I. *Ages in Chaos*, p. 118
24) Fell, Barry. *America BC*, p. 111
25) Pfeiffer C. *Ras Shamra and the Bible*, p. 52
           Oesterley W.O. & Robinson T. *Hebrew Religion*, pp. 148, 182

26) Fell, Barry. *America BC Ancient Settlers in the New World*, p. 94
    Hutchinson R.W. *Prehistoric Crete*, pp. 246 – 247
    Graves R. *Greek Myths* 1 27[1]
27) Graves R. *The White Goddess*, p. 162
    Bailey, James. *The God-Kings and The Titans*, p. 125
28) Graves R. *Greek Myths* 1 98[4]
    Graves R. *Greek Myths* 2 129[1 7 2]
    Ibid. 142[3]
    Brentjes B. *African Rock Art*, p. 59
29) Wolff, Roby. *Animals of Africa*, Litor Publishers Ltd., UK, p. 194
30) Clark R.T. *Myth And Symbol of Ancient Egypt*, pp. 115, 194
    Schapera I. *The Khoisan Peoples of South Africa*, p. 382
    Tyrrell B. *Tribal Peoples of Southern Africa Introduction – South West Africa, Namas*
31) Berglund A-I. *Zulu Thought Patterns and Symbolism*, Chapter 10, p. 363 ff
32) Ibid. pp. 364 ff
33) Ibid. pp. 72 – 73.
    Graves R. *Greek Myths* 1 27[12]
    Ibid. 98[7]
    Ibid. 56[1]
    Berglund A-I, *Zulu Thought Patterns and Symbolism*, pp. 72 – 73
    Frazer, Sir James. *The Golden Bough*, pp. 440 – 441
    Parrinder G. *Sex in the World's Religions*, p. 77
34) Miller P. *Myths and Legends of Southern Africa*, p. 55

Chapter 5   Tsui//Goab and Heitsi Eibib
1) Parrinder G. *Africa's Three Religions*, p. 51
   Parrinder G. *African Mythology*, Paul Hamlyn, London, 1975 p. 75
   Schapera I. *The Khoisan Peoples Of South Africa*, pp. 376 – 379, 380 – 382
2) Ibid. pp. 380 – 382
3) Ibid. p. 381
4) Ibid. p. 381
5) Schwantes S. *The Ancient Near East*, Baker Book House, USA, 1981 p. 48
   Oppenheim A.L. *Ancient Mesopotamia*, p. 197
6) Rundle, Clark R.T. *Myth and Symbol of Ancient Egypt*, p. 89
   Schapera I. *The Khoisan Peoples of South Africa*, p. 377
7) Ibid. p. 41
8) Callaway H. *The Religious System of the Amazulu*, pp. 105ff, 110
   Miller P. *Myths and Legends of Southern Africa*, p. 39

References

9) Schapera I. *The Khoisan Peoples of South Africa*, p. 387
10) Miller P. *Myths and Legends of Southern Africa*, p. 39
11) Schapera I. *The Khoisan Peoples of South Africa*, pp. 383 – 384
12) Ibid. p. 384
13) Ibid. p. 384
    Savill S. *Pears Encyclopaedia of Myths and Legends, Northern Europe and Central Africa*, Pelham Books, 1977 p. 180
14) Schapera I. *The Khoisan Peoples of South Africa*, pp. 373 – 374
15) Ibid. p. 218
    Holy Bible: 1 Kings 9:25
    Lehnert & Landrock. *Egypt*, Guide-Poche Univers, 1976 p. 56
    Oesterley W.O. & Robinson T. *Hebrew Religion*, pp.165, 180
16) Graves R. *Greek Myths* 2 137 [2]
    Berglund A-I, *Zulu Thought Patterns and Symbolism*, p. 131
    Frazer, Sir James. *The Golden Bough*, p. 789
17) Ibid. pp. 331 – 332, 335 – 336
    Graves R. *The White Goddess*, pp. 303, 331
    Mbiti, John. *Introduction to African Religion*, pp. 162 – 163
    Mbiti, John. *African Religion and Philosophy*, pp. 182 – 187
    Seligman C.G. *Races of Africa*, p. 53
    Michell, John. *The Earth Spirit*, p. 17
18) McGowan C. *Female Fertility Themes in Rock Art*, pp. 15, 17, 19
19) Frazer, Sir James. *The Golden Bough*, p. 38
    Wilcock, John. *A Guide to Occult Britain*, p. 284
    Bord, Janet & Colin. *The Secret Country*, Granada Publishing, London, 1976 p. 62
20) Ibid. p. 90
    Rudner J. *Rock Art in South West Africa and the Neighbouring Areas of Angola, Western Botswana and the North West Cape*, SA Archaeological Society, Occasional Paper, 1975 p. 40
    Hitching F. *Earth Magic*, Pan Books, London 1977 p. 3
21) Graves R. *Greek Myths* 2 133 [8]
22) Williams F-N. *Precolonial Communities of Southwestern Africa*, National Archives of Namibia, Windhoek 1991 pp. 98ff
    Oliver R. *The African Experience*, p. 147
    Frazer, Sir James. *The Golden Bough*, pp. 194, 202
    Berglund A-I, *Zulu Thought Patterns and Symbolism*, p. 42
23) Ibid. p. 53
24) Callaway H. *The Religious System of the Amazulu*, pp. 65, 105, 107, 110, 111s
25) Cooper J.C. *An Illustrated Encyclopaedia of Traditional Symbols*, p. 43

Graves R. *Greek Myths* 1 67 ⁶
26) Graves R. *The White Goddess* p. 103
Graves R. *Greek Myths* 1 p. 17
Bovet, Richard. *Pandaemonium*, E.P. Publishing Ltd., UK, 1975 p. 22
Berglund A-I. *Zulu Thought-Patterns and Symbolism*, pp. 183 – 184 & Note 74
27) Mbiti J. *Concepts of God in Africa*, p. 266
28) Michell, John. *The Earth Spirit*, p. 74
Burland C.A. *Myths of Life and Death*, Macmillan, London 1974 p. 12
Bailey, James. *The God-Kings and the Titans*, p. 110
29) Parrinder E.G. *African Traditional Religion*, p. 90
30) Oesterley W.O. & Robinson T. *Hebrew Religion*, p. 59
Parrinder G. *Sex In The World's Religions*, p. 18
31) Tyrrell, Barbara. *Tribal Peoples of Southern Africa*, pp. 61, 122, 124, 148
32) Graves R. *Greek Myths* 1 52 ⁴ ⁵ ⁷, 53 ¹
33) Parrinder E.D. *African Traditional Religion*, p. 52
34) Graves R. *The Greek Myths* 1 52 1 – 4
Wilcock, John. *A Guide to Occult Britain*, p. 281
Dexter, Warren. *Ogam Consaine and Tifinag Alphabets, Ancient Uses*, Academy Books, Vermont, USA 1984
Graves R. *The White Goddess*, pp 114ff
35) Ibid. p. 177
36) Ibid. pp. 114, 199, 281
37) Fell, Barry. *An Ancient Arabic Guide to Ogam on a Sacred Tablet from Zambia Preprint*, Epigraphic Society, Occasional Publications, Vol. 9 No. 209, Dec. 1979
38) Kachur, Victor. *Decipherment of Rune-Like Alekanovo Inscription from Eastern Europe*, The Epigraphic Society, Occasional Publications, Vol. 8 No. 196, Nov. 1979 p.150
39) Callaway H. *The Religious System of the Amazulu*, p. 99
40) Mbiti J. *Concepts of God in Africa*, p. 156
41) Schapera I. *The Khoisan Peoples of South Africa*, pp. 188, 282, 384 – 385
42) Callaway H. *The Religious System of the Amazulu*, pp. 65 – 66
43) Ibid. p. 66
44) Ibid. p. 66
45) Robertshaw P.T. *The First Archaeological Excavation in Southern Africa*, The South African Archaeological Bulletin, Vol. XXXIV No. 129, June 1979 p. 52
46) Schapera I. *The Khoisan Peoples of South Africa*, p. 385
Miller, Penny. *Myths and Legends of Southern Africa*, p. 39

Seligman C.G. *Races of Africa*, p. 24

Chapter 6 Isivavane international
1) Corliss W. *Ancient Man: A Handbook of Puzzling artefacts*, p. 102
2) Ibid. pp. 101 – 102
3) Ibid. pp. 18, 102
4) Ibid. p. 18
5) Bulpin T.V. *Natal and the Zulu Country*, p. 66
6) Clark, R.T. Rundle. *Myth and Symbol in Ancient Egypt*, pp. 43 – 45, 63, 90
7) Hawkins, Gerald. *Beyond Stonehenge*, Arrow Books, London 1977 p. 151
8) West M. & Morris J. *Abantu*, p. 61
   Graves R. *White Goddess*, pp. 410 – 411
   Berglund A-I. *Zulu Thought Patterns and Symbolosm*, pp. 336 – 337
9) Ibid. pp. 292, 331 – 334
10) Callaway H. *The Religious System of the Amazulu*, p. 117
11) Ibid. pp. 434 – 435
    Berglund A-I. *Zulu Thought Patterns and Symbolism*, pp. 231, 336, 364
12) Ibid. p. 335
13) Seligman C.G. *Races Of Africa*, p. 90
14) Ibid. p. 90
15) Ibid. p. 91
16) Berglund A-I. *Zulu Thought Patterns and Symbolism*, pp. 36, 256 – 257, 295 Note 2 & 3
17) Parrinder E.G. *African Traditional Religion*, pp. 20 – 23
18) Seligman C.G. *Races of Africa*, pp. 90 – 92
19) Ibid. p. 91
20) Mbiti J. *Introduction to African Religion*, pp. 10 – 11, 19, 145 – 146
    Mbiti J. *African Religions And Philosophy*, pp. 55 – 56
    Oesterley W.O. & Robinson T. *Hebrew Religion*, pp. 99 – 101
21) Bord J. & C. *The Secret Country*, pp. 52 – 53
    Graves, Tom. *Needles Of Stone*, pp. 90, 122ff
22) Ibid. pp. 118, 154
23) Seligman C.G. *Races of Africa*, p. 91
24) Bord J. & C. *The Secret Country*, pp. 69, 162 – 164
25) Ibid. p. 52
    Graves, Tom. *Needles Of Stone*, 113 – 114
    Oesterley W.O. & Robinson T. *Hebrew Religion*, P. 75
    Vinnicombe P. *People of the Eland*, p. 340

Callaway H. *The Religious System of the Amazulu*, p. 409
Graves R. *Greek Myths* 2 161 ²
26) Schapera I. *The Khoisan Peoples Of South Africa*, p. 373
Graves R, *Greek Myths* 1 60 ⁵, 83 ³
27) Bulpin T.V. *Lost Trails Of The Transvaal*, Thomas Nelson & Sons, Johannesburg, SA 1965 p. 31
Sharkey J. *Celtic Mysteries*, pp. 26, 86
28) Ibid. p. 12
Herm G, *The Celts*, pp. 5, 105 – 106, 238
29) Holy Bible King James Version, Genesis 31:19
Oesterley W.O. & Robinson T. *Hebrew Religion*, p. 106
Gheman H.S. *The New Westminster Dictionary of the Bible*, pp. 545 – 546 Laban, 936 – 937 Teraphim
Bright, John, *A History Of Israel*, p. 79
30) Bouvet R. *Pandaemonium*, p. 172 Note 9
31) Ibid. p. 172 Note 9
32) Graves R. *Greek Myths* 1 73 ¹
Schapera I. *The Khoisan Peoples of South Africa*, p. 373
33) Gordon, Robinson. *Arab Gulf States*, Lonely Planet, pp. 43 – 44
34) Ali-Akbar, H. Bushiri. *The Dilmun Civilization, Its Seals and Sun-God Symbols*, The Epigraphic Society, Vol. 8. No. 183, Nov. 1979 pp, 27ff
35) Brentjes B. *African Rock Art*, p. 52
36) Schapera I. *The Khoisan Peoples of South Africa*, pp. 41 – 43, 59 – 62, 292, 300
Cooke C.K. *Rock Art of Southern Africa*, pp. 140 – 141
Sterling T & Kimble G. *Exploration of Africa*, Cassell, London p. 40
37) Gordon, Robinson. *Arab Gulf States*, Lonely Planet, pp. 276 (map), 277, 329, 331 – 333
38) Nayeem Dr. Muhammed Abdul. *The United Arab Emirates - Pre-History and Proto-History of the Arabian Peninsular. Vol 3.* Department of Archaeology and Museology. King Saud University. Riyadh. UAE. pp. 269 - 286 (no date or publisher info supplied)

Chapter 7   Incwala, The Ancient Swazi Mid-Summer Festival of Regeneration
1) Becker P. *Trails And Tribes of Southern Africa*, William Clomes & Sons Ltd., London 1975 p. 101
2) Graves R. *Greek Myths* 2 161 ⁶
Holy Bible King James Version, Deuteronomy 34: 6

References

3) *Treasures of Tutankhamun* Exhibition Catalogue, Ballantine Books, New York 1978
   Van der Heyden A. *Valley of the Kings*, El Sevier Publishing, Cairo
   Aldred C. *Jewels of the Pharaohs*, pp. 7 – 9
4) West M. & Morris J. *Abantu*, p. 60
   Tyrrell B. *Tribal Peoples Of Southern Africa*, p. 135
   Parrinder E.G. *African Traditional Religion*, p. 69
5) Becker P. *Trails And Tribes of Southern Africa*, p. 103
   Powell T.G.E. *The Celts*, p. 78
6) Parrinder G. *Africa's Three Religions*, p. 91
   Tyrrell B. *Tribal Peoples of Southern Africa*, p. 137
   Holy Bible King James Version, Leviticus 23: 10 – 14
7) West M. & Morris J. *Abantu*, p. 62
8) Becker P. *Trails and Tribes of Southern Africa*, p. 115
9) Ibid. p. 117
   West M. & Morris J. *Abantu*, p. 62
10) Ibid. p. 62
    Tyrrell B. *Tribal Peoples of Southern Africa*, p. 137
11) West M. & Morris J. *Abantu*, p. 62
12) Ibid. p. 62
    Michell J. *The Earth Spirit*, p. 18
13) West M. & Morris J. *Abantu*, p. 62
    Tyrrell B. & Jurgens P. *African Heritage*, p. 43
    Holy Bible King James Version, Leviticus 23: 10 – 14
14) Graves R. *Greek Myths* 1 53 [6]
15) West M. & Morris J. *Abantu*, pp. 61, 64
    Berglund A-I. *Zulu Thought Patterns and Symbolism*, p. 336, 337
16) Mbiti J. *African Religion and Philosophy*, p. 53
17) Clark, R.T. Rundle. *Myth and Symbol in Ancient Egypt*, pp. 41 – 44, 63, 90
18) Tyrrell B. *Tribal Peoples of Southern Africa*, p. 185
    Berglund A-I. *Zulu Thought Patterns and Symbolism*, p.335
19) Ibid. pp. 141 – 144, 237 – 238
20) Ibid. p. 337
21) Ivimy J. *The Sphinx and the Megaliths*, pp. 124 – 125
22) Sullivan B. *Spirit of the Rocks*, p. 75ff
23) Graves R. *Greek Myths* 2 133 [9]
24) Graves R. *Greek Myths* 1 53 [4 7 8]
25) Holy Bible King James Version, Exodus 30 : 1 – 7; 38: 1, 6
    Graves R. *The White Goddess*, pp. 264 – 266
26) Ibid. pp. 264 – 266
27) Ibid. pp. 144 – 145

28) Bailey, James. *The God-Kings and The Titans*, p. 217
29) Aldred, Cyril. *Jewels of the Pharaohs*, p. 40
30) Kunz G.F. *The Curious Lore of Precious Stones*, p. 348
31) Aldred, Cyril. *Jewels of the Pharaohs*, p. 18
32) Kunz G.F. *The Curious Lore of Precious Stones*, pp. 225 – 229
33) Steiger, Brad. *Worlds Before Our Own*, pp. 157 – 158
    Becker P. *Trails and Tribes of Southern Africa*, p. 117
34) Graves R. *The White Goddess*, pp. 440 – 441
35) Ibid. pp. 266, 440
    Oesterley W.O. & Robinson T. *Hebrew Religion*, pp. 28, 148 – 149
36) Graves R. *The White Goddess*, p. 266
37) Ibid. p. 645
38) Schapera I. *The Khoisan Peoples of South Africa*, p. 366
39) Mbiti J. *African Religion and Philosophy*, p. 124
40) Graves R. *The Greek Myths* 1 30 [2]
    Herm. *The Celts*, p. 154
41) Callaway H. *The Religious System of the Amazulu*, p. 59
42) Becker P. *Trails and Tribes of Southern Africa*, pp. 190 – 192
    Laubscher B.J.F. *The Pagan Soul*, Howard Timmins, Cape Town 1975 p. 65
43) Graves R. *The White Goddess*, pp. 105 – 106
    Graves R. *Greek Myths* 1 51 [4]
44) Graves R. *The Greek Myths* 1 83 [4]
45) Powell T.G.E. *The Celts*, p. 78
    Sharkey J. *Celtic Mysteries*, p. 14
46) Parrinder E.G. *African Traditional Religion*, p. 88
    Oesterley W.O. & Robinson T. *Hebrew Religion*, pp. 131, 157
    Holy Bible King James Version, Leviticus 17: 10 – 16
    Mbiti J. *Introduction to African Religion*, p. 59
    Laubscher B.J.F. *The Pagan Soul*, pp. 64 – 65
47) Sharkey, John. *Celtic Mysteries*, pp. 6, 13 – 14
48) Graves R. *Greek Myths* 1 67 [6]
49) Ibid. p. 9 [2]
50) Berglund A-I. *Zulu Thought Patterns and Symbolism*, p. 268
51) Sharkey J. *Celtic Mysteries*, pp. 13, 94
52) Seligman C.G. *Races of Africa*, p. 110
53) Parrinder G. *African Mythology*, pp. 122 – 123

Chapter 8   In honour of Khulu-Khulwané
1) Callaway H. *The Religious System of the Amazulu*, pp. 19 – 21, p. 48, 61 – 63

References

2) Mbiti J. *Concepts of God in Africa*, p. 215
   Seligman C.G. *Races of Africa*, p. 53
3) Graves R. *The White Goddess*, pp. 49 – 50
4) Ibid. p. 50
5) Ibid. p. 49
6) Ibid. p. 49
7) Ibid. p. 49
8) Callaway H. *The Religious System of the Amazulu*, pp. 54, 104
9) Ibid. pp. 40 – 41, 56, 84
   Savill S. *Pears Encyclopaedia of Myths and Legends*, p. 188
10) Callaway H. *The Religious System of the Amazulu*, pp. 41 – 42
11) Ibid. p. 103
12) Ibid. pp. 38 – 39
13) Ibid. pp. 35, 40, 90
14) Ibid. p. 44
15) Ibid. pp. 46, 77, 90
16) Ibid. p. 57
17) Ibid. p. 57 Note 8
18) Ibid. p. 57 – 58
19) Ibid. p. 5

Chapter 9   Olulu, Olulu
1) Brentjies B. *African Rock Art*, p. 52
   Johnstone, Paul. *The Archaeology of Ships*, A Walck Archaeology, pp. 9 – 10
   Joint Scandinavian Expedition to Nubia, Sudan, Upper Nile, Scandinavian University Books, Copenhagen Corpus, V9 – 42, V43 – 69
   Bailey, James. *The God-Kings and the Titans*, pp. 87 – 89
   Gayre of Gayre R *The Origin of the Zimbabwean Civilization*, p. 28
2) Snyder H. *The New Westminster Dictionary of the Bible*, p. 281 Ethiopia
   Murphy, Jefferson. *The Bantu Civilization of Southern Africa*, Thomas Y. Cromwell, New York 1974 pp. 135 – 136
3) Schapera I. *The Khoisan Peoples of South Africa*, p. 240
   Seligman C.G. *Races of Africa*, p. 69
   Graves R. *The White Goddess*, p. 293
4) Bailey, James. *The God Kings and the Titans*, pp.126, 251
5) Gehman H.S. *The New Westminster Dictionary of the Bible*, p. 156
6) Inskeep R.R. *The Peopling of Southern Africa*, p. 127
7) Tyrrell B. & Jurgens P. *African Heritage*, p. 31

West M. & Morris J. *Abantu,* pp. 105ff
8) Ibid. pp. 37, 105
Murphy J. *The Bantu Civilization of Southern Africa,* p.13
Mitchison N. *The Africans,* pp. 119, 132 – 133
9) History Course for Bophuthatswana Tour Guides, University of Bophuthatswana, Department of History pp. 4 – 5
West M. & Morris J. *Abantu,* p. 37
10) Ibid. p. 37
Seligman C.G. *Races Of Africa,* p. 124
11) Bailey, James. *The God Kings and Titans,* p. 181
12) Graves R. *The White Goddess,* p. 177
13) Berglund A-I, *Zulu Thought Patterns and Symbolism,* pp. 176, 183
14) Ibid. p. 183
15) Graves R. *The Greek Myths* 1 60 [8]
16) Ibid. 62 [3]
17) Ibid. 96 [2], 96 [4]
18) Callaway H. *The Religious System of the Amazulu,* p. 40
19) Bryant A.T. *Zulu Medicine and Medicine-Men,* pp. 26 – 27
20) Frazer, Sir James. *The Golden Bough,* pp. 103 – 104
21) Buchan, Dr William. *Domestic Medicine or a Treatise on the Prevention and Cure of Diseases,* D. Schaw & Sons, Edinburgh 1814 pp. 255 – 257
22) Graves R. *The Greek Myths* 1 52 [8]
Graves R. *The White Goddess,* p. 286
23) Callaway H. *The Religious System of the Amazulu,* p. 413 Note 79
24) Graves R. *Greek Myths* 1 27 [2]
25) Graves R. *Greek Myths* 2 158 [4]
Callaway H. *The Religious System of the Amazulu,* pp. 411 – 412
26) Casey, Albert & Downey-Prince, Eleanor. *Odyssey of the Irish Documented by Blood Group and Craniometric Analysis,* The Epigraphic Society, Occasional Publications, Vol. 6 Part 2, 1979 p. 140
27) Powell T.G.E. *The Celts,* p.128, p. 141
Casey, Albert & Downwy-Prince, Eleanor. *Odyssey of the Irish Documented by Blood Group and Craniometric Analysis,* OPES p. 140
28) Ibid. p. 141
29) Private correspondence from Professor Barry Fell to Warren Dexter, dd. 3rd October 1980, and letter to myself from Sanusi Credo Mutwa, dd. 2nd November 1980

Chapter 10   Water Demons and the Dragons of the Drakensberg
1) Green, Lawrence. *There's A Secret Hid Away,* pp. 114 – 115

2) Van der Heyden A. Al Ahram/Elsevier Series, Abydos-Esna-Edfu-Komombo-Aswan-Kalabsha-Philae-Abu Simbal, p. 30
3) Huxley F. *The Dragon*, Thames & Hudson, London 1979 p. 49
   Graves R. *The Greek Myths* 1 100 ²
   Schapera I. *The Khoisan Peoples of South Africa*, pp. 205 – 206
4) Willcox A. *Rock Paintings of the Drakensberg*, p. 32
   Vinnicombe P. *People of the Eland*, p. 231
   Schapera I. *The Khoisan Peoples*, pp. 216 – 217, 410
5) Ibid. p. 84
6) Miller, Penny. *Myths And Legends of Southern Africa*, p. 19
7) Van der Post, Sir Laurens. *The Heart of the Hunter*, p. 256
8) Mbiti, John. *Concepts of God in Africa*, p. 104
   Seligman C.G. *Traces of Africa*, p. 77
9) Cooper J.C. *An Illustrated Encyclopaedia of Traditional Symbols*, p. 146
10) Hitching, Francis. *Earth Magic*, Pan Books, London 1977 p.
11) Graves R. *Greek Myths* 1 90 ⁴
    Cooper J.C. *An Illustrated Encyclopaedia of Traditional Symbols*, pp. 70, 133
12) Ibid. p. 150
    Hutchinson R.W. *Prehistoric Crete*, Penguin Books Ltd., UK 1965 p. 208
    Robinson, Gordon. *Arab Gulf States*, Lonely Planet, p. 46
13) Johnson R.T. *Rock Paintings From the South-West Cape Province*, Rock Art Studies in South Africa, SA Archaeological Society, Occasional Paper, 1975 p. 33
    Schapera I. *The Khoisan Peoples of South Africa*, pp. 21, 101
    Van der Post, Sir Laurens. *The Heart of the Hunter*, p. 69
14) Ross, Kurt. *Codex Mendoza Aztec Manuscript*, Miller Graphics, 1978 p. 19
    Graves R. *Greek Myths* 1 25 ²
15) Ibid. 25 ᵈ ᶠ
16) Ibid. 25 ²
17) Sullivan B. *Spirit of the Rocks*, pp. 61 ff
18) Berglund A-I. *Zulu Thought Patterns and Symbolism*, p. 172
    Callaway H. *The Religious System of the Amazulu*, pp. 12, 140 – 141
19) Ibid. pp. 5, 11, 141
20) Graves R. *Greek Myths* 1 30 ³
21) Mbiti, John. *Concepts Of God*, pp. 104, 265 – 266
    Mbiti, John. *African Religions and Philosophy*, p. 165
    Vinnicombe P. *People of the Eland*, p. 234
22) Oesterley W.O. & Robinson T. *Hebrew Religion*, p. 83

23) Ibid. pp. 159, 177
    Graves R. *The White Goddess*, pp. 335 – 336
24) Mbiti J. *Concepts of God*, p. 104
    Oesterley W.O. & Robinson T. *Hebrew Religion*, pp. 84 – 85
    Parrinder E.G. *African Traditional Religion*, p. 25
25) Graves R. *White Goddess*, p. 103
26) Berglund A-I. *Zulu Thought Patterns and Symbolism*, pp. 60 – 61, 142, 181
27) Ibid. 62
28) Ibid. p. 60
29) Ibid. pp. 183 – 184
    Parrinder G. *Africa's Three Religions*, p. 59
    Bovet, Richard. *Pandaemonium*, p. 22
30) Michell, John. *The Earth Spirit*, p. 18
31) Graves R. *Greek Myths* 1 100 [2]
    Graves R. *Greek Myths* 2 125 [3]
32) Ibid. 125 [3]
    Spence L. *A Dictionary Of Mythology*, Cassell & Co. Ltd., London 1930 p. 156
33) Graves R. *Greek Myths* 2 125 [3]
    Bryant A.T. *Zulu Medicine And Medicine-Men*, pp. 17 – 18
34) Vinnicombe P. *People of the Eland*, p. 233
    Cooper J.C. *An Illustrated Encyclopaedia of Traditional Symbols*, p. 148 (Serpents)
35) Mutwa, Vusamazulu Credo. *Indaba My Children*, Halstan & Co. Ltd., UK 1976 pp. 55 – 56
36) Hromnik C. *Indo-Africa* p. 105
    Inskeep R.R. *The Peopling Of Southern Africa*, pp. 125, 127
37) Ibid. p. 125
    Schapera I. *The Khoisan Peoples of South Africa*, p. 27
38) Inskeep R.R. *The Peopling Of Southern Africa*, p. 128
39) Gayre of Gayre R. *The Origin of the Zimbabwean Civilization*, pp. 206 – 207
40) Inskeep R.R. *The Peopling of Southern Africa*, p. 120
41) Bulpin T.V. *Discovering South Africa*, T.V. Bulpin Publishers (Pty) Ltd., Cape Town 1986 p. 498
42) Bulpin T.V. *Natal and Zulu Country*, T.V. Bulpin Publishers (Pty) Ltd., Cape Town 1977 p. 315
43) Vinnicombe P. *People of the Eland*, Maps 2, 4 – 5
44) Woodhouse B. *The Bushman Art of Southern Africa*, p. 94
45) Woodhouse H.C. & Lee D.N. *Art on the Rocks*, p. 126 Ill. 197

46) Rudner J. & I. *The Hunter and His Art,* p. 34 Ill. 7
47) Bord J. & C. *The Secret Country,* p. 77
48) Massie, Suzanne. *Land of the Firebird,* Hamish Hamilton, London p. 303
    Kunz G.F. *The Curious Lore of Precious Stones,* p. 255
49) Ibid. p. 255
50) Mongait A.L. *Archaeology in the USSR,* pp. 158, 244
    Velikovsky I. *Peoples of the Sea,* pp. 56 – 57, 65 – 68
51) Ibid. p. 66
52) Marshack A. *The Roots of Civilization,* pp. 11, 57
53) Berglund A-I. *Zulu Thought Patterns and Symbolism,* p. 360
54) Woodhouse B. *The Bushman Art of Southern Africa,* p. 32
    Tyrrell B. *Tribal Peoples,* pp. 73, 76, 78, 93, 100, 113, 188, 192, 194
55) Woodhouse B. *Archaeology in Southern Africa,* pp. 125 – 126
    Woodhouse H.C. & Lee D.N. *Art on the Rocks,* p. 117
56) Tyrrell B. *Tribal Peoples,* p. 6
    Fell, Barry. *Ogam Inscriptions from North and South Africa,* The Epigraphic Society, Occasional Publications, Vol. 6. No. 116, January 1979
57) Willcox A.R. *Rock Paintiongs of the Drakensberg,* p. 25
    Schapera I. *The Khoisan Peoples of South Africa,* p. 56
58) Reader's Digest. *South African Yesterdays,* Cape Town 1981 p. 148
    Display in the Johannesburg Museum
    Fell, Barry. *Hunting Inscriptions of the Ancient Libyans,* The Epigraphic Society, Occasional Publications, Vol. 6. No. 126, January 1979
59) Totten, Norman. *Symbolic Field Patterns: Four American Examples,* The Epigraphic Society, Occasional Publications, Vol. 6. No. 131, January 1979

Appendix

The Afro-Celtic Connection
The notes here are linked only to the Afro-Celtic connection and are not to be construed as, or confused with, the Reference Notes

1) Mbiti J. *Introduction to African Religion* p. 24
   Graves R. *The White Goddess* – the whole book.
2) Powell T.G.E. *The Celts* pp. 184 – 185
   Tyrrell *Tribal Peoples* p. 122
3) Powell T.G.E. *The Celts* p. 143
   Berglund A.I. *Zulu Thought Patterns and Symbolism* – see index: Ritual slaughter
4) Graves R. *Greek Myths* 1 24:10
   Herm G. *The Celts* p. 134
   Miller P. *Myths and Legends of Southern Africa* p. 205
   Mbiti J. *Concepts of God in Africa* pp. 188, 191
5) Sharkey J. *Celtic Mysteries* p. 18
   Powell T.G.E. *The Celts* p. 147
   Seligman C.G. *Races of Africa* pp. 60, 128
   Mbiti J. *African Religion and Philosophy* pp. 56, 185
   Shapers I. *The Khoisan Peoples of South Africa* pp. 87 – 88, 94, 96 – 97
6) Powell T.G.E. *The Celts* pp. 144 – 145
   West M. & Morris J. *Abantu* p. 61
7) Powell T.G.E. *The Celts* p. 157
   Laubscher B.J.F. *The Pagan Soul* p. 90
8) Powell T.G.E. *The Celts* p. 157
   Berglund A.I. *Zulu Thought Patterns and Symbolism* pp. 176, 209 – 210
9) Powell T.G.E. *The Celts* p. 150
   Mbiti J. *African Religion and Philosophy* pp. 15, 233
   Mbiti J. *Introduction to African Religion* pp. 145 – 146
10) Ibid. p. 67
    Powell T.G.E. *The Celts* pp. 146 – 147
11) Sharkey J. *Celtic Mysteries* p. 76
    Berglund A.I. *Zulu Thought Patterns and Symbolism* pp. 127 ff, 136 ff.
12) Ibid. pp. 136 – 140
    Herm G, *The Celts* p. 153
13) Callaway Rev. H. *The Religious System of The Amazulu* p. 387

Appendix

Graves R. *The White Goddess*
14) Callaway Rev. H. *The Religious System of The Amazulu* p. 434 – 435
    Berglund A.I. *Zulu Thought Patterns and Symbolism* p. 287
15) Sharkey J. *Celtic Mysteries* p. 6
    Mbiti J. *African Religion and Philosophy* p. 3
16) Parringer E.G. *African Traditional Religion* p. 117
    Berglund A.L. *Zulu Thought Patterns and Symbolism* p. 287
    Callaway Rev. H. *The Religious System of The Amazulu* p. 432
    Graves R. *The White Goddess* p. 49
    Mbiti J. *Concepts of God in Africa* pp. 211 – 212
17) Ibid. p. 265
    Herm G. *The Celts* pp. 54, 150
    Mbiti J. *African Religion and Philosophy* p. 120
18) Herm G. *The Celts* p. 161
    Letter from (Musa) Sydney Ntanzi (19 – 09 – 1979)
    Hadingham E. *Circles and Standing Stones* p. 27
    Miller P. *Myths and Legends of Southern Africa* p. 46
19) Sharkey J. *Celtic Mysteries* p. 16
    Graves R. *The White Goddess* Chapters 10 – 11
20) Chadwick N. *The Celts* p. 46
21) Hern G. *The Celts* p. 58
    Ritter E.A. *Shaka Zulu* pp. 13 – 14
22) Powell *The Celts* p. 139
    Chadwick N. *The Celts* p. 46
    Tyrrell B. & Jurgens P. *African Heritage* p. 44
23) Herm G. *The Celts* p. 253
    Becker P. *Inland Tribes* p. 35
    Tyrrell B. & Jurgens P. *African Heritage* p. 198
    Ibid. pp. 144 – 145, 151 – 152, 156
    West M. & Morris J. *Abantu* pp. 9, 38, 40, 58 – 59, 106
    Herm G. *The Celts* p. 147
    Powell T.G.E. *The Celts* p. 86
23) Ibid. pp. 86 – 87
    Tyrrell B. & Jurgens P. *African Heritage* pp. 161 – 162
24) Ibid. p. 230 ff.
    Powell T.G.E. *The Celts* p. 171
25) Ibid. pp. 105 – 106
    Tyrrell B. & Jurgens P. *African Heritage* p. 218
26) Powell T.G.E. *The Celts* p. 166
    Parringer E.C. *African Traditional Religion* p. 89
    Mbiti J. *Introduction to African Religion* p. 146

27) Tyrrell B. *Tribal People* pp. 114 – 115
    Sharkey J. *Celtic Mysteries* p. 89
28) Ibid. p. 89
    Ritter E.A. *Shaka Zulu* p. 35
    Bulpin T.V. *Lost Trails of the Transvaal* p. 35
29) Herm G. *The Celts* p. 154
    Mutwa, Vusamazulu Credo *Indaba my Children* p. X
30) Powell T.G.E. *The Celts* pp. 127, 135
    Ritter E.A. *Shaka Zulu* pp. 15, 35
31) Ibid. p. 34
    Savill S. *Pears Myths and Legends, Northern Europe, Southern & Central Africa* pp. 13, 34
    Callaway Rev. H. *The Religious System of the Amazulu* p. 438
32) Ibid. p. 166
    Herm G. *The Celts* p. 147
    Sharkey J. *Celtic Mysteries* p. 89
33) Seligman C.G. *Races of Africa* p. 32
    Powell T.G.E. *The Celts* p. 135
34) Ibid. p. 137
35) Ibid. p. 137
36) Laubscher B.J.F. *The Pagan Soul* pp. 67 – 68
    Berglund A.I. *Zulu Thought Patterns and Symbolism* pp. 98, 130, 138, 157, 228 – 229, 238
    Graves R. *Greek Myths* 2 – 105: 7,8
    Graves R. *The White Goddess* p. 252
37) Powell T.G.E. *The Celts* p. 76
    Ritter E.A. *Shaka Zulu* p. 41
38) Becker P. *Trails and Tribes of Southern Africa* p. 103
    Powell T.G.E. *The Celts* p. 78
39) Ibid. p. 78
    Jefferson, Murphy E. *The Bantu Civilization of Southern Africa* p. 12
    Becker P. *Inland Tribes* p. 118
    Seligman C.G. *Races of Africa* p. 128
    Becker P. *Trails and Tribes of Southern Africa* p. 101
42) Seligman C.G. *Races of Africa* p. 126
    Schapera I. *The Khoisan Peoples of South Africa* pp. 84 – 85, 226 – 227
    Powell T.G.E. *The Celts* p. 78
43) Ibid. p. 86
    Mbiti J. *African Religion and Philosophy* p. 2
44) Powell T.G.E. *The Celts* p. 78
    Schapera I. *The Khoisan Peoples of South Africa* p. 290

45) Powell T.G.E. *The Celts* p. 80
    Mbiti J. *African Religion and Philosophy* p. 183
    West M. & Morris J. *Abantu* pp. 61 – 62
    Sharkey J. *Celtic Mysteries* p. 14
46) Mbiti J. *Introduction to African Religion* p. 162
    Graves R. *The White Goddess* p. 303
    Michell J. *Earth Spirit* p. 17
47) Herm G. *The Celts* p. 5
    Bulpin T.V. *LostTrails of the Transvaal* p. 31
    Powell T.G.E. *The Celts* p. 130
48) Sharkey J. *Celtic Mysteries* p. 14
    Callaway Rev. H. *The Religious System of the Amazulu* pp. 212 – 213
49) The board game know in English as "Nine Man's Morris" and to the Zulu as "Umlabalaba"
50) Piggott S. *The Druids* pp. 28 – 29